Lamentations

Living in the Ruins

Lamentations

Living in the Ruins

A Mentor Commentary

John L Mackay

John L MacKay is Professor of Old Testament at Free Church College Edinburgh. He is a internationally respected Old Testament Scholar who has written several Old Testament commentaries including Focus on the Bible commentaries on *Jonah, Micah, Nahum, Habbakuk & Zephaniah*(ISBN 978-1-84550-345-1) and, *Haggai, Zechariah & Malachi* (ISBN 978-1-85792-067-3) and Mentor commentaries on *Exodus* (ISBN 978-1-85792-6419) and two volumes on *Jeremiah* (Vol. 1 ISBN 978-1-857910-9379, Vol. 2 978-1-85792-938-6),

Unless otherwise stated, all biblical quotations are the author's own translations.

© John L. MacKay

ISBN 1-84550-363-5
ISBN 978-1-84550-363-5

10 9 8 7 6 5 4 3 2 1

Published in 2008
in the
Mentor Imprint
by
Christian Focus Publications,
Geanies House, Fearn, Tain,
Ross-shire, IV20 1TW, Great Britain

www.christianfocus.com

Cover Design by Daniel Van Straaten

Printed and Bound by Cromwell Press, Wiltshire

Contents

Introduction

The five chapters of Lamentations may easily be overlooked. Not only is the book brief, but it also nestles between the much larger prophetic works of Jeremiah and Ezekiel. Furthermore, it deals with realities from which we would naturally wish to distance ourselves. Consequently, apart from the affirmation of faith in 3:22-24, the contents of the book are little studied.

However, there is much here to challenge faith and also to build it up. This is the case despite the fact that even a brief glance at the book confirms the aptness of the title for this collection of poems, for they are set in a dark world of catastrophe, misery and apparent hopelessness. Reading them compels us to assess our reaction to such circumstances, and all the more so because what is described here is not some accident which chanced to engulf the city of Jerusalem. Rather this was the deliberately imposed penalty of divine justice on sinful misconduct. Therefore there are many respects in which these events foreshadow God's promised final intervention in human affairs, and constitute a solemn warning to every generation regarding the bitter end which awaits those who stubbornly persist in defying God. 'The time is come that judgement must begin at the house of God: and if it first begin at us, what shall the end be of them that obey not the gospel of God?' (1 Pet. 4:17, AV).

But the book was not written in the first instance to serve as a warning for others, or for that matter as a means of keeping alive the memory of past suffering and disaster in the collective consciousness of the community. Clearly at one level these poems are a tribute to the past in that they recall all that Jerusalem had once been, and act as a reminder of what had been lost in the harrowing tragedy of a protracted siege and its aftermath. However, it is the present which dominates the thought of Lamentations with its repeated portrayal of Zion's pain and grief as the city endured the economic, social and political upheaval of enemy occupation and oppression. Indeed, the audience to whom the work is addressed is obviously the group presently enduring suffering. However, in all their affliction, the paramount question facing the community was religious. Their previous pattern of belief and expectation had been shattered. In retrospect it was evident that the LORD's action against them had been justified, but there remained a lack of clarity as to where that now left them. Had God finally and completely broken off his relationship with them? Would there ever be an end to the indignities imposed on the community? to the agony? to the desolation? Could there possibly be a way forwards to restoration?

Through the measured structure of its poems Lamentations seeks to stem the swirling bewilderment and dismay which afflicted Zion, and to erect a framework in which thought can occur and where, perhaps, hope can be regained. The poet's careful presentation and his astute words of challenge and consolation also enable subsequent generations to extend legitimate comfort in many later situations of disaster, disorder and despair.

A. Historical Setting

Lamentations is written in the traditional style of Hebrew poetry, naming no names and avoiding specific historical references even as it records very personal circumstances and unveils very personal and deeply felt emotions. So to appreciate its message fully we must set it in its original context which was, of course, well known to the poet and his audience. There can be no doubt that the backdrop for Lamentations is the fall of Jerusalem to the Babylonian emperor, Nebuchadnezzar, in 586 B.C.[1] Historical accounts of these events are given in 2 Kings 24–25 and 2 Chronicles 36, and also in Jeremiah, but here we encounter the raw details of the personal tragedies which lay behind the generalised summaries found elsewhere.

Throughout their national history the people of Israel had frequently failed to live up to the requirements of their covenant relationship with the LORD. After the division of the kingdom on the death of Solomon in 931 B.C., conditions in the northern kingdom of Israel declined remorselessly into a syncretistic religion,

---

1. Wilhelm Rudolph (*Das Buch Ruth—Das Höhe Lied—Die Klagelieder* [Kommentar zum Alten Testament 17. Gütersloh: Gerd Mohn, 1962]) argued that the first poem was composed after the first capture of Jerusalem by the Babylonians in 597 B.C. He based this on the fact that the poem does not speak of the destruction of the city or the Temple in the style of later chapters, but only of their capture. However, the first siege of Jerusalem was not a prolonged affair such as is needed to give rise to the descriptions in 1:11, 19.

and indeed halfway through the two centuries of its independent existence outright paganism from Tyre became dominant under Ahab and Jezebel. The prophetic ministries of Elijah and Elisha stemmed the declension in the north for a while, but after the death of Jeroboam II in 753 B.C. there was a precipitate decline into internal confusion which meant that the kingdom could not withstand intensified and relentless aggression from the Mesopotamian superpower of Assyria. Samaria fell to the Assyrians in 723 B.C. and the northern kingdom was no more.[2]

Decline in the south was slower, not least because of a number of reforming kings who initiated measures which checked and reversed a slide into paganism similar to that which had occurred in the north. Certainly such reform was needed after the reign of Manasseh (coregent from 697 B.C.; sole ruler, 686-642 B.C.), for he encouraged old Canaanite traditions including Baal worship and the erection of an Asherah, and tolerated the fertility cult with its sacred prostitution even in the Temple precincts (2 Kgs. 21:4-7; Zeph. 1:4-5). The king went further still by participating in the cult of Molech with its practice of human sacrifice — he offered his own son (2 Kgs. 21:6). Although in later life Manasseh personally repented (1 Chron. 33:12-13, he was unable to reverse the underlying trend in Judah towards paganism.

Manasseh's grandson Josiah (640-609 B.C.) tried in vain to stem the move away from loyalty to the LORD. Official policy promoted the removal of pagan cults and the renewal of the covenant (2 Kgs. 23:1-20). Outwardly at least the people were content to follow their king's lead, if only as an expression of nationalistic fervour. However, there does not seem to have been a genuine heart-attachment to the LORD, and after Josiah's untimely death (2 Kgs. 23:29) circumstances in Judah rapidly worsened, as Jeremiah's prophecy amply testifies (e.g. Jer. 7:1-15). Meanwhile the international

2. While many conundrums in biblical chronology have been successfully resolved, there still remains a number of contested details. The dates used here are those given by Leslie McFall, 'A Translation Guide to the Chronological Data in Kings and Chronicles.' *Bibliotheca Sacra* 148 (1991): 3–45, who refined those established by the seminal work of Edwin R. Thiele, *The Mysterious Numbers of the Hebrew Kings.* (rev. ed.; Grand Rapids: Zondervan, 1983).

situation around them deteriorated, and Judah became trapped in the middle ground between the superpowers of Egypt and Babylon. Babylonian dominance of the area was established by their victory at the battle of Carchemish in 605 B.C., and Judah fell within their sphere of influence. But the regime in Jerusalem under Jehoiakim (609-598 B.C.) was more disposed towards alliance with Egypt, which they felt would impose less oppressive conditions on them. Their revolt against Babylon led to Jerusalem being captured in March 597 B.C., and Jehoiachin, the young, newly enthroned king, was deported to Babylon after being on the throne for only a few months. His uncle, Zedekiah (597-586 B.C.), was installed by Nebuchadnezzar to rule in Jerusalem, but it was not long until he too was induced to revolt against Babylon. When the exasperated Nebuchadnezzar retook the city in 586 B.C., orders were given that it be looted and torched (2 Kgs. 25:8-17). It is against the background of the carnage and destruction experienced in the ruined city that Lamentations was written.

B. Authorship

There are two traditions regarding Lamentations and its authorship. The Massoretes, the scholarly scribes who preserved the traditional text of the Old Testament in the seventh to the eleventh centuries A.D., used the first word of the book as its title, ʾēkâ, 'Ah, how!' (1:1), and placed it not among the Prophets but in the Writings, the third section of the Hebrew canon.. Eventually its location there was standardised in the *Megilloth* ('scrolls') which is a mini-collection comprising five briefer works (Song of Songs, Ruth, Lamentations, Ecclesiastes and Esther). These works were kept together because they were recited at the sacred festivals of the Jews. Lamentations was, of course, read at the time of the remembrance of the fall of Jerusalem, not only that of 586 B.C. to the Babylonians, but also, in the later synagogue, in commemoration of the events of A.D. 70 when the Romans captured Jerusalem. Indeed it was on the *ninth* of Ab (late July/early August), which Jewish tradition associated with the fall of the second Temple to Titus, that there was public mourning and the reading of Lamentations, and not on either of the dates connected with the earlier fall of Jerusalem (the seventh of Ab, 2 Kgs. 25:8-9; the tenth of Ab, Jer. 52:12).

In the Hebrew text as preserved by the Massoretes there is no attribution of authorship for Lamentations.

The other tradition regarding Lamentations is attested in the Septuagint (LXX), the Greek translation of the Hebrew Scriptures made progressively in the century from about 250 B.C. Here the book is entitled *Threnoi*, 'Dirges'. This is unlikely to have been an innovation and probably reflected an even earlier practice. Furthermore, in the Septuagint Lamentations was placed after Jeremiah, among the prophetic writings, and such a position seems also to have been known to Josephus, the Jewish historian of the first century A.D.[3]

More significantly, many manuscripts of the Septuagint have a prologue before the text of Lamentations, which from its style seems to reflect a Hebrew original. It reads: 'And it came to pass after Israel had been taken off into captivity and Jerusalem had been laid waste, that Jeremiah sat weeping and lamented this lament over Jerusalem and said …'. The Vulgate entitles the book, 'Lamentations of Jeremiah the Prophet', and repeats the Septuagint superscription, adding 'with a bitter spirit, sighing and wailing'. A similar position is reflected in the Peshitta (the Syriac rendering made from the second century A.D. on), and in the Targum (an Aramaic translation and commentary, written down from the third century A.D. on but reflecting much earlier synagogue tradition). Jewish views on the matter are also recorded in the Babylonian Talmud (committed to writing in the sixth century A.D.) where it is noted that 'Jeremiah wrote the book which bears his name, the book of Kings, and Lamentations (*qînôt*, 'dirges')' (*Baba Bathra.* 14b-15a). However, it is unlikely that attribution of Lamentations to Jeremiah was part of the original Hebrew text since, in the light of the widespread Jewish acceptance of this tradition, it would then be difficult to account for it subsequently being dropped from the Massoretic Text.

Earlier western scholarship readily adopted the Septuagintal tradition, and it was this acknowledgement of Jeremiah as the author of Lamentations which contributed substantially to him being designated 'the weeping prophet'. In more recent centuries,

3. This would seem to be implied by Josephus' account of the sacred books of the Jews in *Contra Apionem* 1.8.

however, most scholars have doubted that Jeremiah wrote the book. It has been argued that such an attribution merely reflects the scribal habit of assigning anonymous works to well known figures, and that it probably arose through a misunderstanding of 2 Chronicles 35:25: 'And Jeremiah composed/uttered a dirge for Josiah. And all the male singers and the female singers spoke in their dirges for Josiah until today. And they set them as an ordinance for Israel, and behold they are written in the Dirges.' Since the king is spoken of in very positive terms in 4:20, and Jeremiah commends Josiah's character in Jeremiah 22:15-16, some have supposed that chapter 4 is the dirge for Josiah mentioned in Chronicles. However, the reference in 4:20 is undoubtedly to Zedekiah, the last king of Judah, and the content of the chapter as a whole does not match the circumstances of Josiah's reign. Nonetheless the passage in Chronicles does show that Jeremiah was the author of at least one dirge.

Abandonment of Jeremianic authorship led to discussion as to when the book might have been written, with some early critics favouring a date as late as Maccabean times (second century B.C.). It is argued that the author of Lamentations used his extensive imaginative powers to evoke the much earlier situation of Jerusalem's fall. However, the vivid presentation of the devastated city and the absence of references to a return from the Exile or to the rebuilding of the Temple have convinced most commentators that the poems were composed during the exilic period, most probably on the basis of personal participation in the events described. The despairing tone of the work points to an origin between the fall of the city in 586 B.C. and the release of Jehoiachin from prison in 561 B.C., an event which provided a glimmer of hope for the final author of Kings (cf. 2 Kgs. 25:27-30). The poet did not even have that straw to grasp.

However, trends in modern Old Testament scholarship in general have resulted in many favouring multiple authorship of Lamentations. This is often associated with a liturgical origin for the poems, possibly among the temple singers.[4] Certainly Jeremiah 41:5 does refer to public mourning shortly after the catastrophe,

---

4. Cf. Johan Renkema, *Lamentations* (Historical Commentary on the Old Testament; Leuven: Peeters, 1998), 52–53.

and it is clear that mourning and fasting in the fifth month, Ab, had been instituted from an early date after the fall of the city (Zech. 7:3-5; 8:19). However, the poems have no obvious signs of an official or priestly origin but seem to arise out of personal reflection, though that does not preclude their subsequent use in a liturgical setting. Furthermore, there is no clear evidence of multiple authorship, and so in view of the many features shared by all the poems it remains reasonable to assume that one figure has been responsible for all five compositions as well as for the sequence in which they are now preserved.

But is the individual responsible for Lamentations to be identified as Jeremiah? The evidence is finely balanced. In favour of the identification is the similarity in tone and language to be detected in the two books. Instances include the use of the phrase 'daughter Zion' (see discussion at 1:6), references to eyes running with tears (1:16; 2:11; 3:48-49 as compared with Jer. 9:1, 18; 14:17), 'terrors from all around' (2:22 as compared with Jer. 6:25; 20:3, 10), the forgetfulness of Zion's lovers (1:2 compared with Jer. 30:14), and the cup of God's wrath being passed to Edom (4:21 compared with Jer. 49:12). No single occurrence provides irrefutable evidence of Jeremianic authorship, but cumulatively they do point to the author as someone who, at least, was familiar with Jeremiah's writings.

On the other hand, there seem to be substantive differences in theological perspective between Jeremiah and Lamentations. One might note that the evidence of 4:17 — that 'we' looked in vain for help from foreign alliances — is at variance with Jeremiah's known views (cf. Jer. 2:18; 37:5-10). The great expectations entertained of the king (4:20) also reflect a different attitude from that of Jeremiah (cf. Jer. 37:17). Further it would seem from 4:19 that the author took part in the flight from the city recorded in 2 Kings 25:4-5, and that could not have included Jeremiah who was languishing in prison at that juncture (Jer. 38:28). It may well be questioned if Jeremiah have written 2:9 quite as it stands. While these differences might be accounted for by supposing that Jeremiah is presenting the outlook of the people in general, not his own, it is more natural to surmise that the author is someone whose viewpoint is closer to that of the populace as a whole than Jeremiah's would have been.

Jeremianic authorship is much more plausible than modern commentators are generally willing to concede, but it is not asserted by the text itself or elsewhere in Scripture. The point does not substantially affect the interpretation of the book provided the same general setting is maintained as would apply if Jeremiah was the author. However, I have adopted the more cautious practice of referring to the author as 'the poet', and assume him to have been one who was an eyewitness of the fall of the city, deeply affected by the suffering which occurred, and influenced by Jeremiah's ministry in his subsequent interpretation of events. Under the inspiration of the Spirit the poet was given profound insight into the underlying causes of the judgement which had come upon his nation, and he was guided in leading his contemporaries to a true appreciation of their situation and of how hope might yet spring from the misery which engulfed them.

C. Literary Structure

One advantage of referring to the author of Lamentations as 'the poet' is that it keeps reminding us that we are studying a work not only of deep theological significance but also of consummate literary craft, which is deployed to enhance the presentation of the message. Though it is not always possible to bring these literary features across in a translation, some understanding of the art and skill involved enhances our appreciation of the book. Indeed, the time and mental energy which the poet had obviously invested in composing his work functioned as a means of assuring his audience that he did not dismiss or minimise their agony. Their situation demanded careful treatment. The use of poetry rather than prose suggested the need for emotional therapy rather than (or, more probably, in addition to) philosophical or theological argument as the way to soothe shattered lives.

It is appropriate to mention here some of the techniques the poet used in achieving his aims.

(1) Basic Structure

The book of Lamentations consists entirely of poetry, with each of its five chapters being a separate poem. The first three chapters of Lamentations are of a similar length, but the verse structure is

---

The Poetic Structure of Lamentations

Chapter 1	Chapter 2	Chapter 3
acrostic	acrostic	acrostic
22 verses of three lines	22 verses of three lines	66 verses of one line with three verses per letter

Chapter 4	Chapter 5
acrostic	not acrostic
22 verses of two lines	22 verses of one line

---

different. Though there are some variations, the verses of chapters 1 and 2 consist of triplets of lines, each line of which is a bicolon, that is, it has two distinct parts or cola.[5] Chapter 3 is organised in three line stanzas, with each line numbered as a separate verse. Chapter 4 consists of couplets of bicola, whereas in chapter 5 each verse is simply a bicolon.

Many of the bicola in Lamentations exhibit the parallelism which is characteristic of Semitic poetry, in that the second member (colon) of a line (bicolon) echoes or modifies the first. Because of this parallelism, the poetic structure of the book is not merely a matter of artistic skill and embellishment, but it also provides significant indications as to how the work is to be read and understood. In chapter 5 almost every verse (only three are exceptions, and two of these, 5:9 and 5:10, appear to be in parallelism with each other) displays balanced parallelism.

---

5. The translation presented here adopts the convention of indenting the second colon in a bicolon (as also the second and third cola in a tricolon, such as those found in 1:1). This helps to bring out the original poetic structure.

(2) Alphabetic Acrostics

Apart from chapter 3, each chapter has 22 verses, the same as the number of letters in the Hebrew alphabet, and in chapters 1, 2 and 4 the first word of each verse begins with a different letter of the alphabet in sequence.[6] In chapter 3 the acrostic pattern is more elaborate in that verses occur in groups of three, with each letter of the alphabet in initial position three times in succession. This intensification of the acrostic device focuses attention on the chapter and underscores its thematic (as well as its literary) centrality. In chapter 5, however, all that remains of the acrostic form is the number of verses.[7] As indicated below, this may contribute to a final plaintive note in the book.

Various proposals have been put forward to account for the use of an acrostic pattern. Its prevalence certainly gives to the book as a whole a coherence which might not otherwise easily arise between five separate poetic compositions. Acrostic devices were by no means innovative, and various sorts are widely attested in both Egyptian and Mesopotamian literature. They are also to be found partially or wholly worked out in other Biblical poetry (cf. Psalm 119).

But why did the author adopt it in Lamentations? Some have suggested that it was incorporated as an aid to memorisation of the poems. Others have proposed that it was simply a device for displaying literary proficiency. Yet again, others have emphasised that the technique contributed to the sense of the work, as well as the aesthetics of the composition, by embodying the idea of completeness (in a way comparable to our expression 'from A to Z'), and so presenting a claim that no aspect of the nation's trauma was exempted from this expression of its grief. Additionally, the use of acrostics may have commended itself to the poet as a means of establishing emotional control in the fraught and bewildering circumstances of Jerusalem. Certainly this literary feature does not

---

6. At 2:16-17, 3:46-51 and 4:16-17 there is a reversal of the order of the letters *pê* and *'ayin*, but not in chapter 1. For discussion, see on 2:16.

7. The fact that Psalms 33, 38 and 103 also consist of precisely 22 lines may indicate that this length was deliberately chosen on occasions even when there was no alphabetical constraint.

impart a sense of artificiality to the poems, but rather heightens their impact. Its use is quite compatible with the book being composed during the immediate aftermath of the great catastrophe.

Further, since acrostics are generally considered to be literary rather than oral devices, their repeated employment in these poems may well indicate a written origin for them.

(3) Qînâ

Of necessity scholars remain far from certain as to how Hebrew poetry originally sounded, but there is agreement that many of the lines of poetry in Lamentations are in two parts, of which the first has more stressed syllables than the second, predominantly three stresses in the first colon and two in the second. This imbalanced structure is often termed *qînâ* ('lament') metre, though it is by no means confined to laments, and there are laments which do not employ it (most notably David's lament over Saul and Jonathan, 2 Sam. 1:17-27). This rhythm is best exemplified in chapter 3, and it is the dominant pattern throughout the book with the exception of chapter 5 which consists largely of the much more common balanced 3:3 rhythm.[8] The numbers are of the major word-stresses in each colon, with a *qînâ* pattern being typically 3:2, but 4:3 and 4:2 would also qualify.

The *qînâ* rhythm with its falling away in the second colon is often considered to have a limping effect, which may have made it appropriate for laments. While recent studies have shown how varied the stress patterns employed in Lamentations are, it is possible to see this as part of the craft of the poet and to consider that the *qînâ* provides 'an underlying structural control'.[9]

---

8. In fact 5:2 is an excellent illustration of the 3:2 stress pattern, and also of the synonymous parallelism (a correspondence of equivalence) between the two cola (half-lines) which is a notable feature of Semitic poetry. Hyphens join words which represent one stressed Hebrew term.

> Our-inheritance has-been-turned-over to-strangers,   (3 stresses)
> our-houses to-foreigners.   (2 stresses)

9. Delbert R. Hillers, *Lamentations: A New Translation with Introduction and Commentary* (Second edition. The Anchor Bible. New York: Doubleday, 1992), 22.

(4) Concentric Analysis

In an intriguing proposal Shea claimed that use of the *qînâ* pattern might helpfully be extended from analysis of the poetic line to the form of Lamentations as a whole. He considered that the complete book may be structured in a *qînâ* pattern of 3:2. The first colon would correspond to chapters 1–3, ending with the strong beat of chapter 3, and the second colon would correspond to chapters 4–5 with its abbreviated rhythmical form concluding the book as a whole with a sigh.[10] Further the more elaborate complete acrostic pattern of chapter 3 sets it apart from the two preceding chapters, so that here again there is evidence of the long:short pattern that is characteristic of the *qînâ*. The pattern might, Shea argued, also be reasonably detected in chapters 4 and 5, because the first of these, with its double verses, is twice the length of the second.

He also proposed that 'the book of Lamentations was written in … the *qinah* or lament pattern which "dies away", because it was written in remembrance of Jerusalem, the city that died away.'[11] This, he concluded, is a strong argument against the view that chapter 5 comes from a later author than the first four acrostic chapters. However, focusing on the *qînâ* pattern as the only macrostructural constraint in the book does lead to deemphasising chapter 3 with its central message of hope and gives a more downbeat, pessimistic edge to the presentation in which hope is submerged beneath the pressing realities of suffering, mere survival, and the silence of God.

Many commentators argue that an alternative structure for analysing Lamentations is provided by concentric analysis, with a focus on chapter 3. Such an approach frequently leads to a more optimistic perception of the overall message of the book. For instance, Johnson identified seven units in Lamentations which he argued are arranged chiastically around 3:21-42 which functions as the focus of that chapter and also of the book. He also argued that chapters 1 and 2 are each composed of 'fact' halves (1:1-11; 2:1-11) and 'interpretation' halves (1:12-22; 2:12-22), an arrangement

10. William H. Shea, 'The *Qinah* Structure of the Book of Lamentations,' *Biblica* 60 (1979): 103–7.
11. Shea, '*Qinah* Structure,' 107.

which is also echoed in chapter 4 (fact, 4:1-11; interpretation, 4:12-22).[12]

An elaborate literary structural analysis of Lamentations is presented by Johan Renkema.[13] He considers that it is misguided to analyse the construction of the individual poems and of the book as a whole in a linear fashion, expecting a climax at the end of each poem and at the end of the book. Rather the most significant poetic technique employed is a concentricity, and he provides evidence for this from verbal repetition throughout the poems. Renkema also subjects the individual poems to detailed analysis and division, and utilises the device of 'responsion' to trace verbal and thematic links between similarly located verses in different poems. Various aspects of these latter features seem somewhat artificial, and are not adopted in this commentary. However, concentricity is established as a key aspect of the structure of Lamentations, and Renkema's work in this respect is referred to in the discussion.

No analysis can claim finality, however, because the poet did not rigidly restrict himself to one technique. Instead, he combined a variety of methods in a skilfully wrought and subtle blend which gives structural coherence to the work as a whole.

(5) Genre

Form criticism does not seem to have much to offer in that, with the possible exception of chapter 5, most scholars consider the poems in Lamentations to be of mixed form. Even Hermann Gunkel, who initiated modern form critical studies, concluded that a mixture of several different literary genres were to be found in the book. Chapters 1, 2 and 4 were funeral songs, chapter 3 was an individual lament, and chapter 5 was a communal lament. But the

---

12. Bo Johnson, 'Form and Message in Lamentations,' *Zeitschrift für die Alttestamentliche Wissenschaft* 97 (1985): 58–73. For a more detailed concentric analysis of Lamentations, see David A. Dorsey, *The Literary Structure of the Old Testament: A Commentary on Genesis–Malachi* (Grand Rapids: Baker, 1999), 246–52.

13. Johan Renkema, 'The Literary Structure of Lamentations (I–IV),' in *The Structural Analysis of Biblical and Canaanite Poetry* (JSOTSup 74; ed. Willem van der Meer and Johannes C. de Moor; Sheffield: JSOT Press, 1988), 294–396.

individual poems fail to conform to the patterns expected in such categories.

The word *qînâ* is used in the Old Testament of a dirge, which is uttered at a funeral or as a memorial, and is addressed to those who are mourning. A dirge is thus a narrower category than a lament which expresses grief over some tragic event, not necessarily a death. A complaint not only expresses grief but, as in so many of the psalms, seeks redress from God for the distressing situation. While chapter 1 possesses some of the features of a dirge with the introductory 'Ah, how!', the third person speaker in most of 1:1-11, and the description of reversed fortunes, it is still not a response to an actual death[14] nor does it call on those addressed to engage in mourning rites. Further, as regards chapter 3, direct address to God does not occur until its very end, and so it is difficult to view that poem simply as a complaint.

Consequently it is appropriate to maintain that throughout Lamentations there are elements of both lament and complaint. There has been irreparable loss, and yet Zion is in some sense still alive. In that the city has fallen to the enemy and been destroyed, its fate now seems irreversible, and yet there is petition and complaint with respect to the ongoing situation, seeking that the physical and spiritual agony of its remaining inhabitants be ameliorated. The mixture of these elements reduces the applicability of form critical categories and analysis in studying Lamentations.

(6) City Laments

Laments were not unique to the literature of ancient Israel. Many scholarly analyses of Lamentations focus on the genre of the individual poems and in this way try to establish their relationship to other ancient Near Eastern writings. Despite the extensive discussion involved it is unclear how helpful it is to understanding the poems to label them communal laments or whatever, and to compare them with Mesopotamian laments over a ruined sanctuary

---

14. As Mintz perceptively remarks, 'An image of death would have purveyed the false concept of finality; the dead have finished with suffering and their agony can be evoked only in retrospect' ('The Rhetoric of Lamentations and the Representation of Catastrophe,' *Prooftexts* 2 [1982]: 3).

or over the destruction of a city.[15] We do not know to what extent the Mesopotamian examples were known about in Israel, or whether there were similar laments over fallen cities in their literary tradition. It is the case that they share the characteristic of the personification of a destroyed and catastrophe-stricken city, described from the point of view of the conquered — but such an event was an all too frequent occurrence in the world, ancient or modern. Both genres express similar emotions. In Mesopotamia the collapse of the city is attributed to the wrath of the god or to a capricious decision of the divine assembly. Often a deity is depicted as leaving his or her temple because the situation facing the city was so overwhelming that no assistance could be offered. In Lamentations the LORD has given over his city to punishment, but no mention is made of a divine return to a rebuilt sanctuary, which differs essentially from Mesopotamian examples.[16] Further, in Lamentations there is acceptance of human sin as precipitating the crisis. So, beyond a broad cultural similarity, the literary relationship of Lamentations to other ancient writings is not self-evident, and this line of analysis adds little to our understanding of Scripture.

D. Message of the Book

Why was Lamentations written? Discovering the message of the book depends on identifying the target audience for whom it was originally composed and on assessing their circumstances as they first heard the work. It was not written as a eulogy with which to pay tribute to the past, nor was it initially designed to be a liturgical resource for present and future generations to ponder the experiences of the past; rather it addressed the needs of those who survived the collapse of Jerusalem as they struggled to cope with their interminable suffering and their intense grief. Each chapter of the book is set against this sombre background of catastrophe and agony.

---

15. For arguments in favour of the existence of an ancient city-lament tradition within Israel, see Hillers, *Lamentations*, 32–39.

16. For a useful discussion of Mesopotamian parallels, see F. W. Dobbs-Allsopp, *Lamentations* (Interpretation. Louisville, Kentucky: John Knox Press, 2002), 6–12.

Consequently, it has to be admitted that there is a general same-
ness of outlook pervading the poems of the book, but that is not to
imply that the five poems portray what is essentially the same scene
from different viewpoints. Even though the physical situation of
Jerusalem is the same at the beginning and at the end of the book, it
was the poet's intention that his hearers' perspective on their
predicament should have changed.

Chapter 1 describes the destruction and misery of Jerusalem,
particularly in contrast to her former glory. Chapter 2 emphasises
that the catastrophe had occurred because of the LORD's wrath, and
so the only hope of relief for the city must originate with him.
Chapter 3 has a more personal formulation, arguing the relevance
of the poet's own experience. Though repeating many of the
themes found elsewhere in the book, it especially centres on the
existence of divine 'steadfast love', which gives a genuine basis of
hope for the future (cf. 3:22). The chapter draws on the experience
of the psalms of individual lament in which, despite suffering from
harrowing circumstances, an individual attains a new sense of
orientation towards God. Chapter 4 seems to descend from the
pinnacle of faith achieved in the previous chapter by plunging back
into the harrowing details of the catastrophe. It does end, however,
with an anticipation of future reversal of the circumstances of
oppressed and oppressor (4:21-22). Chapter 5 is prayer throughout,
ending with an affirmation of the LORD's eternal rule and his
righteousness, and with the plea that he intervene effectively. The
external circumstances of Zion remain unchanged, and cannot
provide a basis for hope. But they are now approached in a spirit of
prayer, with a renewed affirmation of the character of the LORD
and with an acceptance that he alone can provide the way forward.
Even so, it has to be recognised that the resolution of Zion's
quandary presented in Lamentations does not rise as high as that
found in the lament psalms which usually end by anticipating a
future time of praise (e.g. 'I shall sing to the LORD, for he shall
have dealt bountifully with me,' Ps. 13:6). The uncertainty which
obscured Zion's view of the LORD's purposes has not been totally
dispelled.

(1) The Need for Sympathy

The repeated elaboration in Lamentations of the many aspects of Zion's suffering incorporates an explicit recognition of the magnitude and severity of the situation. The poet does not attempt to provide a superficial remedy by downplaying the calamity the city was enduring, but places himself sympathetically alongside the community he is addressing. He is not speaking at them; instead he speaks as one who shares their experience and comes at it from the inside (3:1-18). In doing so, the poet is aware of the extent to which hearing about their trauma may play a part in a process which will enable the city's inhabitants to grapple with the disaster. A coherent, powerful verbalisation of their grief may indeed fall short of effecting healing for the broken, dysfunctional community, but it moves them on from the distraught, disjointed utterances of personal heartache. Setting out the shattered fragments of their lives was a necessary preliminary to the process of recovery because it forced each individual to recognise the many pieces which constituted the jigsaw of their experience. So too facing up to the fact that others around them had endured the same harrowing disintegration of their lives would induce them to abandon the inward self-absorption which can be characteristic of those overwhelmed by tragedy. In this way they could come together once more as a community in the face of their shared grief.

It is significant to note what the poet does not invite us to do, and that is to sit in judgement on Jerusalem. He makes no attempt to condone her past rebellion and sin. The justice of what the LORD has imposed on her by acting against her is accepted (though not it would seem its severity and prolongation). What the poet does do — and invites us to participate in — is to feel along with her, and in an attitude of sympathy and love to see if anything can be done to relieve her distress by pointing out a way back to the enjoyment of a harmonious relationship with God. It was a time of uncertainty, and the poet does not allow that uncertainty to be resolved by easy words. The future would be determined by the character and purposes of God.

(2) The Justice and Wrath of God

The poet is not taken wholly up with the intense anguish which has plunged the people into despair. With keen theological insight he does not let go of the fact that in the situation before him there is another constant factor besides the grief of the people. There is the abiding reality of the wrath of God. The misery of the people is the consequence of the outworking of the wrath of God against their sin. Analysing the present and understanding what possibilities the future may hold depends how these two factors interact.

The wrath of God is the inherent divine reaction to the presence of sin. Zion has experienced the day of the LORD in which he has intervened in the flow of world history and imposed on the people the penalty which sovereign justice requires. However, the collective offence of the city is not spelled out in Lamentations. The allegation that 'she gave no thought to her end' (1:8) does indeed show that there was a reckless unwillingness to recognise the gravity of her situation. The existence of her 'lovers' and 'friends' points to entanglement in foreign alliances and possible involvement in pagan cults (1:2). Mention is made too of the failure of influential figures in the community to promote loyalty to the LORD (2:14; 4:13). Though various factors are indicated as contributing to the LORD's displeasure with Zion, they do not become a major focus in the book. What is emphasised is the severity of the LORD's judgement.

Zion's agony raises the question of human suffering in general. It is part of the fallenness of the world since Genesis 3. When responsible creatures rebel and turn away from God, they plunge themselves into an existence which is inevitably one of suffering caused by God-abandonment. Only by reason of the moderating influence of divine grace acting generally towards our fallen world is there any limit to the extent of its misery. To eliminate God is to eliminate blessing; to rebel is to embrace a state of unmitigated woe. And divine punishment judicially assigns to intransigent rebels the woe which they have in fact selected for themselves.

But God does not use suffering only to inflict punishment on the fallen world. It is also part of his disciplining of his people. Along with other aspects of God's providential governance of his fallen world, there is much here that is unfathomable to human minds (cf. Job 9:10; Isa. 55:8-11). However, the LORD's action with respect to his covenant people is in terms of his stated commitment. The execution of divine judgement on them is the fulfilment of the warnings given centuries before by Moses. After a delay in gracious forbearance, destruction and exile have been imposed as the curse of the broken covenant (Deut. 4:26-27; 28:32-37; 29:23-27; 30:17-18). No longer could the people enjoy security in the inheritance which they have rendered unclean by their misbehaviour, and so they were 'vomited out' of the land of promise (Lev. 18:24-30).

Lamentations, however, does not concern itself with the fate of the exiles, nor does it question the appropriateness of the LORD's action in overthrowing the city. Both the poet and his audience accepted that the people had not conducted themselves correctly before God and that his verdict against them was just (1:18). What perplexes them is not that God has judged, but the interminable duration of the judgement and the severity of the blows which have come upon the community. They do not assert their innocence; rather they are overwhelmed by their continuing misery and frustrated that there does not seem to be any way to shorten it. Why had they been left to suffer in this way? Would there ever come an end to their agony? Would they not have been better off dead (4:9)? The protracted nature of their suffering left them in a situation worse than that which Sodom had undergone (4:6). In their distress the people are clamouring for their pain to stop, but there is no reply to their entreaties. The God who has spoken in judgement is silent when they cry out to him. Would there ever be a termination to this disaster?

(3) Zion Theology

It is inevitable that acute suffering raises questions as to why such things occur. This is especially the case when it is the believing community which is undergoing such trauma. Why has God allowed this to happen to his people? Will he at some point relent and bring comfort? Lamentations was written for the theologically confused, and is concerned with exploring how the people should now view their standing before God.

This involved the community abandoning their false expectations and regaining a true theological understanding of what was entailed by their relationship with the LORD. For centuries they had been warned that their misconduct meant that divine judgement was impending (2 Kgs. 24:3; 21:12). The southern kingdom of Judah had been given the vivid lesson entailed in Samaria's overthrow. But delayed judgement led to indifference. They saw no need for repentance, and the measure of national restoration of religion under Josiah had left them quite satisfied with their conduct. Certainly, the religious state of the land was not as bad as it had been in Manasseh's reign. The Temple and its worship had been purged of idolatrous abominations. The people therefore expected to enjoy the blessings of the covenant, but that had not happened. However, the reform movement had been superficial, and the community had focused on outward features, not heart reorientation. Consequently their sense of security was not based on the actual facts of the situation (Jer. 6:13-14; 7:1-4). So when catastrophe struck, the people were stunned. The popular religion prevalent in Jerusalem so lacked in depth and insight that it could not provide any interpretative framework for comprehending the disaster which the LORD had imposed.

Their lack of spiritual perception had also been reinforced by an associated phenomenon, which has been termed 'Zion theology'. At one level this was an expression of biblical truth: that God had promised to bless the city. But this promise had seemingly been absolutised in the wake of the deliverance of the city from Sennacherib in 701 B.C., and there had arisen a blind optimism that, no matter how the people conducted themselves, the LORD was irrevocably and unconditionally committed to bless the city. Psalms such as 46, 48 and 76 could be cited to reinforce this point of view. That this forms an element in the religious underpinnings of Jerusalem is evident from the references/allusions to be found in 2:15; 4:12, 20; 5:19. Their thought world came crashing down when reality clashed with this theory. In absolutising the promise of the covenant, they had forgotten the two-sided nature of the covenant relationship and so had neglected the need for loyal commitment and obedience as their response to the blessings conferred on them. Repeated breaches of their covenant obligations had led inexorably to the withdrawal of God's protection from them.

(4) Personal and Communal Suffering.

Lamentations records the experience of a community undergoing protracted anguish, and this raises questions as to how the approach and teaching of the book may be applied at the level of personal affliction and trouble. It is often recognised that there are two extended Old Testament treatments of human suffering, in the book of Job and in Lamentations, but it is argued that the situations being examined are significantly different. In Job the focus is on the individual whose suffering is *personal* and *undeserved*. As in many of the psalms, Job's affliction does not derive from any directly attributable fault of his own. Also, as in the psalms of suffering, there is a timeless quality about the presentation of Job's circumstances with no clear specification of time or place. This is not to say that his problems are dealt with in some abstract, generalised fashion but, while the Scriptural record recognises the intensity of the personal experience involved, it presents the matter in a way which is open to application in other situations.

Lamentations too in its presentation is lacking specification of time and place. Undoubtedly we are intended to hear it against the background of 586 B.C. but, since this is never really spelled out (cf. Edom in 4:21-22), the poet in effect invites us to ponder if these events and the reaction to them have a wider significance. But Lamentations differs from Job in that it focuses on the impact of suffering which is both *national* and *deserved*. The people as a whole are experiencing the divine imposition of penalty upon them as an errant community.

However, while it has to be recognised that the experience which underlies Lamentations is 'irreducibly collective',[17] it is nonetheless the case that the suffering of the community is the aggregate of the suffering of the individuals who comprise that community. While the corporate aspect of the experience heightens its intensity and magnitude, there is nothing in Lamentations to suggest that the experience of the community is qualitatively different from that of an individual sufferer. Indeed, the poet presents his material in ways that indicate essential continuity between the individual and the community in this regard.

---

17. Mintz, 'Rhetoric,' 2.

This essential continuity may be seen in the figure of 'daughter Zion' in chapters 1 and 2. This personification involves attributing to the non-human entity — the city — the qualities of a human personality, a widow, once beautiful and prosperous, but now ravaged by the enemy, abandoned by her former friends, and sitting alone and forlorn at the road side. The figure of a ravaged widow, subject to continuing victimisation, evokes sympathy, and allows us to grasp the overwhelming nature of the catastrophe which has occurred. A general presentation emphasising the great numbers involved would have been more impersonal and less poignant. But at the same time the personalised approach assumes the legitimacy of correlating national tragedy and individual suffering.

The same logic is also evident in chapter 3 where the 'man' speaks of his personal experience of affliction (3:1-18) and generalises from it as regards other individuals in similar circumstances (3:28-39) and also as regards what is now an appropriate reaction on the part of the community acting together (3:40-42). Their collective response to the tragedy should not be disjoined from the response of the individuals who comprise the community.

However, it has to be recognised that in Lamentations we are dealing with deserved suffering, imposed as divine judgement on the nation. Even so, it is not appropriate to view Judah as just one among many nations, any more than it is appropriate to think of Job as any sufferer. Here it is the covenant nation which is undergoing God's chastisement. What is in view is the fate of the nation with privileged knowledge of, and access to, God. Since it has undervalued its special access to God and has thought little of its heritage, he has in retribution withdrawn those blessings from them. Many of the inhabitants of the land had been led off into exile, and from them and also from those who survived in the land the LORD had withdrawn his presence and they were having to endure the silence of divine unresponsiveness to their entreaties. It is this spiritual dimension which sharpened the cutting edge of their sufferings. As a nation they had forsaken God, and he has now left them to experience the consequences of their desertion by abandoning them to their enemies.

(5) The Future Prospect

It is not to downplay the pain of Zion to assert that the poet is concerned with more than giving audible expression to the city's agony. He wishes to enable the community to move on. He points out that there is already a measure of hope present in the fact that 'we have not been brought to an end' (3:22). It was not through oversight, but with a purpose, that the LORD had preserved them as survivors in the ruins of Zion. Nevertheless, more than mere survival is needed to heal fragmented and shattered lives. Lasting recovery requires recognition of the character and purpose of God, and also the response of repentance from a community which had so drastically failed to maintain its covenant allegiance.

Particularly in chapter 3 the poet applies the Pauline therapy of extending comfort to any in affliction because of his prior personal experience of the comfort extended to him by the Father of mercies and the God of all comfort (2 Cor. 1:3-5). He presents his own history as a paradigm which shows that even guilty sufferers may approach the LORD. It had been renewed recollection of the character of the LORD which triggered his release from the depths of despair (3:18). So throughout the book the poet insistently points to God. It is not a major element in terms of a word count, but it is strategic in terms of stimulating a renewal of faith and of giving cohesion to the thinking of the disoriented community. This forms the theological backbone to the poet's presentation.

1:18 The LORD is indeed righteous.

2:17 The LORD has done what he planned; he has fulfilled his
       word which he commanded long ago.

3:22 The LORD's acts of steadfast love

3:25 The LORD is good to those waiting for him.

5:19 But you, O LORD, sit enthroned for ever; your throne endures
       to generation after generation.

The nation's destiny was not in the hands of blind fate. Rather the people were experiencing the reality of the personal reaction of God in wrath against their sin. It was the LORD's response to their persistent defiance of his requirements which had led to the present crisis, and he alone was able to intervene to alleviate their misery. But that would not occur unless they recognised how wrong their

previous lifestyle had been and turned with confession of their sin
to him (3:39-42).

The covenant bond between God and his people is also presented as a ground for hope (3:24), but this again points to the
ambiguity of the situation for the survivors in Zion. The extent of
the devastation imposed on their land forced them to recognise how
heinous their sin had been in God's sight. Had their misconduct
then effectively annulled the covenant? Faith struggled to find a
chink of light in the face of outward desolation. The ongoing
silence of God to their prayers gave no warrant for supposing that
there would be a future positive relationship. Their circumstances
all militated against optimism.

So the poet does not present a confident picture of what will
happen next. The community which had been overcertain of its
standing in the courts of heaven is not encouraged to engage in further reckless presumption. Indeed, the poet does not claim to know
the path by which the LORD will lead his people back into his
favour. He does not even assert that there is a path. What he sees,
and sees clearly, is that if there is a path to recovery it must be
divinely provided (5:21-22).

The poet does not point forwards to a period of restoration. This
is often regarded as a divergence from the message of Jeremiah. It
must be noted, however, that Jeremiah's message of restoration was
principally focused on a return to the land. The Book of Consolation (Jer. 30–33) is structured round the theme of reversal of exile.
'For, behold days are coming,' declares the LORD, 'when I shall
restore the fortunes of my people Israel and Judah,' says the LORD,
'and I will bring them back to the land which I gave to their fathers
and they shall possess it' (Jer. 30:3; cf. Jer. 50:4-5). In Lamentations, however, the focus is not on the exiled community in
Babylon, but on the survivors left in Jerusalem. There is no awareness of the timescale on which they may expect relief but, because
they are in the hands of the LORD who is essentially benevolent and
merciful, the poet's outlook is tentatively positive. There will be an
end to the agony of their punishment.

E. Application

Is it possible to move from Lamentations into a New Testament context? One notable feature of the situation is that while there may be New Testament allusions to Lamentations there is no direct application of a passage in the New Testament.[18] Connections have therefore to be sought at a more general level.

We may firstly locate the experience recorded in Lamentations in terms of the outworking of God's purposes for his people in history. There is a note of hope in the book, but it is faint. In time a measure of relief was afforded to Zion by the return of some of the exiles from captivity. But the restoration did not exhaust what had been promised. It was only a small portion of the promised land which the people were permitted to occupy, and that was only achieved as subjects of a series of foreign rulers. Many Jews continued to reside in foreign lands, and widespread spiritual blessing was not realised. The focus of God's plan was moving on from the outward forms which dominated the Old Testament era, and so the record of those times finishes on a note of incompleteness, awaiting the Messiah and the resolution he would bring to the problems facing the people.

Further, we must note that the descriptions Lamentations gives of the suffering of Zion function as a perpetual reminder of how heinous sin is in God's sight. That serves to correct our human propensity to minimise sin and its impact. At the same time it must be kept in mind that these poems depict the deserved suffering of those who consider themselves to be God's people, but who have been untrue to their commitment to him. There is therefore an ongoing challenge to every congregation and denomination in the Christian church not to fall in with what is popular and currently appealing in matters of religion, but always to seek what is divinely warranted as true. The relevant New Testament perspective may be derived from the warnings issued to Ephesus as a church which had abandoned its first love and which, if it did not respond to the exhortation to repent, would find the Lord coming and removing its

---

18. It is possible to detect linguistic similarities between 3:15 in the LXX and Acts 8:23; between 3:45 and 1 Cor. 4:13; and between 1:15 and Rev. 14:20, 19:15, but none of these provide a significant interpretative key.

lampstand from its place (Rev. 2:5). Equally there is the Lord's warning about the Father who dresses the vine and who takes away every branch that does not bear fruit and who also prunes the branches bearing fruit that they may bear even more (John 15:1-8).

The Zion of Lamentations is a portrait of divine discipline in Old Testament times when the polity of the people of God involved a closer integration of church and state than now prevails. But the threat of the removed lampstand still exists, as does the pruning of the heavenly vinedresser. Indeed such action may be detected in the spiritual ineffectiveness of the church in the west today. Under the influence of Enlightenment thought the church largely abandoned being submissive to God's word and instead arrogated to itself the right to sit in judgement on Scripture (rather than being judged by it). Consequently God has imposed condign punishment on the church which has devalued his word. The church now finds its pronouncements ignored, its voice silenced, and its labours unavailing because in so many places all that it has left to present is an ersatz message which it has generated for itself and substituted for the whole Scriptural counsel of God. It is no longer by military means that the Lord imposes his verdict on his people, but there is the spiritual frustration of being condemned to live in a pagan-dominated society which constantly minimises the church's position and ruthlessly seeks to eradicate the legacy of its past testimony.

The way forwards, then and now, is the pathway of repentance with its recognition of past wrongdoing and its plea for divine restoration. The example for a church which has abandoned its first love is the godly grief which produces a repentance that leads to salvation without regret (2 Cor. 7:10). Paul's characterisation of the Corinthians' response to his rebuke sets the standard for other communities of the faithful who have been diverted from single-minded sincerity in following the Lord.

Lamentations does not present any trite or easy answers as to how moving back into fellowship with God may be effected. The poet might have, like Isaiah, looked for a second Exodus in which the LORD would act mightily to deliver his people. Though he does not do so, in the light of the New Testament we have a greater understanding of God's dealings with his people. The poet makes

INTRODUCTION 33

no direct mention of the coming of the Messiah, but now we can
see how the LORD's steadfast love worked itself out in the Son's
payment of the penalty of his people's sin so that the anger of God
against them may justly come to an end. Furthermore, it is now
perhaps easier to appreciate (if not to endure) God's fatherly
chastisement of those who, as his sons, are subject to his discipline
(Heb. 12:5-11).

Ultimately, the message of Lamentations calls for us to centre
our theological thinking on the character of God himself. It
confronts us with the reality of the wrath of God, and reminds us
that the tensions which arise from God's holy revulsion against sin
cannot be resolved apart from the cross of Christ. God as the divine
warrior has set himself against sin and the powers of darkness to
the extent that he wages war even against his people when they fall
into sin. It is only because Jesus Christ has defeated the enemy that
the victory has been won (1 Cor. 15:57; Col. 2:15) and reconciliation with God accomplished (Eph. 2:16; Col. 1:22).

F. Translation

The translation of Bible passages throughout this commentary is
my own except where a specific English version is identified as the
source. The style of translation I have adopted here is deliberately
wooden in an attempt to bring out certain features of the original.
The many modern renderings of Lamentations into English will
provide an interested reader with more idiomatic presentations of
the sense of the text and ought to be consulted alongside this
commentary.

It is appropriate to mention one problem which arises in trans-
lating Lamentations, and Hebrew poetry in general, because of
differences in linguistic structure between Hebrew and English.
That question relates to how the perfect form of Hebrew verbs
should be rendered. The perfect does not primarily indicate *when*
an action takes place, but rather the *mode* in which an action is
viewed. The perfect form views an action in its entirety and so
presents it as complete; the complementary form, the imperfect,
views an action as incomplete. In prose passages, appropriate
renderings for these verb forms are generally English past and
future tenses respectively, but in poetic passages there is much

greater variety. In this translation I have usually employed a present perfect rendering for potentially ambiguous uses of the Hebrew perfect form, to convey the combination of past occurrence and ongoing consequence. An instance of this is the verb, 'she has become', in 1:1. This relates to a past event, but one which still conditions the present. However, the earlier verb in 1:1 is also a perfect, but 'she has sat' does not convey adequately the present impact of this verb and a present tense is used to describe the city as having sat down in the past and consequently still remaining seated.

Lamentations 1

OUTLINE

A. Grief Observed (1:1-11)

    (1) Bitter Reversal (1:1-3)

    (2) Abandoned and Afflicted (1:4-6)

    (3) Jerusalem's Agony (1:7-9)

    (4) Despoiled and Famished (1:10-11)

B. Grief Felt (1:12-22)

    (1) Zion's Plea for Sympathy (1:12-16)

    (2) Overwhelmed by Sorrow (1:17)

    (3) Zion's Admission (1:18-19)

    (4) Zion's Plea for Divine Intervention (1:20-22)

The book of Lamentations plunges straight into its theme with a heart-wrenching presentation of the catastrophe which engulfed the city of Jerusalem in the early sixth century B.C. when it fell to the Babylonians after a prolonged siege. Once it had been ransacked, its major buildings burned, and its leading citizens deported, those who were allowed to remain had to endure the harsh conditions imposed on the people by their conquerors. The human dimension of the tragedy is emphasised by describing the despoiled city not in political, economic or architectural terms but, using the device of personification, as a widow who, having lost family and possessions, is left destitute and forlorn.

The intricacy of the portrait of Zion's grief and despair found in this poem displays to the full the artistic skill of the poet who composed it. The presentation is structured by the use of an alphabetic acrostic in which the first word of each verse begins with successive letters of the Hebrew alphabet.[19] Each verse comprises a stanza, generally of three lines each of which has two parallel cola (but see 1:1, 7). The lines are often in the imbalanced *qînâ* rhythm (three stressed syllables followed by two in the second shorter half-line), though a balanced 3:3 structure also occurs.

It is possible to detect an overall concentric structure in the stanzas of the poem. Renkema has pointed to the following carefully placed elements which combine to create this effect:[20]

1:1	full of (< *rab*)	1:22	many (< *rab*)
1:2	no one comforting … enemies	1:21	no one comforting … my enemies
1:3	distresses	1:20	distress
1:4	her priests	1:19	my priests
1:5	the LORD … have gone into captivity	1:18	the LORD … have gone into captivity
1:6	Zion	1:17	Zion
1:7	none to help … the foe	1:16	a comforter is far … the enemy
1:8	who honoured her [?]	1:15	my mighty men
1:9	LORD	1:14	the Lord
1:10	stretched out	1:13	stretched out
1:11	see … and observe	1:12	observe and see

19. This is indicated in the following translation by affixing to each verse the corresponding letter of the Hebrew alphabet.

20. Renkema, 'Literary Structure,' 296–97.

Not all of these verbal echoes are equally convincing (Renkema admits that the correspondence between 1:8 and 1:15 is particularly weak) but, taken together, these indicators validate the conclusion that the poet has deliberately deployed his material in a concentric fashion. In that case, the key theme of the poem is found at its centre (1:11-12), which Renkema terms its 'kernel', and whose message he sums up as 'God, men! Look at our misery.'[21]

However, such a literary structure analysis needs to be supplemented by one derived from thematic considerations, that is, from the content (what is said) rather than the form of the poem (its actual vocabulary and poetic structure). A key feature in thematic analysis of Lamentations is the way in which changes occur in the viewpoint of the poem when different speakers are introduced. In chapter 1, this leads to a basically similar bipartite analysis. In the first part of the poem (1:1-11) the speaker is predominantly the poet who, acting as a narrator, describes the horrendous scene before him, though there are also incorporated two sound bites from Zion in 1: 9c, 11c. In the second part of the poem the personified city of Jerusalem speaks on her own behalf, though again there is a brief change of perspective in 1:17. It should be noted, however, that the two voices do not speak to each other: the narrator addresses an unidentified audience; daughter Zion addresses those who pass by, and later God. Still there is substantial agreement between their viewpoints. Jerusalem is isolated and suffering ongoing hardship, and there is no one comforting her in her adversity (1:2, 9, 16, 17, 21; cf. 1:7).

A general bleakness of tone pervades the poem in that the series of pictures of the grief and desolation affecting the city brings out the dejection of those who have suffered such dreadful loss. Still the switch in the second half of the poem from third person to first person narrative does provide a measure of movement in the presentation. While speaking sympathetically, the narrator conceals his personal reaction and involvement. On the other hand, Zion speaks openly of her anguish and pain. This heightens the emotional impact of what is described and draws the reader further into empathising with the experience of the community.

---

21. Renkema, 'Literary Structure,' 297.

Although the LORD is addressed in the poem, he does not speak. The city lacks solace from human sources and also from God. He is silent, and it is the absence of any indication from God as to how he now views the community that casts an air of uncertainty over the whole poem. Zion's distress is compounded by the realisation that she does not know if it is possible to reestablish contact with the God who has imposed his judgement on her. What will happen next? Is there a way out of this misery? No answers are yet revealed.

Why then was the poem written? One possibility is that the intent was cathartic, an attempt to vocalise the anguish of the remaining inhabitants of Jerusalem so as to give vent to their grief, and thus perhaps assuage it. However, the careful structuring of the poem militates against it being read as simply an outpouring of sorrow. The poet is seeking to guide the community away from utter prostration and despair. His initial presentation shows that he is not engaged in blind optimism. He is not denying the horrors and the hardships experienced in the city, but the reality of where they are need not be an end but a beginning. Although he does not attempt to lighten the gloom that dominates the city, yet the very fact that there remains life of a sort amid the ruins is an anticipation of a measure of hope which will be spelled out later (3:22). Solemn though this poem is, it is not yet Zion's obituary.

A. Grief Observed (1:1-11)

(1) Bitter Reversal (1:1-3)

א 1:1   Ah, how she sits alone!
                  The city ⌐which was⌐ full of people,
                  has become like a widow.
              She ⌐who was⌐ great among the nations,
                  a princess among the provinces,
                  has become a forced labourer.

The structure of the first verse is not immediately evident. In the rest of the poem the dominant pattern is that of a verse/stanza consisting of three lines (bicola). That provides substantial justification for adopting a similar configuration here, and it is in fact found in most English translations which present a stanza consisting of three contrasting situations. However, the Massoretes, the scribes from the first millennium A.D. through whom the Hebrew text has been transmitted, marked the verse as consisting of two tricola (lines of three segments). Though the Massoretes were active much later than the date of composition of Lamentations, their views are not to be lightly dismissed since they stood in the same poetic and cultural tradition as the writer of Lamentations, and they were not innovators but deliberate conservators of the traditional understanding of passages. They evidently did not consider a divergence from the prevailing binary pattern of the chapter a great breach of poetic etiquette; indeed, they might well have viewed it as adornment. On that approach the reversal of the fortunes of the unnamed city is being described in two ways. In the first line it is the change in the size of its population which is emphasised; in the second line it is the change in its political status.

For the interpretative introductions to the verse presented by the Septuagint and the Vulgate, see *Introduction: B. Authorship.* It is improbable that these additional comments were part of the original text, because it is difficult to see why or how they would have been subsequently omitted.

The word rendered *Ah, how!* is an exclamation of shock, an incredulous gasp behind which lurks a question: how ever did this change come about? This word often introduces a dirge, a mournful poem composed as a tribute to the dead (cf. 2:1; 4:1; 2 Sam. 1:19; Isa. 1:21, a very similar passage; Jer. 48:17), and so the presentation is characterised by sadness, not criticism or attribution of blame. The situation in view here is not so much the death of the city but the devastating loss which it has suffered. It is characteristic of the poems in Lamentations that they focus on Jerusalem rather than the land of Judah as a whole. At this point, however, the poet has not yet disclosed the identity of the city.

Sits/'has sat down and so remains sitting'[22] on the ground was a static posture often adopted by one grieving (cf. 2:10; 3:16; Gen. 23:2; 2 Sam. 12:16; 13:31; Ezek. 26:16; Est. 4:3), but here more is implied in that *alone* alludes to the phrase, 'he will sit/dwell alone',

---

22. For the rendering of the perfect verb 'sits', see *Introduction: F. Translation.*

which is used in Lev. 13:46 of the leper. The city is presented as ostracised from the community of nations. It is a scene of passivity and dejection as she remains where she has already collapsed on the ground. Possibly there is also a touch of ironic contrast in that 'alone' might also be used to imply security (cf. Deut. 33:28; Jer. 49:31). Jerusalem no longer enjoys freedom from aggression, but is desolate and isolated.

The fact that the community in grief is pictured as a woman implies a link between communal reactions to suffering and those of an individual. The personification is not merely a poetic fancy, but a device which links the experience of the community with that of each grief-stricken individual within it. Also, the personification of the city as a mother emphasises the relationship between it and its inhabitants. It is a metropolis, a mother city (cf. 'her young women', 1:4; 'her young children', 1:5; 'her people', 1:7). Such female personification of the city was common throughout the ancient Near East.

Although it is possible to take the phrase *full of people*/'great (< *rab*, 'many'; cf. 1:22) with people' as indicating 'a superior among her own people' that is, an illustrious capital city,[23] there is much to be said for the traditional understanding which identifies the contrast as between the city's present isolation and her former thronged state. Indeed, she *has become like a widow*. There are three implications in this comparison which builds on the metaphor of the city as a woman.[24] Though 'widow' does not imply absence of family, it is often associated with it. So this metaphor points to the loneliness and misery of one who has lost her husband. Associated with this is the vulnerability of a widow who no longer has a legal protector, but lives precariously, open to exploitation by the unthinking and the unscrupulous (cf. Ps. 94:6; Mal. 3:5). Additionally, the figure of a widow evokes a response of pity, unlike the language of divorce where the underlying accusation of unfaithfulness leads to the attribution of blame (cf. Hos. 2:2).

---

23. Cf. Th. F. McDaniel, 'Philological Studies in Lamentations,' *Biblica* 49 (1968): 29–31.

24. For further details on the use of this metaphor in relation to cities, see Chayim Cohen, 'The "Widowed" City,' *Journal of the Ancient Near Eastern Society of Columbia University* 5 (1973): 75–81.

It is difficult to decide how far the simile 'like a widow' should be pressed. The thought may simply be general: the ruined city is defenceless and the population required to rebuild her and effect a recovery no longer exists. But it is at least possible to raise the question: if the city is likened to a widow, who might her husband have been? A case may be made for the analogy being worked out in terms of the king and the leaders of the community as her husband, and they were, of course, now dead, captives or fugitives (cf. 1:6). But the use by Hosea and later by Jeremiah of the breakdown of marriage as an analogy for the deterioration of the relationship between the LORD and his people (cf. Jer. 3:8; Hos. 2:2) makes it probable that here (and later on throughout the poem) it is her relationship with the LORD that underlies the poet's probing and her own questioning of her status and present condition. Hence the comparison, '*like* a widow'. The LORD is not indeed dead, but the outcome seems no different from what would prevail if he were, because the city no longer enjoys the benefits of a protective and caring relationship with him. This note of uncertainty as to where the city now stands before God recurs throughout the book right up to its concluding verse (5:21).

The second line of 1:1 employs two similarly structured epithets for Jerusalem. The city had formerly enjoyed the status of being **great among the nations**, a phrase which might well be the Hebrew equivalent of a superlative. This may look back to the days of David and Solomon, or to the resurgence of the kingdoms of Israel and Judah under Jeroboam II and Uzziah respectively. It may even cover the measure of independence Judah enjoyed in the century before her fall, when surrounding nations acknowledged that Judah played a key role in the affairs of the region (for example, it was in Jerusalem that ambassadors of other nations gathered for the conference recorded in Jer. 27). As the capital of the kingdom, Jerusalem enjoyed prestige and respect from the smaller nations around her.

The term **princess** does convey the idea of exercising authority, and therefore the **provinces** will not be those of the Assyrian or Babylonian empire but areas of Judah controlled from the capital. There were also other territories which had come under the sway of Jerusalem for longer or shorter periods and, when it functioned as an administrative centre, wealth and resources flowed into the capital.

But that has all gone. Jerusalem's fortunes have been reversed and the city is a *forced labourer*. The capital, like other conquered territories, is compelled to pay tribute and provide compulsory labour for her conquerors. The city has moved from royal status to slavery.

ב 1:2   Bitterly she weeps in the night,
          and her tear ⌐is⌐ on her cheek.
      She has no one comforting ⌐her⌐
          among all her lovers.
      All her friends have dealt treacherously with her;
          they have become her enemies.

The presentation of Jerusalem's situation zooms in from a distant view of a despondent figure sitting on the ground, and now we can see how wretched she is because her face is wet with her forlorn tears. *In the night* suggests that her grief was so intense that daytime alone was insufficient to express it and the time normally allotted to sleep and recuperation had also to be used for mourning.

The middle line of the verse shows that the intensity of Zion's anguish is increased by a lack of sympathy. This theme recurs throughout the poem: the absence of one bringing comfort (cf. 1:9, 16, 17, 21; note also the expression in 1:7). 'Comfort' is extended to others in time of sorrow and bereavement. It is an act of sympathy in which words and also, on occasion, presence express encouragement to one undergoing difficult circumstances (cf. Job 2:11). The narrator and Zion herself agree that the absence of comforting words has heightened Zion's misery. While comfort may not usually be extended by strangers, the situation is different here in that mention is made of *all her lovers* (cf. Jer. 4:30; 30:14). It is not clear whether this is a political term for the nations with whom Judah had entered into an anti-Babylonian alliance (cf. Ezek. 16:33),[25] or whether the word has religious overtones in connection with the pagan gods she had worshipped (cf. Hos. 2:5). In terms of the issues raised in the poem and the book the latter is less likely,

---

25. Cf J. A. Thompson, 'Israel's "lovers",' *Vetus Testamentum* 27 (1977): 475–481.

but both are in reality linked because alliance with foreign powers often entailed dalliance with their gods. This hints at another theme of the book: Zion's faithlessness. Her policy had been to turn to others rather than relying on the LORD (cf. Isa. 30:1-7; 31:1-4), and so she is not an innocent victim of a catastrophic accident. Zion's misery was the consequence of divine judgement on her rebellious conduct.

The use of *all* in the last two lines of the verse is a feature of the poem occurring sixteen times to emphasise the devastating totality of Zion's experience (found also in 1:3, 4, 6, 7, 8, 10, 11, 12, 13, 15, 18, 21, 22). She cannot discern any ray of light in the gloom of her depression.

Zion is suffering from more than the absence of her former allies and erstwhile supporters. *All her friends* she used to have *treacherously* failed to live up to the undertakings they had entered into. 'Treachery' is used of perfidious behaviour in connection with marital infidelity (Jer. 3:20), betrayal by family and associates (Jer. 12:6) or break up of a political relationship (Judg. 9:13). Not only did her former allies fail to provide comfort to Zion in her distress, they had been actively ranged against her. This animosity was particularly exhibited by the Edomites (cf. 4:21; 5:2) who had attended the Jerusalem conference (Jer. 27:3) but who were not slow to annex Judean territory after the Babylonian victory. Zion was isolated, abandoned, and exploited.

ג 1:3   Judah has gone into exile from affliction
             and from an abundance of servitude.
       She is dwelling among the nations;
             she has not found a resting place.
       All who pursue her have overtaken her
             in the midst of distresses.

The presentation now zooms out to include the whole nation of *Judah*, which is also personified as a woman. The verb *has gone into exile* comes from a root meaning 'to uncover', 'to lay bare', and its use has traditionally been explained as arising from the perception that when people migrate from their land they expose it to the enemy. There is difficulty in connecting the verb with the following phrases, *from affliction and from an abundance of servitude.* 'Affliction' refers to mental or physical anguish, generally caused by an adversary's hostile action, whether in open warfare or by oppressive acts in occupied territory. 'Abundance of servitude' shows that, while the people allowed to stay in the land were not technically slaves, they were virtually so because the occupying forces imposed many burdens on them. Terms from the same roots had been used in connection with the oppression in Egypt before the Exodus (cf. Gen. 15:13; Exod. 1:11-13; Deut. 26:6), and the thought is that similar circumstances had returned.

It is, however, the significance of the repeated preposition 'from' which is problematic. If the exile referred to is that imposed by the Babylonians, 'from' can hardly be equivalent to 'away from' because conditions in Babylonia still involved hardship and forced labour. It might be employed in an instrumental sense 'through', 'by means of': Judah has gone into exile through affliction and enslavement. But the fact that in Lamentations the expression used for the experience of enforced deportation is 'captivity' (< *šābâ*, cf. 1:5, 18), not 'exile' (< *gālâ*), opens up the possibility that this reference is to refugees escaping to other lands to avoid Babylonian rule (a sense possibly found in 2 Sam. 15:19; Ezek. 12:3). Another option is that 'from' is used in a temporal sense, 'after' (cf. NIV), and that the reference is to the previous troubled and insecure twenty-five years of Egyptian and Babylon invasion and control.[26] Most probably, this last possibility ought to be adopted: after a distressing period of foreign interference and invasion Judah's circumstances have not got better, but worse, because now her people have been forced to leave their land.

If the first line of the verse talks of the people of Judah deported from their land, then they are viewed subsequently as *dwelling*/

---

26. A further option is that suggested by Renkema (*Lamentations*, 107–8). He changes the pointing of the verb from *gālətâ* to pual form *gullətâ*, and takes the sense from the primary meaning of the root as Judah has been 'stripped'/'laid bare' like a woman humiliated and exposed because of enemy oppression. Though this yields a plausible sense in this context, it does involve changing the vowels of the existing text. It is generally the case that it is preferable to retain the Massoretic pointing when an appropriate sense can be derived from it.

'sitting' (the same form as in 1:1)[27] *among the nations* (cf. 2:9), scattered wherever they were directed to go. They have been deprived of *a resting place*, which the land would have provided for them. In the covenant curse upon disobedience the LORD had warned that the people would be scattered among the nations and that 'there would be no resting place for the sole of your foot' (Deut. 28:65).

Pursue and *overtake* picture marauding armies going throughout Judah and surrounding territories to capture groups of people seeking refuge and rounding them up for deportation. *Distresses* is a plural form denoting the intense anxiety of a constricting, life-threatening situation (cf. 'the distresses of Sheol', Ps. 116:3; or a time of national attack, Ps. 118:5).[28] Judah experienced terrible conditions during and after the Babylonian invasion, and there was no possibility of escape.

(2) Abandoned and Afflicted (1:4-6)

¶ 1:4   The ways to Zion are in mourning
            because no one is coming to the appointed
                festivals.
         All her gates are desolate;
            her priests are groaning.
         Her young women are grief-stricken,
            and, ⌊as for⌋ herself, her lot is bitter.

Zion is named for the first time. This designation emphasises the religious significance of the city as the place where the Temple was located and the worship of the LORD was focused, 'my holy hill' (Ps. 2:6), 'the mountain where God has desired to dwell, ⌊where⌋

---

27. In 'dwells now' (ESV) the 'now' is a translator's supplement to bring out the ongoing force of the perfect verb: she has sat down and remains sitting. Hillers advocates taking the perfect as a true past, 'She dwelled among the nations' as an independent state (cf. 4:20), but did not enjoy the blessings associated with the land (*Lamentations*, 66–67).

28. The allusion to the circumstances of the Exodus makes plausible an intended play here between 'distresses' (*məṣārîm*) and 'Egypt' (*miṣrayim*). No longer is divine deliverance to be found from the Egypt of her distress, but further misery will overwhelm her because those pursuing her have caught her.

the LORD will indeed reside continually' (Ps. 68:16). So at this
juncture the poet highlights the cultic impact of the catastrophe
which had befallen the city: the worship of the sanctuary has been
abandoned. *The ways to Zion* are the roads by which ordinary
worshippers and the priests in their courses would go to the city. In
a fine example of personification the empty roads are said to *be in
mourning*, observing the behaviour customary at a time of bereavement, here probably referring to an absence of activity rather than
to giving vent to emotion in dirges and wailing. This was especially
evident at the three times in the year when *the appointed festivals*
were held, and the population of the land would go to Jerusalem to
worship at the Temple. That no longer takes place; the roads are
deserted.

The ways led to the gates, either those of the city or those of the
Temple, with the latter giving access to the courtyards surrounding
it. The city gates would normally be a bustle of activity as they
were the site for transaction of official and commercial business;
the Temple gates would be thronged by pilgrims. Instead, in a
further personification (cf. Isa. 3:26), it is said that the *gates are
desolate*, a term with several aspects.[29] Objectively, it can refer to a
settlement being destroyed and rendered uninhabitable. Subject-
ively, it also refers to the human reaction of being appalled at
witnessing such devastation. In English, 'desolate' comes close to
conveying both the idea of abandonment and absence of people and
that of being made utterly sad and wretched. It seems the Temple
gates are particularly in view, because the parallel colon points out
that *her priests are groaning*. They had subscribed to the popular
belief, if indeed they had not propagated it, that while the Temple
stood the city would be inviolate.[30] The Babylonians did not generally destroy the temples of conquered nations, and they would
probably not have done so with the Jerusalem Temple had it not
become such a symbol of national intransigence and resistance. The
priests express their misery at the devastation which had been
wrought. Not only was their income lost and their daily routine
disrupted, but their cherished hopes for the land and the outworking
of God's purposes in their midst had been shattered.

29. šômēmîn, 'desolate', has an Aramaic style ending in *n*, cf. *tannîn* in 4:3.
30. See *Introduction*, page 26.

Young women represents a term often translated 'virgin' (cf. 1:15), but that usually is too specific a rendering. It refers to girls of marriageable age who are as yet unmarried, and is coordinated with 'my young men' in 1:18. While the young women would not be official Temple personnel, they customarily engaged in singing and dancing at the festal gatherings (cf. Ps. 68:25). But now instead of the intense joy of such occasions, they are *grief-stricken*, an ongoing condition.[31] Elsewhere in the book (1:5, 12; 3:32, 33) the root is used of the LORD bringing grief through inflicting adverse circumstances, and it may well be that is implied here also. It is not just the absence of times of rejoicing which causes them distress, but the fact that this calamity had been divinely imposed.

The focus switches from the particular to the general. As for the city herself, that is the population as a whole, *her lot is bitter* (literally, 'bitter to her'). For the city as feminine, see on 1:1, 6. This is the destiny of the community which has offended the covenant King and is consequently experiencing the penalty he imposes for misconduct. 'The sound of the day of the LORD will be bitter' (Zeph. 1:14; cf. Amos 8:10).

ה 1:5   Her foes have become the head;
        her enemies are at ease,
        for the LORD has brought grief on her
        because of the abundance of her rebellions.
        Her young children have gone
        ᴸintoᴸ captivity before the foe.

The condition of the city (referred to five times by 'her') is in marked contrast to that of her powerful conquerors. *Her foes have become the head* may well reflect the reversal envisaged in the covenant curse, 'he will be the head, but you will be the tail'(Deut. 28:44). Since their triumph has put them in military and administrative control, the new masters of the land feel unthreatened and *are at ease.* How could anyone effectively resist Babylon?

---

31. An ESV footnote records that the Septuagint and the Old Latin read *dragged away.* This reflects a form such as *nāhûgôt*, from *nāhag* (I), 'to drive off, lead away' (cf. 3:2). The MT *nûgôt*, a niphal participle from *yāgâ*, 'to grieve', is an unusual form, but, as the more difficult reading, it should be retained.

It was, however, more than Babylon and Nebuchadnezzar who were active in the situation. The poet provides a theological commentary on what has occurred, and in doing so discloses that he accepts the accuracy of Jeremiah's warnings. 'A leopard is watching over their cities; everyone going out from them will be torn apart, for their rebellions are many, their backslidings are numerous' (Jer. 5:6; cf. Jer. 7:12-15; 14:10; 21:14). The real enemy of Zion who had determined her lot was none other than the LORD himself (cf. 2:5); he had brought this disaster upon his city. So what had happened was not a sign of divine weakness or lack of concern, but proof of the LORD's commitment to the standards of his covenant. He had clearly warned the people about the dire consequences of infringing the covenant. **Brought grief** reflects 'grief-struck' in the previous verse. **Rebellions**/'acts of rebellion' was initially a political term, but it is used metaphorically in the religious sphere to refer to deliberate violations of the statutes of the covenant, actions which cannot be regarded as momentary aberrations or easily rectified mistakes. There is no specification as to how the people had rebelled because they knew very well what had gone wrong, and the poet's focus is on the grievous consequences of their behaviour. The link between their guilt and their continuing suffering is further explored in 1:8, 14, 18. Still the fact that this negative exercise of the LORD's covenant jurisdiction accounts for their current condition at least leaves open the possibility that he might reverse the situation in the future (cf. Deut. 30:1-10).

The third line of the verse further reflects on the appalling catastrophe which had come upon the city in that it had been emptied of **her young children**. Although this term elsewhere occurs along with infants (cf. 2:11), here it stands on its own, and so may refer to youngsters aged between five and ten years. They have not been spared the agonies of the city's fall (cf. 2:11-12, 19-20; 4:4), but have been rounded up as slaves. When they are taken into exile, the future of the city goes with them because they are sent **into captivity before the foe**. This too was part of the curse that fell on the community because of their covenant rebellion (cf. Deut. 28:36, 63-68). The scene evokes sympathy: but was there divine sympathy? Can the suffering and grief which the LORD had brought on his people be all that they are to expect from him in the future?

א 1:6   And[32] there has departed from daughter Zion
         all her splendour.
         Her rulers have become like deer;
         they have not found pasture,
         and have gone without strength
         before the pursuer.

The term **daughter Zion** refers to the city itself. The older rendering 'daughter of Zion' suggested that there are two parties mentioned, Zion and her daughter, whereas more recent opinion favours understanding the nouns as being in apposition so that both refer to the population as a whole. 'Daughter' is not used in its primary sense, but more broadly as 'young woman', and has overtones of affection and sympathy. The idiom is part of a widespread personification for a city or a land in female terms (cf. Isa. 23:10, 12; Jer. 50:42; 51:33),[33] and in Lamentations it additionally serves to make clear the nature of the metaphor used to describe the city. The focus is not on the physical destruction of the buildings of the city but on the personal, individual sufferings of its citizens. Daughter Zion may be more appropriate as a collective term for the people as a worshipping community, whereas daughter Jerusalem looks more to their political and social identity.

Everything that contributed to the standing of the community, **all her splendour**, no longer exists. 'Splendour' may be used to refer to the LORD himself (Pss. 29:4; 104:1; 111:3), and here what is in view is primarily what his presence had contributed to the significance of the city. This had centred on the Temple, but it now lay in ruins (cf. 4:1) because the LORD's glory had departed from his house and his city (cf. Ezek. 9:3, 10:19; 11:23).

---

32. As remarked by Hillers, *Lamentations*, 67, the initial *waw*, 'and', is awkward since there is no close connection with what precedes. It has arisen from the need to conform to the pattern of the alphabetic acrostic. *Waw* is similarly employed in 2:6; 3:16-18; 4:6 because very few Hebrew words begin with that letter.

33. Twenty of the 45 occurrences of a phrase involving 'daughter of ...' occur in Lamentations, and 16 of the others are to be found in Jeremiah. It was, however, a long-standing idiom, being also found earlier in Micah and Isaiah (e.g. Isa. 1:8; 52:2; 62:11; Micah 1:13; 4:10). The earliest occurrence is in Ps. 9:14.

While *her rulers* might include 'princes' in the modern sense of members of the royal family, the primary reference is to the influential figures who formed part of the civil or military administration in the city (cf. 4:4-5). *Deer* ordinarily pictures effortless ease and speed of movement, but here there is a contrast with what might be expected because these deer *have not found pasture*. They are sickly and emaciated, just as even the prominent citizens of Jerusalem had become during the intense siege (cf. 1:11; Jer. 14:3). So, though they desperately tried to escape, they were *without strength*, and unable to evade the pursuing Babylonian hunters. They were captured, and either executed or deported.

(3) Jerusalem's Agony (1:7-9)

▼ 1:7   Jerusalem remembers[34]
              ⌊in⌋ the days of her affliction and wanderings
          all her precious things
              which were ⌊hers⌋ from days of old.
          When her people fell into the hand of the foe
              and there was none to help her,
          her foes saw her;
              they mocked at her downfall.

Since Lamentations was written while Jerusalem was still experiencing distress, it is appropriate to take *the days of her affliction and wanderings* as a temporal phrase rather than as the object of the city's remembering. 'Wanderings' (cf. 3:19)[35] may well be set against a background of homelessness where her destitute people have been forced to scatter in various directions as they seek shelter. 'Affliction' (cf. 1:3) takes its sense from its context. It may

---

34. The perfect of verbs of mental perception regularly conveys the idea of present awareness.

35. The word *mərûdeyhā* has been variously understood. It occurs three times (here; 3:19; Isa. 58:7). 'Bitterness' (RSV) substitutes a second *rēsh* for the *dāleth*, and identifies the root as *mārar*, 'to be bitter', but that is unnecessary. Derivation from *rûd* would imply a wandering that is imposed on an individual, frequently associated with poverty and homelessness. The plural noun is one of intensity, and the combination 'her affliction and wanderings' is a hendiadys (a figure of speech in which one thought is expressed by two coordinated terms) for 'her miserable wanderings'.

be the misery endured by widows and orphans (Isa. 10:2) or, more
generally, of those deprived of necessities including a home (Isa.
58:7). Spiritually, being bowed down by affliction should lead to a
greater sense of dependence on the LORD. Here this is additionally
motivated by remembrance of *all the precious things* which he had
formerly bestowed on her. The term is used again in 2:4 to denote
material possessions (but note 1:10, 11). Probably in this verse it
focuses on the Temple and the palace complex at the heart of the
city which constituted such a major part of her splendour (cf. Ps.
48:3, 13-15).

But when the city remembers the heritage she previously
enjoyed, this only serves to throw into more stark relief her recent
trauma. When the foe attacked, Zion was left without assistance.
There was none to help her is a variation of the refrain first found
in 1:2. At a political level this applied to her allies' failure to rescue
her from Babylonian aggression (cf. 4:17), but crucially it was the
support of the LORD which had been missing. Zion had confidently
expected that God would help her in her difficulties ('God will help
her at the break of day', Ps. 46:6). However, since her conduct had
effectively undermined her covenant claim on the LORD for
protection, there had been no last minute intervention. As a result
her foes saw her exposed in her weakness, and poured scorn on the
claims that she had previously made regarding her God. Her
downfall/'cessation'[36] was witnessed by her enemies, and their
mockery intensified Zion's misery (cf. 1:21; 2:16; 3:46, 61-63;
5:1).

This verse consists of four lines, and not three as is the norm in
the poem. This has led commentators to suggest that either the second or the third line is a marginal comment which at some stage
has been wrongly incorporated into the text. Yet the early textual
traditions support the verse as it is. However much it may offend
our notions of the regularity which should characterise poetic patterns, it does seem that ancient poets felt free to incorporate such
an elaboration as an ornamentation of their basic structure (cf.
2:19). Renkema suggests that such a conscious irregularity of style
was selected to give literary expression to the way in which the

36. The root of 'downfall' (*mišbāt*) is the same as that in Sabbath (*šabbāt*),
and hence the rendering of 'Sabbaths' in the Vulgate and AV.

LORD's behaviour had knocked Zion off balance.[37]

ח 1:8   Sinned grievously has Jerusalem;
              therefore she has become impure.
          All who honoured her have despised her,
              for they have seen her nakedness.
          She herself also has groaned
              and turned backwards.

The poet interposes into the description of Jerusalem's agony and
shame an explanation for her suffering. No argument is advanced to
justify this assertion; it is presented as agreed and accepted. **Sinned
grievously** is literally 'a sin she sinned', and points to grave failure
to achieve a norm, either by deficiency or excess, resulting in
injury to the interests of a person or community. Whereas 'rebellion' (1:5) focused on their relationship with the LORD, 'sin' is a
more comprehensive term in that it also includes the impact of their
misconduct on one another. However, in the case of the covenant
people such disorder in society was ultimately a matter of failure to
match the norms that the LORD had stated for them and so infringed
on his majesty and authority. Zion's downfall is presented as the
result not of confrontation with superior military force, but of
God's reaction to her breach of his covenant standards.

The consequence of her sin (**therefore** = 'on account of that')
was that she became **impure**. There are several possibilities regarding the translation of this word which occurs only here. It may be
derived from a root meaning 'to move about' or 'to shake', and so
could mean either 'she wanders' (cf. LXX, AV) or, in reference to
the gesture of nodding the head to and fro in scorn (cf. Ps. 44:10;
Jer. 48:27), 'she has become a mockery', an object of derision (cf.
NRSV). Alternatively, the word may be a variant spelling of a term
meaning 'menstrual impurity' (cf. 1:17; cf. ESV, NIV, RSV).
Whereas 'a mockery' would look back to the previous verse,
'impure' fits in with the following description, and is marginally

37. Renkema, *Lamentations*, 132. For a different justification for retaining
the four lines of 1:7 based on syllable counts, see D. N. Freedman, 'Acrostics
and Metrics in Hebrew Poetry,' *Harvard Theological Review* 65 (1972): 367–
92. For a discussion favouring elimination of one of the lines, see Hillers,
Lamentations, 68–69.

more probable.[38] But an additional allusion to expressions of contempt should not be excluded.

All who honoured her probably refers to the city's former political allies who had acknowledged her prestige and accorded her respect (cf. 1:2). *Despised* comes from a root meaning 'to be of little value, to be contemptible' (cf. 1:11). Her former allies have treated her as no longer having any significance or influence, and have written her off as a thing of the past because *they have seen her nakedness*. At a personal level such exposure was a source of utter shame and disgrace, especially for women in the ancient world (cf. Ezek. 16:37; Hos. 2:3). Applied at a metaphorical level to Jerusalem as a community, the nakedness of the land reveals its weakness and vulnerability to attack (cf. Gen. 42:9, 12). In that it is imposed by the LORD himself, it is a punitive and shaming sanction on the land for its misconduct. The description is similar to that of the fate awaiting daughter Babylon in Isaiah 47:3: 'Your nakedness will be uncovered; also your shame will be seen. I will take vengeance and I will spare no one.'

As well as the reaction of Jerusalem's enemies to her degradation and abuse, *also* introduces the fact that her recent experience has undermined her self-image (cf. 1:11). In her dejection at her state all she can do is to *groan* (cf. 1:4) in her misery and *turn backwards*. In this way she avoids having to endure their disdainful looks at her condition.

ט 1:9   Her uncleanness was in her skirts;
        she did not remember her future.
    So she has come down appallingly;
        there is no one comforting her.
    'See, O LORD, my affliction,
        for the enemy has triumphed!'

---

38. (1) The noun *nîdâ* might be derived from the root *nûd* in the sense 'to shake the head'. (2) The LXX and the medieval Jewish rabbi Rashi identify it as coming from the same root, but in the sense 'to wander'. (3) Taking the noun as a byform equivalent to *niddâ* (or indeed changing the text to that form, though this is less likely) yields 'unclean'/ 'impure', that is, a menstruating woman. This is reflected in Aquila, Symmachus, and the Peshitta, and is favoured by many modern translations.

Based on the figure of the city as a woman, *uncleanness* refers to her menstrual flow. She has been so taken up with the circumstances affecting her that she has become forgetful of her appearance and has not noticed that *her skirts*, the lower parts of her clothing, had become stained. Such ritual impurity led others to avoid contact with her. It has been argued that this is a typically priestly analysis of Jerusalem's downfall, and therefore has its provenance elsewhere than Jeremiah, but that is based on an unwarranted degree of division between prophetic and priestly circles. All who truly acknowledged the LORD respected every aspect of his covenant law.

Jerusalem had lived as if there were no tomorrow, no time in which she would be called to account for her behaviour. So she had acted irresponsibly without caring about what would happen next. *Remember* seems an unusual choice with respect to the future, but the verb can be used in an extended sense of calling to mind and acting appropriately (cf. Isa. 47:7; Eccl. 11:8). *Her future* (literally, 'her end') is not simply a matter of the interplay of impersonal forces; it is the outcome determined by the LORD (cf. Amos 8:10; Jer. 5:31). Jerusalem had latched on to the blessings of the covenant and the expected day of the LORD without realising the blessings were conditioned on obedience, and had suppressed in her mind the fact that curse would follow disobedience. Her thoughtless insensitivity had set in train the events which led to her downfall.

As a consequence of her reckless conduct, *she has come down* from her position of prestige and favour. *Appallingly*/'amazingly' renders an ironic use of a term usually employed for extraordinary displays of divine power, particularly those associated with the LORD's saving intervention on behalf of his people (cf. Exod. 15:11; Pss. 77:11, 14; 89:5). But here there are no positive associations. It was true that what the LORD did was not what they had expected, but it was destruction he had imposed, not salvation. Furthermore the disaster which came on them was unmitigated. *There is no one comforting her* (cf. 1:2), not just from among her lovers, but the LORD himself was absent also.

There then follows a sound bite in which Jerusalem herself is heard speaking, and we are reminded that we are not discussing an impersonal tragedy. In her anguish she can at first stir herself only briefly as she directs her prayer to God. She knows that the LORD himself is the only one who can reverse the judgement which he has imposed on her and mitigate her intolerable pain; so in a plea for comfort and help she implores him to see *my affliction*. For 'affliction', see on 1:7. The collocation of the imperative 'see' and a vocative, 'LORD', is a feature of Lamentations (cf. 1:11, 20; 2:20). It expresses the extremity of Jerusalem's condition in which the urgency of her situation makes for forceful speech as she pleads on the basis of her unbearable anguish, not her merit. The LORD is one who responds to the cry of the needy (cf. Exod. 2:23; Judg. 2:18; Pss. 22:5; 81:8; 107), and he has promised his help in time of trouble (Pss. 50:15; 91:15). There is no doubt about Zion being in trouble because *the enemy has triumphed*/'become great'. Surely the LORD cannot let that situation continue. Was it not true in the past that 'the LORD was moved to pity by their groaning because of those who afflicted and oppressed them' (Judg. 2:18)?

(4) Despoiled and Famished (1:10-11)

﹅   1:10   The foe has stretched out his hand
               over all her precious things,
            for she has seen ⌊how⌋ nations
               have entered her sanctuary,
            those of whom you commanded:
               they shall not enter your assembly.

Despite Zion's outburst, the narrator's voice continues in an apparently neutral tone as he elaborates in verses 10 and 11 on the people's misery, first through the depredations and sacrilege of the enemy, and then through the impact of famine.

The focus is first on the way in which, contrary to the popular belief that the LORD had unconditionally guaranteed the security of Jerusalem, the enemy had in fact *stretched out his hand* to grasp the wealth of the city as it was plundered and its sacred places violated. Elsewhere we are provided with lists of the official booty carried off to Babylon (2 Kgs. 25:13-17), but *all her precious things* (cf. 1:7) extends beyond what was looted from the Temple and the palace to include the jewellery and personal effects of the inhabitants of the city.

Here again the dominant concern is the religious dimension of the invasion. **Nations**, that is, heathen nations, **entered her sanctuary**/'holy place'. The reference is to the Temple, not just the outer courtyards but right into the heart of the complex, the Holy of Holies (cf. Jer. 51:51). This was not just an affront to the conquered people; it was a violation of the express command of the LORD. Moabites and Ammonites had been forbidden ever to enter the assembly of the LORD (Deut. 23:3), and there may well have been contingents from these nations present during the sack of Jerusalem. There was also a two-generation ban on Edomites and Egyptians doing so (Deut. 23:7-8). Possibly these are specific instances of, and qualifications of, a general outright ban — and if that was so for the sacred assembly in the outer courts of the Temple, how much more so for the inner sanctuary where only the priests might enter. Moreover the outrage was compounded by the fact that the entry in view here is not that of those intending to worship, but of those who have come to pillage.

ב 1:11 All her people are groaning,
  as they are seeking bread.
 They have given their precious things for food
  to revive their life.
 'See, O LORD, and observe,
  for I have become worthless.'

In addition to the shame and perplexity of the community, there is now mention of a theme which will recur extensively — the gnawing, weakening impact of famine on the populace (e.g. in 2:11; 4:10; 5:9-10). Even though food would have been stockpiled in anticipation of Nebuchadnezzar's siege, its protracted nature meant that severe famine conditions had prevailed within the city before it fell (cf. Jer. 37:21). But the focus here is on the aftermath of the siege. The intolerable conditions persisted; relief supplies were unknown. It was ongoing misery under which the people were **groaning** (cf. 1:4). Life was an unremitting search for **bread**, which here stands for food in general. The city gates might be open, but the surrounding land had been devastated by the invading armies, and the farm labourers had been slain or enslaved. An agricultural economy would take years to recover from such an invasion. But it was not just a matter of economics. Famine was theologically significant; it was a sign of God's displeasure and his withdrawal of support (cf. Jer. 24:10; Ezek. 7:15; 14:13; Amos 4:6).

In the chaotic conditions after the capture of the city some may have been spared the full extent of enemy pillaging, or they may have managed to hide their wealth more successfully. They would need all their gold, silver and jewels to purchase anything in the rampant inflation and scarcity which would prevail after the fall of the city. Though the term *precious things* (cf. 1:7, 10)[39] may be used with a personal reference (Ezek. 24:16; Hos. 9:16), the description is unlikely to be of the sale of children for food. For a potential purchaser children would be just more mouths to feed, and the Babylonians could have enslaved any they wanted. Material wealth is the only currency in such disastrous conditions. *Revive* ('to cause to turn back') might also be rendered 'prolong'. The picture is of an emaciated population which is barely alive and which has to use whatever resources remained to them to satisfy their overwhelming need for food.

Against this background the poet again lets Jerusalem speak for herself as she pleads with the same intense expression as is found in 1:9, 'See, O LORD'. To the request *see*, there is added *observe*, which is often a synonym of 'see' (cf. 5:1), but especially in the combination found here it conveys the thought of more penetrating observation, of paying close attention, probably with a view to action. A possible background for this plea is to be found in the saying of Habakkuk, 'Your eyes are too pure to see evil, and you cannot observe wrongdoing' (Hab. 1:11), where vision and observation imply toleration or even sanction. Surely then if the LORD really took cognisance of what was happening in Zion, he could not approve of it.

In calling for the LORD's scrutiny and action, Zion repeats the verb 'despised' from 1:8, but now it is not in a form that expresses the negative evaluation of others regarding the city. Here we have her own self-evaluation as she looks at herself with loathing. She is

---

39. The qere substitutes *maḥămaddêhem* for the kethibh *maḥămôdêhem*. This would align the spelling with that found in 1:10, but there was yet another spelling, *maḥămudeyhâ*, in 1:7. Possibly there are two words involved, *maḥmād* (the more common) and *maḥmōd*, but there is no discernible difference in their meaning.

no longer able to function as she once did, but has *become worth-less*. She recognises that she has squandered her resources and opportunities, and considers herself to have become of little value, a nobody. It is her consequent misery and need that she wishes the LORD to see; perhaps they will induce him to act in mercy.

We note that there is no third voice in this presentation. The LORD does not reply. He has withdrawn his presence from the city.

Reflection

* Zion's ruin and despair were such that mourning is an activity which permeates the setting of Lamentations (cf. later 2:10). The sadness to which the city gave expression was not merely a consequence of physical deprivation and pain. Zion was the community of God's people on earth. Their experience of joy was ultimately derived from worshipping the LORD in the Temple as they offered sacrifice and praise to him (Pss. 42:4; 122:1). The obverse experience of grief was intensified by the loss of spiritual access to the LORD, which was made physically very obvious by the destruction of their appointed place of worship, the Temple. They could no longer gather together there to worship him and, when they did pray to God, they were not aware of any answer (cf. Ps. 28:1). How presumptuous they had been when life was easy! How deep their dismay now that God had hidden his face (cf. Ps. 30:6-7)! While Christians are not immune from circumstances in life which naturally engender heartache and distress, yet their grieving ought always to be markedly different from that of the world because of the hope which is theirs in Christ Jesus (1 Thess. 4:13).

* Impurity (1:8) and uncleanness (1:9) are not terms which ordinarily figure in our religious thinking. They derive from the ritual laws associated with Israel's sanctuary but, though that now seems to be part of a bygone era, these regulations illus-trated vital spiritual truth. Initially they dealt with the need for physical purity and cleanness on the part of those who would participate in the worship of the LORD who was present at the sanctuary. Physical purity symbolised the need for spiritual purity in those who would worship the LORD. Defilement rendered individuals unfit to come into the sanctuary, and in an

extended sense it made the people unfit to remain in the promised land for it too belonged to the LORD. 'You shall not render unclean the land in which you are staying, in the midst of which I am dwelling, for I the LORD am dwelling in the midst of the people of Israel' (Num. 35:34). Sin, especially the worship of idols, polluted the land (cf. Jer. 3:9; 16:18; Ezek. 36:17-18). For the impact of such defilement on the original inhabitants of Canaan, see Leviticus 18:24-28. Psalm 106:34-41 sets out how as a result of Israel's misconduct the LORD handed them over to the nations and let their foes rule them.

• The basic principles are still the same. God cannot tolerate moral impurity, and his people, as the temple of the living God, must separate themselves from such defilement if they are to enjoy his welcome and serve him acceptably (cf. 2 Cor. 6:14–7:1; 1 John 3:3).

• The ministry of extending comfort and consolation is one which is patterned after the activity of 'the Father of mercies and God of all comfort, who comforts us in all our affliction, so that we may be able to comfort those who are in any affliction, with the comfort with which we ourselves are comforted by God' (2 Cor. 1:3b-4). It is specifically as the 'Father of our Lord Jesus Christ' that he does so, because spiritual solace is founded on the salvation achieved by the Son and made real to believers by the Holy Spirit. This 'comfort of the Holy Spirit' (Acts 9:31) may come through divine ordering of events, including the use of individuals as the channels to convey blessing, for instance, as Paul was comforted by the coming of Titus (2 Cor. 7:6). It may also be generated by meditating on and appropriating the promises of Scripture, which inspire hope and banish dejection (Rom. 15:4).

• The refrain 'no one comforting her' points to the isolation of suffering, both as regards an individual and a community. It can be alleviated by the presence of those who sympathise with the sufferer (Job 2:11) and also by the extension of forgiveness to one who has repented for causing offence (2 Cor. 2:6-7). Ultimately, however, heart comfort is only achieved by the establishment of a true relationship with God and, as Zion found out, there may be much to be worked through before that can be achieved.

- There is no simple correlation between calamity and personal guilt (Luke 13:1-5). We must not fall into the thinking of Job's comforters that, because he was suffering so severely, he must be guilty of some heinous offence. On the other hand, however, we must not forget that much suffering is the consequence of sin. A right relationship with God requires self-examination to ascertain what may have gone wrong (1 Cor. 11:28, 31-32; 2 Cor. 13:5). Recognition of what is amiss ('Sinned grievously has Jerusalem', 1:8) leads to correction of what is contrary to his desires. Such repentance is not just a turning from a sinful lifestyle in general. It requires an examination of the specifics of the past and due amendment of life, laying aside '*every* weight and the sin which so easily ensnares' (Heb. 12:1). Those whom Christ loves he reproves and corrects so that they may be incited to repentance and holiness (Rev. 3:11; cf. 2 Chron. 6:26).

B. Grief Felt (1:12-22)

The second half of the poem follows on closely from what precedes, but now the tragic circumstances of the people are presented from an inside perspective. It is implied that the preceding prayer to the LORD has received no answer, and so the city turns to seek sympathy from others (1:12); but, as she tells them that she is suffering in this way because of the LORD's anger against her sin (1:13-16), she is reduced to silence by the enormity of the blow that has been dealt her, and the poet as narrator intervenes to comment on the scene (1:17). When Zion again speaks, she recognises that the LORD has acted appropriately in the light of her sin (1:18a), and once more draws attention to her ongoing suffering and misery (1:18b-21b). There is then a concluding petition in which she pleads for divine action against her oppressors (1:21c-22).

(1) Zion's Plea for Sympathy (1:12-16)

ל 1:12 Is it nothing to you, all you who pass along the way?
        Observe and see
      if there is any suffering like my suffering,
        which is being inflicted on me,
      ⌞with⌟ which the LORD has brought grief on ⌞me⌟
        on the day of his fierce anger.

In the light of 1:17 the speaker is to be identified as Zion, the community of those bound by covenant with the LORD, which is still being personified as a helpless widow sitting on the ground at the roadside. The initial words, 'not to you', are difficult to interpret. It is unlikely that, as an ancient Jewish view supposed, they constitute a wish that others will not be affected with such a calamity as has come upon Zion: 'May this not be your fate!' In the intensity of her suffering Zion is focused on her own needs, not on the situation of others, and so it seems preferable to read the words as an unmarked question, *Is it nothing to you?*,[40] in which Zion upbraids those *who pass along the way* for their heartlessness (cf. Jer. 15:5). The travellers are not identified; essentially they are just any who happen to come close (cf. 2:15; Pss. 80:12; 89:41), but who would rather pass by on the other side (cf. Ps. 31:11).

The combination, *observe and see* — the same words as in 1:11 but in reverse order — calls on them to do more than look. The city does not, however, ask them to *do* anything; it is a sympathetic ear that she desires. It is improbable that this is to be viewed as Zion reverting to her former ways in which she sought help from anyone and anywhere apart from the LORD (cf. 1:2). The city is aware that so immense is the crisis in which she is engulfed that she cannot cope without outside assistance. Since there has been no answer from the LORD, in her despair she turns to any who may come within earshot. Perhaps they will help; perhaps asking them to listen will induce the LORD to break his silence.

Zion calls on those who pass by to consider not her past glory or her present shame, but her agony: *if there is any sorrow like my sorrow* (cf. Dan. 9:12). The scope of the word rendered 'sorrow' is unclear. It may include outward manifestations of suffering, or point more specifically to inner anguish. Probably it is wrong to try to differentiate between physical and mental affliction in this context. Zion's cry for sympathy wishes her whole situation to be taken into account: what the observer can see and what she herself testifies to as her inward response.

---

40. The Hebrew expression *lô* *ʾălêkem*, 'not to you', is obscure. Many modern commentators seek to emend it, but the early versions all seem to reflect the Massoretic text. The traditional Jewish understanding is found in the Talmud (*Sanhedrin* 104b) as well as in later works.

Her agony is intense because of the origin of her suffering which *is being inflicted* (cf. 1:22; 2:20; 3:51) on her. She recognises this is not the outcome of an accidental, impersonal process, but *the LORD has brought grief* on her (cf. 1:5) so that her present suffering is the result of *the day of his fierce anger* (cf. Isa. 13:9, 13; Jer. 4:8; 30:24). 'Fierce' suggests 'hot' or 'burning', and fits in well with a situation in which Jerusalem was consumed by fire. This is an aspect of 'the day of the LORD', the time in which he no longer restrains his wrath but acts judicially against the rebellion of mankind (cf. 1:21; 2:1, 16, 21, 22). But Zion now recognises that the day of divine retribution has come upon her, and the question she poses is whether she is able to survive the aftermath of what the LORD has imposed on her.

נ 1:13 From on high he has sent fire into my bones,
    and it has overcome them.
He has spread a net for my feet;
    he has turned me back.
He has made me desolate,
    faint all the day.

Zion presents a series of vivid pictures to bring out the powerlessness of those who experience the imposition of divine wrath. *From on high* refers to God's dwelling place in heaven, and reinforces Zion's acceptance of the divine origin of her calamity. *He has sent fire* may have in mind the destruction of the cities of the plain, which epitomised for Israel God's judgement on unforgivable sin (cf. 4:6; Gen. 19:24; Isa. 1:9-10). *Into my bones* is an idiomatic expression for 'throughout my body'. Here it must be part of the personification. Just as a fever would inflame and weaken the whole of an individual's constitution, so the whole of the city was affected by the fire of divine judgement.

Metrical considerations lead many to take the phrase 'into my bones' with the following part of the line. Furthermore *and it has overcome them* (literally 'her' with the verb from a root 'to trample' or 'to rule over') conceals an awkward use of a singular form to refer back to the plural 'bones' as well as a difference in gender between the subject of the verb and its presumed antecedent 'fire'. Assuming that the initial consonants of the verb form have been transposed and identifying the root as 'to come down' leads to a translation such as 'into my bones he made it come down', which is favoured by many English versions (e.g. ESV, NIV).[41] The overall picture is substantially the same on either reading. In the second line the picture switches to that of a hunter who **has spread a net for my feet** (cf. Ps. 57:6). The mesh of the camouflaged net would catch the feet of an animal causing it to stumble and providing an opportunity for the hunter to pull the net together to trap his prey. Alternatively the net may have been spread over a concealed pit into which an unwary animal would fall. The same technology was also a recognised military technique to trap men (cf. Ezek. 12:13; 17:20; 19:8-9; Hos. 7:12). Being caught like an unsuspecting beast was not an outcome which Zion had ever seriously contemplated because she had expected the LORD to be the one to free her from the nets of others (cf. Pss. 25:15; 31:5). But in the event **he has turned me back** shows that the LORD prevented her from taking the escape route she desired.[42] He left no way out from the fiery judgement he was imposing.

He has made me desolate ('he has given me' to this state; for 'desolate', see on 1:4, 16) denotes the divine imposition both of physical destruction and of psychological disorientation so that Zion is overwhelmed by the magnitude of the catastrophe and no longer able to function properly. **Faint all the day** is a second aspect of the divine punishment. Though 'faint' may be connected with the indisposition of menstruation (cf. Lev. 15:33), and so be appropriate to the feminine personification of Zion,[43] it is in fact a word of quite general use (cf. Isa. 1:5; Jer. 8:18). Zion has collapsed, weak and demoralised; she cannot resume normal living.

---

41. The Hebrew verb is *wayyirdennâ*, a *waw* consecutive with a 3rd person masculine singular imperfect qal form of *rādâ*, 'to rule over'. Switching the initial consonants and repointing the form as an imperfect hiphil from *yārad*, 'to come down', would yield a form such as *yôrdennâ*, but an imperfect with reference to past time is awkward after an initial perfect.

42. Though the verb is a form of *šûb*, 'to turn back', English translations are rightly agreed that it is not here used as a spiritual metaphor (cf. 5:21) but in its basic sense of physical movement. (Contra Walter C. Kaiser, Jr., *A Biblical Approach to Personal Suffering* [Chicago: Moody, 1982], 52–53.)

43. This is argued for by Barbara B. Kaiser, 'Poet as "Female Impersonator": The Image of Daughter Zion as Speaker in Biblical Poems of Suffering,' *Journal of Religion* 67 (1987): 164–82.

ℶ 1:14 The yoke of my rebellions has been bound;
         by his hand they are intertwined.
      They went up on my neck;
         he has caused my strength to fail.
      The Lord gave me into the hands
         of ⌐those before whom⌐ I am unable to stand.

The verb *has been bound* is not found elsewhere but it may
plausibly be understood as a technical term for fastening a yoke to
the neck of an animal.[44] The past *rebellions* of the people (cf.
1:5) have had ongoing effects which are likened to a yoke set on a beast
of burden. The LORD had securely attached the penalty of their sin
to the necks of the people so that there was no way they could
extricate themselves. *Intertwined* envisages the many iniquities of
the people as divinely plaited into a rope which is used to attach the
wooden yoke to the neck of the animal. They *went up* (that is, they
were set on[45]) refers to Zion's many transgressions and their consequences being imposed as an overwhelming burden on her. *He
has caused my strength to fail*/'to stumble' is an idiomatic
expression for weakness and incapacity. Zion has found herself
unable to continue through the penalty imposed on her.

The Lord (*ʾădōnāy*) is used here for the first time instead of the
LORD (Yahweh). This effects a shift of focus from God as Yahweh,
the covenant King, to the absolute sovereignty and authority of
Adonai, a title derived from a noun commonly used to address a
superior with respect. While the Lord (Adonai) may be used as
virtually a synonym of the LORD (Yahweh), it often has overtones
of distance, even of coldness or formality in the relationship. Its use
here reflects the degree of uncertainty Zion felt regarding where
she really stood in the LORD's purpose after the harsh sentence he
had imposed on her when he *gave* her *into the hands* of an empire
of such political and military might that she was unable to resist

44. Some Hebrew manuscripts read *ʿal*, 'upon', for *ʿōl*, 'yoke', as do the
LXX and Vulgate. By changing the verb from the *hapax legomenon*, *śāqad*, to
šāqad, it is possible to read 'watch has been kept on my rebellions' (cf. LXX),
but this substitution has probably arisen from scribal misunderstanding of the
unusual original. Cf. Renkema, *Lamentations*, 163–64.
45. The use of 'went up' (*ʿālû*) is explained by the play on the Hebrew sound
of 'upon' (*ʿal*) and the verb 'to go up' (*ʿālâ*).

them. Indeed, Zion testifies: *I am unable to stand.* The calamity has not ended, and she is prostrate under the continuing exactions imposed by the enemy occupation of her land.

ם 1:15   He has tossed aside all my mighty men —
            the Lord in my midst.
         He has summoned an assembly against me
            to break my young men.
         The Lord has trodden ⌊as in⌋ a winepress
            virgin daughter Judah.

The verb in the first line of the verse is of rare occurrence and uncertain meaning. One suggestion is that it implies 'heap up', 'pile up', and so in the light of the agricultural imagery later in the verse it is a scene of divine harvest — but then it would be the crop that is heaped up.[46] More plausibly, the word may be related to a similar Akkadian root meaning 'to treat as worthless', 'to reject' (a sense which also fits in with the use of the term in Ps. 119:118). *All my mighty men* refers to the influential leadership of Jerusalem. The Lord (cf. 1:14) had assessed their capacity to resist the Babylonian onslaught, and brushed them aside as insignificant. *In my midst* suggests that what is in view is not action in the field of battle, but helplessness when the city was under siege. The Lord, not the enemy, is in the midst, and he has subverted the defensive strength and strategies of Zion's military leaders.

An assembly generally referred to an appointed time of festival, but here ironically the Lord has decreed that there is to be a gathering *against* Zion which has as its aim *to break my young men.* For 'break', see on 2:9; 3:4. 'Young men' refers to fully-grown but unmarried males, the epitome of vigour and strength (cf. 1:18; 2:21; 5:13). They would be the warriors who constituted the bulk of her troops. They, as well as their leaders, face the same destiny, one that leaves Zion helpless with none to assist or console her.

The scene widens somewhat to consider the fate of the land as a whole, which had been conquered before the armies invested

---

46. 'Heap up' takes the verb *sālâ* as a byform of *sālal*, 'to heap up' (cf. Jer. 50:26). 'Trample' (NKJV) seems to reflect the rendering of the Syriac Peshitta, and also presents a harvest image. The verb is not the same as the one found in the third line of the verse.

Jerusalem. A winepress was essential apparatus for any vineyard. It might be a container made of wood, but frequently it consisted of two hollows, hewn out of the bedrock. When the grapes were harvested, they were placed in the larger, higher vat where several workers, supporting themselves by means of wooden poles inserted into sockets at the side of the vat, squashed the grapes by foot. The juice from the trodden grapes then flowed along a channel into the lower, deeper container, from which, after settling overnight, it would be put into jars for transportation and storage. Treading a winepress is an image of the Lord's imposition of his anger which is found elsewhere (cf. Isa. 63:1-6; Jer. 25:30), with the juice of the grapes as they are processed at harvest time being likened to the flow of blood as hostile forces sweep through the land. ***Daughter Judah*** is subject to the same fate as the capital city. For the construction with 'daughter', see on 1:6. The addition of ***virgin***, a young woman of marriageable age, who should still have her future before her (cf. 1:4), adds to the poignancy of the scene in which the Lord sovereignly brings such devastation upon her (cf. Jer. 14:17).

ע 1:16 On account of these things I am weeping;
           my eye, my eye, is running down with water,
       for a comforter is far from me,
           one to revive my life.
       My children have become desolate,
           for the enemy has prevailed.

On account of these things sums up the description of the preceding verses. The dreadful events of the past and their ongoing consequences have reduced Zion to a plaintive figure who can do little other than weep at the calamities which surround her. ***My eye, my eye*** is a poetic repetition to emphasis Zion's dire condition.[47] It is not one tear she sheds, but an unending stream (cf. 3:48-49; Ps. 119:136; Jer. 9:1, 18; 14:17).

That there is no let up to her grief is explained by the fact that ***a***

---

47. In 4QLamᵃ *ʿênî*, 'my eye', occurs only once (so also LXX, Peshitta, Vulgate), suggesting that the MT is an instance of dittography, that is, an accidental writing of a word twice. Even so, it is possible to make sense of the MT, and the variants may have arisen from elimination of a poetic expression of intensity.

comforter is far from me. It is not that she has a comforter who is unfortunately at some distance from her; rather she has no one with whom to share her burden — no one to assuage her grief. *Far from me* is a variation on the formula 'there is no one to comfort her' (1:2, 9, 17, 21). 'Far off' is used elsewhere to describe the felt absence of the LORD (cf. Pss. 10:2; 22:1, 11, 19; 35:22; 38:21; 71:12). It would seem that the focus here is on him as the one alone has the ability *to revive my life* (cf. 1:11). As far as Zion can see he has become unavailable, but her prayer is that this will be reversed.

My children/'my sons' probably refers to all the remaining inhabitants of the city. They too are unable to extend any assistance to her because they *have become desolate* (cf. 1:4, 13), not just bereft of physical resources in the ruins of the city, but also drained, bewildered, overwhelmed by their own fate. The unthinkable had happened to them: *the enemy has prevailed*. Jerusalem, which they were convinced had been granted a divine guarantee of inviolability, had been taken and sacked. What was more, this had occurred at the initiative of the LORD himself. How then could there be any scope for hope?

(2) Overwhelmed by Sorrow (1:17)

ב 1:17   Zion has spread out her hands,
               ⌊but⌋ there is no one comforting her.
          The LORD has commanded concerning Jacob
               ⌊that⌋ his neighbours be his foes.
          Jerusalem has become
               an unclean thing among them.

At this point it would seem that Zion is overwhelmed by emotion and is, for the moment, unable to speak. So the poet interposes his description of the scene, which again begins with Zion's isolation. *Zion has spread out her hands*[48] in a plaintive gesture, pleading for a glance of pity, a word of sympathy, probably while she uttered the preceding words. While the gesture may be employed as an accompaniment to prayer (cf. Ps. 143:6; Isa 1:15; Jer 4:31), it is also used more generally (cf. Isa. 65:2). However, the familiar

---

48. Literally, 'has spread out with her hands', that is, has made an expansive, appealing gesture with (*bêth* of instrument) her hands.

refrain sums up the lack of response: ***there is no one comforting her***. Neither those who pass by nor the LORD himself displays any concern to relieve her plight.

The reason for the LORD's attitude is evident. ***Jacob*** is not essentially a political entity but the covenant people, and the LORD, their covenant suzerain, has been so displeased with them as to ***command*** their downfall before their enemies. The thought probably goes beyond the fall of Jerusalem in 586 B.C. back to the fall of Samaria in 723 B.C. Neither kingdom had been exempt from the penalty incurred through displeasing the LORD. In the popular theology of the times, military defeat was a sign of the powerlessness of a nation's gods. Here it is asserted that the God of Jacob was in such control of events that his people's defeat had been directly ordained by him. ***His neighbours***/'those surrounding him' were the LORD's instruments to accomplish his purpose.

The LORD's abandonment of Jerusalem has led to her loss of status among the nations. Again ***has become*** points to changed circumstances, a reversal of fortune. ***Unclean thing*** (a word closely relate to the term 'impure' in 1:8) refers to the ritual status of a woman during menstruation (cf. Lev. 12:2, 5; 15:19-33), from whom others keep apart. So too Jerusalem: her neighbours treat her as one to be avoided so that they do not come to share in her defilement (cf. Isa. 30:22; 64:6; Ezek. 7:19-20, 36:17; Ezra 9:11). Zion is on her own: isolated and without friend or comforter.

(3) Zion's Admission (1:18-19)

ש 1:18 The LORD is indeed righteous,
            for I defied his command.
        Hear, all you peoples,
            and see my suffering.
        My young women and my young men
            have gone into captivity.

When Jerusalem recovers her composure sufficiently to speak again, there is a different tone in her words. No longer is she simply appealing for sympathy from any and all, though that is still present in her speech. The focus is now much more on the theological aspect of the situation, as her opening words indicate.

The LORD is indeed[49] *righteous* emphasises this permanent characteristic of God, that he is true to himself and his own inherent standards of what is correct and just. He therefore cannot be charged with inappropriate action or arriving at inequitable verdicts. In particular his righteousness governs his relationship with his covenant people. Because he has committed himself to be their defender, divine righteousness often displays itself in their liberation and salvation from situations of peril, but it is not simply to be equated with release and victory. Fundamentally, it is the LORD being true to himself and to the commitments into which he has entered. The covenant is twofold: it bestows blessing on obedience, but it curses the disobedient. Zion acknowledges that her suffering constitutes the just desert of her misconduct (cf. 'that you may be righteous in your words', Ps. 51:4; cf. also Neh. 9:33). *I defied his command* (literally, 'his mouth'; cf. 1:20; 3:42). In penitence Zion admits that, though she had been well aware of what the LORD had required of her in his law, she had in fact wilfully disobeyed his authority and acted contrary to his direct and explicit requirements, which had been presented to her more than once through the preaching of the prophets.

It is no longer travellers passing by the city who are addressed as in 1:12. The command to *hear* what is being relayed to them regarding Jerusalem is now directed at *all you peoples*,[50] seemingly without exception. They too are called on to witness Jerusalem's agony. It is summed up in various features. Firstly, *my young women and my young men have gone into captivity.* For 'young women', see on 1:4; for 'young men', see on 1:15. Those who survived the sword and famine have been removed from the land to serve their conquerors elsewhere (cf. 1:5). It is not just the severance of the ties of love and the loss of their contribution to the present well-being of the community that are sources of grief. Their departure casts a dark shadow over Zion's survival because they are the next generation and they have been taken away. Is there also

---

49. There is a decided emphasis in the statement, *ṣaddîq hûʾ YHWH*, which 'indeed' attempts to bring out.

50. The qere *hāʿammîm*, 'the peoples', adds the article to the kethibh, *ʿammîm*, 'peoples'. This seems to be a scribal addition to make clear the vocative nature of the expression, but that is already implicit in the text.

a warning here to the nations as to what might befall others who
defy the LORD?

פ 1:19 I have called to my lovers,
              ˻but˼ they have deceived me.
        My priests and my elders
              have perished in the city
        while they sought food for themselves
              to revive their life.

The second factor in Zion's misery is the treachery she had experienced at the hands of others. *I have called to my lovers* reflects on
1:2, but the form of the word for 'lovers' is somewhat different.
Here it is more clearly an improper relationship which is referred to
(cf. Jer. 22:20; 30:14; Ezek. 16:33, 36; 23:5, 9, 22; Hos. 2:7-15).[51]
Whether Zion's confidence had been in the surrounding nations or
in their gods, it had been misplaced and she now admits that her
policies in this regard had been misconceived for *they have
deceived me.* Their words of friendship had been worthless, for in
her hour of need they had been found wanting.

A third feature of the situation was the lack of leadership that
remained in the city. At the opposite end of the age scale from the
young of 1:18, the *priests and elders* had perished. The priests
were the LORD's appointed religious officials who were in charge
of the worship of the Temple and who had responsibility for edu-
cating the people in the demands of the law (cf. 2:9, 20; 4:13, 16).
The elders were the traditional leaders of the community who
through age and experience were equipped to direct affairs (cf.
2:10; 4:16; 5:12, 14). The unrelenting pressure of famine both
during and after the siege had brought on by their deaths, and so the
city had been deprived of needed counsel and guidance. Even such
prominent members of the community had *sought food … to revive
their life* (cf. 1:6, 11), to keep themselves alive. That they had to do
so *for themselves* denotes the levelling effect of conditions in the
stricken city, and that their death came 'while' they were doing so
was a sign of their weakness. In the city personal survival, not
concern for the community, had become the overriding priority.

---

51. The difference is between the qal participle in 1:2 and a piel participle
here. Cf. Renkema, *Lamentations*, 183.

(4) Zion's Plea for Divine Intervention (1:20-22)

ר 1:20   See, O LORD, for I am in distress;
            my stomach is in turmoil.
         My heart has been turned upside down within me,
            for I have been utterly defiant.
         From outside the sword has bereaved;
            in the house it ⌐is⌐ like death.

Yet again, in her desperation, Zion entreats the LORD to *see* (cf.
1:9, 11). It is a measure of her faith that she realises that there is no
other source of help. The one who possessed the authority and
power to impose this penalty was the only one who was in a position to remove it.

   Zion pleads on the basis of her need. She is *in distress*, hard
pressed by adverse circumstances.[52] It is not the past disaster which
is now in view so much as its ongoing consequences, particularly
the deprivation and heartache which are afflicting the community.
My stomach is in turmoil (cf. 2:12). The reference to her inward
agony and agitation is a standard Hebrew metaphor for the
emotions. It is not clear whether the sensation referred to is one of
searing heat or of agitation, but the idea is clearly that of an
uncomfortable and disquieting feeling. *My heart has been turned
upside down within me* also reflects Zion's consternation (cf. Hos.
11:8). Her life and expectation have been flipped over, and that is
reflected in her inner disposition. Furthermore the verb 'turn upside
down' is one that is repeatedly used of the overthrow of Sodom and
Gomorrah (cf. Gen. 19:21, 25, 29; Isa. 1:7; Jer. 20:16). Zion may
be saying that the judgement she has undergone is like theirs, or
even worse. And the reason was not hard to find: *for I have been
utterly defiant*. Not once but repeatedly, not in some minor matter
but in the whole tenor of her life, she had defied the LORD and
repudiated his commands and his warnings. It was by this attitude
that the LORD characterised that generation of the people of Judah
as a 'defiant/rebellious/disobedient house' (Ezek. 2:5, 8).

---

52. There is an obvious play on *ṣar*, 'distress', arising from the actions of
ṣar, 'foe' (1:5, 7, 10, 17). There is a similar echo of *mārâ*, 'to be defiant', in
the poalal form, *ḥŏmarmārû*, 'is in turmoil'.

The result was utter catastrophe for the nation. *From outside the sword has bereaved.* Around the city and in its streets there had been no safety as the invaders spared none, and exposure to their violence left families mourning their lost. It was an aspect of the covenant curse of which the LORD had warned: 'From outside the sword will bereave, and indoors terror' (Deut. 32:25; cf. also Jer. 14:18; Ezek. 7:15). *In the house it has been like death.* This is probably a reference to the impact of famine, with 'like' not quite equating the situation with death,[53] but still pointing to weakening sickness which meant that death was inevitable before long.

ל 1:21 They have heard that I ⌊am⌋ groaning;
            there is no one comforting me.
        All my enemies have heard of my trouble; they
            have become glad;
        but you yourself had done ⌊it⌋.
        You have brought the day you called for;
            and let them be as I am.

Though many commentators and some translations (e.g. RSV) emend the Hebrew text to an imperative, 'Hear!', addressed to God, the text as it stands is not without meaning. *They have heard* may be an indefinite reference to people in general, or it may anticipate the following mention of Zion's enemies. It was no secret that Zion was *groaning* in her misery (cf. 1:4, 8), and the reason was equally evident: *there is no one to comfort me*. Although the primary reference is to her earlier situation, nothing has occurred to alter Zion's isolation and misery.

The dire nature of her circumstances was intensified by the gloating reaction of her enemies. Translations generally take the verb *they have become glad* with the second part of the line, implying that Zion's enemies joyfully acknowledged 'that you yourself had done it'. The Massoretic accents, however, place the break after 'they were glad'. Although this leads to a long first colon, it does have the advantage of avoiding the attribution of an advanced

---

53. Another possible understanding is that the inseparable preposition *kə* functions as '*kāph* veritatis', to emphasise the reality of a situation, as well as to set up a comparison (cf. 2:5; 5:3): 'Death has been indeed (or, truly) in the house.'

level of understanding to the surrounding heathen nations. *My trouble*/'misfortune' (cf. 'evildoing', 1:22) refers to the continuing suffering of Jerusalem. When those hostile to her had become aware of how desperate the situation in the city had become, they spontaneously expressed their satisfaction and delight.

Such a malicious response caused Zion even greater hurt, but at the same time she was able to interpret the situation differently. *You yourself had done it.* The emphasis is on the LORD, and by bringing him into the picture another assessment of the facts could be arrived at. The LORD was in control, and he had *brought the day you called for.* This is a reference back to the day of his fierce anger (1:12). Since over the centuries Zion had repeatedly ignored the prophets' warnings about the impending day of the LORD's intervention in judgement (cf. 2 Kgs. 17:13; 2 Chron. 36:15-16; Jer. 25:3-7; 35:15), the patience of the LORD was finally exhausted and he acted just as he had announced he would.

The final statement in the verse, *and let them be as I am*, has led commentators to identify the day the LORD announced as one still in the future when judgement would come on the nations. On this basis they follow one early version and read an imperative, 'Bring on the day you have announced'.[54] However, it is more probable that Zion is expressing bewilderment that the LORD's predicted day of judgement has been only partially fulfilled. It was a time when he would impose his order on the affairs of earth and punish those who opposed his ways. Zion acknowledges the righteousness of his action against her but, if the LORD is acting as judge of all the earth, why has he not carried his task out to completion? Why should others be exempt from punishment when Zion has suffered so terribly? Why should her enemies be permitted to go on tormenting Zion with impunity?

---

54. The verb is a perfect form which translators have understood in a variety of ways. A reference to a past action ('You have brought') is favoured by the LXX and ESV, but treating the form as a prophetic perfect yields a future translation as in AV, ASV ('You will bring'). Most translations favour a volitive form, either an optative, 'Oh, that you would bring the day' (NASB; cf. NIV), or an imperative 'bring' (NLT, NKJV, NRSV). This may be justified on the grounds either that the verb is to be understood as a precative perfect or that the imperative form found in the Peshitta is to be adopted.

ת 1:22 Let all their evildoing come before you,
               and afflict them
           as you have afflicted me
               on account of all my rebellious acts,
           for my groans are many
               and my heart is faint.

Zion's final plea follows on closely from the thought of the previous verse. The LORD is righteous, and therefore the nations should be punished as well. Zion asks the LORD to *let all their evildoing come before you*, that is, that he as judge should scrutinise their deeds, which Zion confidently characterises as contrary to his standards. 'Evildoing' is the same word as 'trouble' (1:21), but the reality is being viewed from a different perspective: 'trouble' as regards those who experience it, and 'evildoing' as regards those who perpetrate it. This is significant for the conclusion of the petition. On the basis of the evidence provided by the conduct of her enemies, Zion argues that action should follow: *afflict them as you have afflicted me on account of all my rebellious acts*. 'Afflict' is from the same root as 'being inflicted on' (1:12) and 'bring deep pain' (3:50). Zion does not pretend that she is without fault. She has openly confessed her rebellion (cf. 1:20) and the appropriateness of the LORD's response. But surely divine equity required that the misconduct of others be not overlooked?

That this is not a disinterested plea for equity is seen more clearly in the concluding line. *For my groans* (cf. 1:21) *are many* (< *rab*, cf. 1:1) *and my heart is faint.* Though Zion has acknowledged the righteousness of the LORD's dealings with herself, she is not yet able to see how what has been imposed on her may be lifted. However, it may be eased. Daily she suffered and wept because of the cruelty of the occupying forces of Babylon and the incursions of her hostile neighbours. If they receive their just deserts, then some of the pressure on her would be eased, some of the hurt would be removed, and she would no longer be 'faint' (cf. 1:13), unable to withstand the pressure of their malice and oppression. Her prayer is not yet for restoration, just for relief.

But still there is no reply.

Reflection

- There is a deep instinct in mankind to crave sympathy in suffering. This should be readily obtained from a friend, but words of consolation voiced by a stranger are equally effective if only they are genuinely uttered and are not merely conventional politenesses. An expression of heartfelt understanding and compassion can bring solace in difficult situations. 'Weep with those who weep' (Rom. 12:15) is conduct patterned on that of Christ (John 11:33-35). His compassion extended to all who were harassed and helpless (cf. Matt. 9:36; 14:14; 15:32).

- The day of the LORD is a theme which recurs throughout the prophets. It denotes the open intervention of the LORD in the affairs of this world so as to right wrongs and vindicate the justice of his rule. Amos had to counter Israel's expectation that it would affect only other nations who lived in hostility to the LORD (Amos 5:18-20). Divine action would come as dark judgement upon the covenant people also if they continued in their rebellion against God (cf. Isa. 2:12; Jer. 46:10; Ezek. 7:19; Joel 1:15; Zeph. 1:7-18). Specific judgements in the course of human history are anticipations (and forewarnings) of the final day of the LORD in which he will ultimately consume from his creation all that is stained by rebellion. 'But the day of the Lord will come like a thief, in which the heavens will pass away with a roaring noise, and the elements will be burned up and destroyed, and the earth and the works that are done on it will be exposed' (2 Pet. 3:10). In looking back at the doom which came upon Zion, we must be mindful of what is yet to come.

- It is to the credit of Zion that her attitude is not one of complaint against the justice of the LORD's action. She sees beyond the secondary causes of her tragedy, and genuinely accepts not only that her situation has come from the hand of God, but that it has been justly imposed on her. 'The LORD is indeed righteous' (1:18). Krašovec points to three passages which are very similar to this, namely, Exodus 9:27; Ezra 9:15; Nehemiah 9:33. The argument is clear. When an individual or a people would place God on trial because of a disaster which they are having to face, and they ask, 'How can God allow this to happen?', they must always recognise the guilt of mankind. God is in the right, and it is not possible to undermine the correctness of his actions. As the people are brought to realise their true situation before God, they become newly aware of their personal indebtedness to God. 'Accepting God's justice by recognizing their guilt is seen by the poet as essential to the change of heart needed by Israel for her deliverance.'[55] We must never lose sight of the fact that 'all his ways are right' (Deut. 32:4; cf. Jer. 12:1).

- Zion is intensely aware that her rebellion has separated her from God. The devastation of the city makes equally evident his estrangement from her. The people plead with God not on the basis of their merit, but on the grounds of their distress (1:20) and groaning (1:22). They are struggling to overcome divine silence, and are implicitly appealing to what he is in himself, the God of grace and compassion (cf. Isa. 63:15).

- But does their call for action against their enemies reveal an unworthy spirit of revenge from which a New Testament believer ought to dissociate himself? Is not Zion's plea at the same level as the rejoicing of her enemies? Undoubtedly the people express themselves with an eye to the relief they would enjoy if the oppression of their enemies was halted, but there is also a genuine perplexity as to how the LORD is righteous and yet has not taken action against such perpetrators of evil. They desire to see God vindicate his name, and their attitude is not dissimilar to that set out by Paul in his compendium of Christian conduct, 'Beloved, never avenge yourselves, but leave it to the wrath ⌊of God⌋, for it is written, "Vengeance is mine; I will repay", says the Lord' (Rom. 12:19). Zion does not seek to take vengeance herself, and in this respect also knows the outcome of her situation to be in the hands of God.

---

55. Jože Krašovec, 'The Source of Hope in the Book of Lamentations,' *Vetus Testamentum* 42 (1992): 225.

Lamentations 2

OUTLINE

A. **Under the Cloud of the LORD's Anger (2:1-10)**

    (1) The Lord's Unrestrained Anger (2:1-3)

    (2) The Lord's Hostility (2:4-5)

    (3) Destruction of the Temple (2:6-7)

    (4) Destruction of Zion and Its People (2:8-10)

B. **Distressed at Jerusalem's Plight (2:11-17)**

    (1) The Heart-Wrenching Tragedy (2:11-12)

    (2) Probing the Extent of Zion's Calamity (2:13-17)

C. **Zion's Plea (2:18-22)**

    (1) Plead for the Sake of Your Children (2:18-19)

    (2) The Prayer of Daughter Zion (2:20-22)

The poem which constitutes the second chapter of Lamentations shares many structural and thematic features with the initial poem of the book. In form it too is an alphabetic acrostic, with each of its 22 verses beginning with successive letters of the alphabet (though there is a switch at 2:16-17). Each verse also usually consists of three poetic lines, and the poem retains a generally concentric structure, though thematic considerations indicate that the main division occurs after verse 10, and not absolutely in the centre of the poem. The poet displays his artistic skill by deploying similar terms in verses equidistant from the centre.[56]

2:1	in the day of his anger	2:22	on the day of the anger of the LORD
2:2	he has not shown pity … to the ground	2:21	on the ground … you have not shown pity
2:3	has consumed	2:20	eat (same verb)
2:4	he has poured out	2:19	pour out
2:5	the Lord (Adonai)	2:18	the Lord (Adonai)
2:6	the LORD (Yahweh)	2:17	the LORD (Yahweh)
2:7	an enemy … as on a day	2:16	your enemies … the day
2:8	daughter	2:15	daughter
2:9	her prophets … vision	2:14	your prophets … have envisioned
2:10	daughter Zion … young women	2:13	virgin (young woman) daughter Zion
2:11	has been poured out … faint … in the streets	2:12	faint … in the streets … is poured out

Several of these correspondences may seem weak when viewed individually, but taken together they constitute an impressive network woven into the fabric of the poem, and giving coherence and also focus to the central theme of the suffering of Zion, particularly as it affects the young of the city.

The second poem shares many themes with the first because it continues to describe the same situation. There are, however, developments which advance the poet's treatment. This is noticeable in the extent to which concepts such as 'the day of his fierce anger' (1:12) and 'the day you called for' (1:21) are expanded in

56. This analysis is drawn from Renkema, 'Literary Structure,' 307–8.

2:1-10 to show that the city is suffering because of the LORD's judgemental imposition of the catastrophe which has engulfed Zion. Equally, although in 2:1-10 we continue to hear the same, almost detached, tones of the narrator as in the initial section of chapter 1, in 2:11 he is unable to maintain this stance and displays his personal grief — a feature which prepares the way for the in-depth presentation of chapter 3.

An analysis of the chapter may then be derived from paying attention to thematic transitions in the perspective of the poem, particularly where the speaker changes. The first section is a third person description by the narrator of the LORD's punishment of Zion (2:1-10). The LORD has shown no restraint in the outpouring of his anger (2:1-3), and has acted like an enemy against the city (2:4-5), even though this has entailed the destruction of sacred institutions (2:6-7) and has brought devastation and misery to the city and its inhabitants (2:8-10). There is then a switch to first person language in which the poet sets out his personal reaction to what he has witnessed of the city's trauma (2:11-12) and goes on to address the city itself (2:12-17), seeking some way in which comfort may be extended to it. There is a clearer indication of those who are responsible for precipitating this crisis in Zion (2:14), but explanations for the past do not relieve present distress. In the face of the LORD's determination to punish the city, the only source of solace and redress must be the LORD himself. After the poet has again urged Zion not to spare herself in reminding the LORD of her agony (2:18-19), she addresses God, resuming her earlier pleas for divine attention because of her intense need (2:20-22). Throughout the second part of the poem concern is especially expressed for the suffering of the young in the city (2:11-12, 19, 20, 22).

A. Under the Cloud of the LORD's Anger (2:1-10)

The focus is still on the horrendous ordeal of Zion. It is made very clear that this has come from the hand of God, but no attempt is made to show how justified the LORD was in his response to the misconduct of his people. It is the dire nature of their experience of the LORD's unrestrained anger which has seared itself into the poet's consciousness. 'It is a fearful thing to fall into the hands of the living God' (Heb. 10:31).

(1) The Lord's Unrestrained Anger (2:1-3)

א 2:1   Ah, how he is covering with a cloud in his anger,
            the Lord, daughter Zion!
         He has cast down from heaven to earth
            the beauty of Israel.
         He has not remembered his footstool
            in the day of his anger.

The funereal tone of the introductory *Ah, how!* begins the poem in
a very similar fashion to the first (cf. 1:1), but a somewhat different
perspective is brought out by the juxtaposition of *the Lord,
daughter Zion* at the end of the first line. Unlike the first poem
where Zion's destiny had been generally described in isolation,
now the stress is very much on the interaction between the
Sovereign Lord (*'ădōnāy*, cf. 1:14) and his people (cf. 1:6). The
term 'the LORD' is avoided in 2:1-5 because the scene is not one of
covenant blessing. *He is covering with a cloud*/'beclouding'[57]
describes an ongoing situation in which the city is enshrouded by
the storm cloud of divine *anger* (cf. 1:12). The ominous implications of the unrelieved darkness and gloom hanging over the land
are reinforced by the repetition of 'his anger' at the end of the
verse. Such darkness is a feature of theophanies (cf. Ps. 18:11; Isa.
8:22; Zeph. 1:15), but here there is an inversion of the expected
covenantal order, and divine judgement has been imposed on Israel,
not on their enemies (cf. Amos 5:18-20).

   The summary of the Lord's action given in the initial line is
then unpacked in 2:1-8 in a series of verbs, for each of which God
is the subject. In this way it is emphasised that there can be no
doubt about his decisive involvement in Zion's overthrow. While
the beauty of Israel might refer in general terms to all that their

57. This is the only occurrence of the verb *'wb*, which has traditionally been
explained in terms of a connection with the noun *'āb*, 'cloud' (cf. LXX,
Peshitta). In the abstract, covering with a cloud might suggest providing relief
from the heat of the sun, but this is contextually ruled out: the scene is one of
judgement. Another possible translation supposes the root to be linked to a
cognate Arabic term meaning 'to treat with contempt', a rendering which may
be supported by 'despise' in the Targum (cf. NIV margin; NRSV; *NIDOTTE*
3:332–34).

status as the covenant people of the LORD bestowed on them, it is probable that here it is Zion, and particularly the Temple, that is in view ('an object of fame and beauty for all the lands', 1 Chron. 22:5). This was where the heavenly rule of the LORD had been visibly and splendidly disclosed on earth ('Strength and beauty are in his sanctuary,' Ps. 96:6). By purposefully casting this glorious disclosure down *from heaven to earth* the LORD had severed this link, and so the covenant people, *Israel* (the term is used only here and in 2:3, 5), no longer enjoyed the privilege of his presence in their midst and his sanctuary was exposed to the ravages of the enemy.

The thought of divine abandonment is continued in the final line of the verse. *Has not remembered* describes an ongoing attitude of practical neglect: deliberate oversight rather than amnesia (cf. 5:1). It too is a reversal of the covenant privilege by which the LORD remembered and saved his people (cf. Exod. 2:24; 6:5; Pss. 105:8; 106:45; 111:5). A footstool was a needed accompaniment of the elevated thrones of the ancient east. *His footstool* may refer to the Temple complex on Zion (compare Ps. 99:5 with Ps. 99:9) or more particularly to the ark of the covenant which was the religious focus of the sanctuary (cf. 1 Chron. 28:2). It is difficult, and probably unnecessary, to choose between these two references because the one is based on the other. The later history of the ark is not documented, but it may well have remained in the Temple until it was destroyed in 586 B.C.[58] The loss of the ark, whether hidden, burned or looted, is alluded to here as an indication of the intensity of the LORD's anger against his people. Even this sacred symbol of his presence was not exempt *in the day of his anger* (cf. 1:12, 21), a phrase which recurs in 2:22 to form an inclusion[59] bracketing the whole poem.

ב 2:2   The Lord has swallowed up — he has not shown
         pity —
         all the pastures of Jacob.

---

58. For further discussion regarding the ark at this period, see John L. Mackay, *Jeremiah* (Fearn, Ross-shire: Mentor, 2004), 1:192–93.

59. 'Inclusion' was an ancient authorial technique whereby at the end of a work, or of a section of it, words and themes from the beginning of the section were repeated to indicate closure to the hearers or readers.

He has thrown down in his wrath
the strongholds of daughter Judah.
He has hurled to the ground — he has profaned —
a kingdom and its rulers.

Five successive lines in Hebrew (2:2abc, 3ab) begin with third person masculine singular perfect verbs,[60] and the initial repetition of this form contributes to the overwhelming sense of the sovereign action of *the Lord* (*ʾădōnāy*, cf. 2:1). *Swallowed up* implies an act of destruction that is swift and seemingly irreversible (cf. 2:5, 8, 16). What is overthrown may possibly be re-erected, but what is swallowed up seems gone for ever. To the irreversibility of the Lord's action, there is added his implacability. *He has not shown pity*[61] emphasises how, contrary to what might have been expected from the LORD's previous attitude of longsuffering despite the misbehaviour of the people, they had now exhausted his forbearance, and so he has sovereignly acted without hesitation or mercy, sparing them none of his indignation (cf. 2:17, 21; 3:43). The objects of his wrath are specified as *all the pastures of Jacob*. 'Jacob' is used not in reference to the northern kingdom but to the entire land. 'The peaceful pastures' (Jer. 25:37) represent the economic prosperity of the whole country, which was mainly based on agriculture. Since the term 'pastures' basically denotes 'resting places' and can also be used to refer to settlements, the scene is that of the devastation wrought throughout fields and villages of the countryside by the invading forces of Nebuchadnezzar.

But the impact of divine judgement spread further. *Wrath* refers to the intense displeasure of God before which nothing can stand (cf. Isa. 13:9; Ezek. 22:31). Here it is recalled how the Lord had also used the enemy forces to demolish *the strongholds of daughter Judah*. Various strategic sites throughout the land had been fortified to withstand external aggression. As the Babylonians tightened their grip on Jerusalem, we are told that of these fortified cities only Lachish and Azekah remained standing at one stage (Jer.

---

60. For discussion of repeated terms in this poem, see Hillers, *Lamentations*, 27, footnote 30.

61. The qere *wəlōʾ* adds the conjunction to the negative of the kethibh. This is probably a scribal addition to smooth out the staccato effect of the original (cf. 5:3).

34:7), and once they were overwhelmed, the land was defenceless. For 'daughter Judah', see on 1:15.

Both the ruin of the economy and the demolition of the fortresses were part of the LORD's action against his rebellious people by which he levelled the land of promise.[62] *He has profaned* refers to the land being deprived of its special sacral character, when the LORD acted to sever the sacred link between himself and the covenant people (cf. Ps. 89:38-45, especially v. 39b, 'You have profaned his crown on the ground'). *Kingdom* refers to more than just the last king of Judah. It is the kingdom of David, the line of covenant promise, which is overthrown along with *its rulers* who directed the affairs of the kingdom (cf. 1:6). By depriving the land of its special significance and devastating it economically and militarily, the LORD had completely ruptured his special relationship with it and with its people. The warnings he had delivered through the prophets, his covenant spokesmen, had not been idle threats.

א 2:3   He has cut off in the heat of his anger
            every horn of Israel.
        He has taken back his right hand
            in the face of the enemy,
        and has burned against Jacob like a flaming fire
            which has consumed all around.

Further specification is given of the way in which the Lord has destroyed the strength of his people *in the heat of his anger.*[63] The strength of a wild animal was embodied in its *horn*, and this image

---

62. The Massoretic Text punctuates the verse so as to include 'he has hurled to the ground' with what precedes. 'He has thrown down in his wrath – the strongholds of daughter Judah he has hurled to the ground. He has profaned a kingdom and its rulers.' Though C. F. Keil, *Jeremiah, Lamentations* (trans. J. Martin; 1872; Commentary on the Old Testament; repr. Grand Rapids: Eerdmans, 1975, 383) argues for the suitability of this punctuation, it does leave only a single colon in the last line, and that seems improbable.

63. Renkema notes that the phrase used here (*bāḥŏrî-ʾap*) is not precisely the same as that used elsewhere, *ḥărôn ʾappô* (1:12). He comments that the latter expression is used only for divine anger, whereas the term *ḥŏrî* is also used of human anger, and suggests that the language here is more anthropomorphic (Renkema, *Lamentations*, 226).

was transferred to individuals and communities as a symbol of their power or pride (cf. Deut. 33:17; Pss. 75:10; 92:10). The focus here is on the military strength in the community. Israel's soldiers had been deprived of the ability to attack others or to defend themselves, and the impact of that continued in the defeated nation.

The *right hand* of the LORD symbolises his strength, which is usually exerted to defend and protect his people (cf. Ps. 98:1). Here, however, *he has taken back* his right hand.[64] This is not in preparation for striking their enemies; rather this represents the withdrawal of his protection from his people despite the fact that they are being attacked (*in the face of the enemy*).

Furthermore, the LORD's action in the situation confronting them is not merely withdrawal; it is the imposition of his wrath. *He has burned against Jacob* (cf. Ps. 2:12; Isa. 30:27). The LORD is compared to an all-consuming fire in his relationship with his covenant people. There is no quenching its ferocity; no escape from its flames.

(2) The Lord's Hostility (2:4-5)

ת 2:4   He has bent his bow like an enemy;
              his right hand was at the ready like a foe.
         He has slaughtered
              all that was delightful ⌊to the⌋ eye.
         In the tent of daughter Zion
              he has poured out his fury like fire.

The poet looks back on the devastation the Lord has wrought in Jerusalem. Though the initial onslaught of his wrath is now in the past, its consequences continue to be sorely felt. The Lord is presented as a hostile archer who *bent his bow* (cf. Ps. 7:12-13). The comparisons using *like* avoid terming the Lord an outright enemy, because, if he were unequivocally and absolutely their enemy, there would then be no possibility for hope. Even so there is no attempt to downplay the severity of his actions.

---

64. The expression is ambiguous, and 'his' might refer to Israel in that the LORD turns back Israel's strength so that they are incapacitated before their enemies (cf. Hillers, *Lamentations*, 98). However, the reference in 2:4 to the LORD's right hand favours the same reference being intended here.

The second colon of the first line is awkward,[65] but it probably conveys the idea that the Lord has taken up position with respect to his right hand as an enemy archer who has trodden on his bow to fit its string and now holds an arrow in place ready to shoot at his chosen target. The *right hand* which the previous verse described as being withdrawn is now ready to strike. The LORD's strange and alien work in punishing the people for their misdeeds (cf. Isa. 28:21) inverts their expectation of how he would treat them.

Although the line *he has slaughtered* is very short and some translations set out the verse as lacking half a line (cf. ESV), there is no textual evidence to support another reading. This specifies the impact of Yahweh's arrows of judgement (cf. Num. 24:8; Deut. 32:42; Pss. 7:14; 18:15; 38:3; 64:8). But where did they lodge? While the term *delightful* and associated words may refer to physical objects such as the Temple (Ezek. 24:21) or the magnificent architecture of Jerusalem (Ps. 48:14), the associated verb 'slaughtered' makes a personal reference to the children of Zion more probable here (cf. Ezek. 24:16; Hos. 9:16).

The impact of the Lord's anger is further spelled out in the third line of the verse. Though 'tent' may be used to describe the Tabernacle (cf. Exod. 28:43) or the Temple (cf. 1 Chron. 9:23), the latter is not yet the focus in the poem (cf. 2:7) and it would scarcely be termed *the tent of daughter Zion*. 'Tent' refers to the city as a whole (cf. Isa. 33:20; 54:2), and particularly as composed of dwellings. 'Fury' comes from a root meaning 'to burn', and the Lord's *fury* is compared to a flaming liquid which has been *poured out* (cf. 4:11; Pss. 69:24; 79:6; Jer. 6:11; 7:20), and has spread with devastating effects into the homes of the city.

ה 2:5   The Lord has become like an enemy;
            he has swallowed up Israel.
        He has swallowed up all her palaces;
            he has ruined all his strongholds,
        and he has increased in daughter Judah
            mourning and lamentation.

---

65. The term 'right hand' is feminine, but the accompanying participle 'placed', 'positioned' (and so 'be at the ready') is masculine.

This verse emphatically reiterates several features of the preceding description. The phrase *like an enemy* is again used (cf. 2:4),[66] and *the Lord* (cf. 2:1) is directly identified as the referent. *Swallowed up* repeats the expression of 2:2 to stress the utter ruin the Lord's hostility has brought on the covenant people, *Israel* (cf. 2:1), for their sin. There is a contrast between *her palaces* — that is, the complex of royal and temple buildings, and possibly also the residences of the influential in daughter Zion (referred to as 'her') — and *his strongholds* (cf. 2:2), the fortresses throughout Israel ('his', since 'Israel' is usually masculine). But their fate is the same. Sudden destruction and ruin have been brought by the Lord, contrary to the consensus of popular theology. In imposing this penalty on them, God has increased *mourning and lamentation* (*taʾăniyâ waʾăniyâ*; cf. Isa. 29:2). The play on the similar sounds in these two words is often brought out by a rendering such as 'mourning and moaning' to describe the sadness and wailing which were present throughout *daughter Judah* (cf. 2:2).

(3) Destruction of the Temple (2:6-7)

❶ 2:6   He has done violence to his booth like a garden;
         he has ruined his festal meeting place.
         The LORD has caused to be forgotten in Zion
             festival and Sabbath;
         and in the fierceness of his anger he has spurned
             king and priest.

The description of the penalty imposed on Zion is heightened in intensity by focusing on its impact on the holy institutions of the city. The enormity of what occurred is emphasised by the change of the designation of God to the LORD (cf. 1:14). The targets of his

---

66. In 2:4 the preposition *kə* in the term *kəʾôyēb* has undoubtedly the force of a comparison. It is possible to argue that in 2:5 the comparison has advanced to the stage of correspondence ('*kāph* veritatis', 'indeed became an enemy'; cf. David J. Reimer, 'Good Grief? A Psychological Reading of Lamentations,' *ZAW* 114 [2002]: 548, note 16), but, after 2:4, it is more probable that the construction still stops short of identifying the Lord as an enemy (which use of the preposition *lə* would have implied), and instead indicates that his actions were like those of an enemy without actually asserting that he was.

wrath are the covenant institutions he had personally designed for his people. The verb to *do violence* usually refers to unprovoked assaults on individuals. Translators of this passage have tended in various ways to tone down its implications here, but none is needed for this describes how the people perceived the LORD's attitude towards them when he came against them as an enemy. It was like being mugged in the street, or becoming the victim of a terrorist incident. In this verse, however, the object of the attack is a place rather than persons. The term *his booth* occurs only here with this spelling, but it certainly refers to the Temple as the LORD's own place of residence (cf. Pss. 27:5; 76:3). Divine violence is directed against divine property. The addition *like a garden* does not make much sense as a comparison, but Hebrew is known to omit the preposition 'in' in such phrases, and 'as in a garden' conveys the sense that just as easily as a temporary garden hut may be demolished, so the LORD tore down the Temple (cf. Isa. 1:8).

The destruction of the Temple has had consequences for the rituals that should have been carried out at the sanctuary, which are summed up in terms of the pilgrim festivals and the weekly Sabbath. The same word (*môʿēd*, 'that which is appointed') refers to the designated place for Israel's worship (*festal meeting place*), the time at which they were to be held, and the manner in which such a *festival* was to be celebrated. This was all at the heart of Israel's God-instituted religion, constituting the core of their devotion to their covenant God. It is therefore startling that it is the LORD, the covenant God, who *has caused* them *to be forgotten in Zion*. That is not to say that absolutely no memory of them was retained; after all, the poet is here talking about them. But the ruins of the Temple could no longer accommodate the former appointed solemnities.

Fierceness/'indignation' introduces another dimension of anger that goes beyond inner feelings of fury to outward expression, which in the case of mankind takes the form of uttering curses against another (cf. 'will be cursed by peoples, will be denounced/ the object of curses/indignation by nations,' Prov. 24:24; cf. Num. 23:7-8) and which as regards God is the imposition of the penalty in reality (cf. Isa. 66:14; Jer. 10:10). Here it is *king and priest* who have been officially *spurned* (cf. Jer. 14:21) as the LORD dismissed them from his service and, either by death or exile, no longer permitted them to fulfil their appointed roles in his kingdom or in the Temple which was his palace. The Temple also served as the chapel royal for the kingdom, and so the worship maintained by the king is implicitly rejected also. The priests no longer officiate in the sanctuary because it no longer exists; indeed, the priests have also perished.

❡ 2:7   The Lord has rejected his altar;
            he has disowned his sanctuary.
           He has surrendered into an enemy hand
            the walls of her palaces.
           They raised a shout in the house of the LORD
            as on a day of a festival.

The dismissive repudiation implied by *rejected* is usually reserved for persons. The mention of *his altar* has then probably a reference both to the holy ordinances connected with sacrifice, and to those who officiated at the altar. Their misconduct had exposed their rebellion against the Lord (*'ădōnāy*, cf. 2:1), and he can no longer tolerate their hypocrisy. This rejection need not, however, be final (cf. 3:31; Zech. 10:6). However, for the present there can be no doubt about the fact that *he has disowned his sanctuary*, no longer acknowledging it as dedicated to his service. As it has ceased to be the object of his affection and protection, it is fitly consigned to hostile possession.

While the term employed in *her palaces* usually designates dwellings of the king or of persons of prominence in the land, it is probably used here of the Temple and its surrounding complex of buildings, which included the royal palace. This was the heart of Zion, and in his rejection of the people and of their worship the Lord has sovereignly given control of the walls of Zion, particularly the walls around the Temple and its associated buildings, into control of the enemy. It was an invitation for them to pillage and to burn. This constituted the ultimate challenge to the Zion theology which had been popular in Jerusalem in the century before its fall. The belief was prevalent that, because the LORD had been pleased to presence himself in the Temple, both it and the city in which it lay were perpetually inviolate. They confessed that the LORD was stronger than any enemy, and so were assured that his presence guaranteed that Zion would never fall. Yet it had: not because of divine powerlessness, but by divine leave.

The horrific result was that the enemy *raised a shout in the house of the LORD as on the day of a festival* (cf. 2:6). This, however, was not a holy shout of acclamation for the LORD, but an act of mockery and sacrilege as the exultant enemy expressed their joy at the conquest of the city, the capture of the Temple, and what they took to be the impotence of the LORD. The unthinkable had occurred.

(4) Destruction of Zion and Its People (2:8-10)

ח 2:8   The LORD determined to ruin
        the wall of daughter Zion.
    He stretched out the measuring line;
        he did not withhold his hand from swallowing up.
    So he caused rampart and wall to mourn;
        they wasted away together.

The three lines of this verse tell a story: first, God's decision to destroy, then the action he took, and finally the result of what he did.[67] The *ruin* (cf. 2:5, 6) which the LORD brought on Zion was not some wanton act which had inadvertently run out of control. It was the result of deliberate calculation as to what was to be achieved. When divine forbearance was exhausted, what took its place was planned and structured (cf. 2:17). *The wall of daughter Zion* was that which provided her with safety and security. It had to be taken away, and so God carefully and purposefully *stretched out the measuring line* (cf. Amos 7:7-9). His aim was not to construct but to demolish (cf. 2 Kgs. 21:13) through a deliberate act of divine power in which he showed no hesitation: *he did not withhold his hand*. For *swallow up*, see on 2:2, 5.

The *rampart* was probably a lower outer fortification against enemy assault. Both it and the city *wall* are said *to mourn*. This personification probably comes from the custom of a mourner sitting on the ground grief-stricken (cf. 1:1). After the walls had been penetrated by the enemy, they were largely demolished (2 Chron. 36:19), leaving the city open to attack. *Waste away* generally refers to plants, or by extension to people who are weak and languishing.

---

67. Since the narrative here relates historical facts, it is appropriate to render the perfect verbs by past tenses in English.

Applied to walls, the thought may well be that breaches in them
had so weakened their structure that further material fell from
them.

ᴜ 2:9   Her gates have sunk into the ground;
          he has destroyed and broken her bars.
        Her king and rulers are among the nations;
          there is no ˻priestly˼ instruction.
        Her prophets too have not found
          any vision from the LORD.

The scene of the previous verse is further elaborated. *Her gates,*
which once would have provided stout resistance to any force
trying to enter the city, have been unhinged and lie collapsed on the
ground among the rubble. The LORD has ***destroyed and broken her
bars***, that is, the strong pieces of wood that served to keep her gates
closed. These beams, however, could only function properly if the
LORD maintained their effectiveness, but here he has acted to
nullify their intended purpose. They are shattered, and so is Zion's
security.

    The focus switches from the physical consequences of the fall
of the city to its impact on communal life. No group has escaped
disaster, and as a result the social cohesion and effectiveness of
Jerusalem have been undermined. ***King and rulers*** (cf. 2:2) alike
are no longer kept secure by the LORD. Instead they have been captured and carried into exile, so that there is no political or military
leadership left in the land. The king in exile is probably a reference
to Jehoiachin, the second last king of Judah who, along with the
administrative and military elite of the land, was taken into exile by
Nebuchadnezzar in 597 B.C. (2 Kgs. 24:14-15). The absence of
instruction or 'law' (*tôrâ*) might be construed as descriptive of the
locality to which the rulers have been deported as being a lawless,
Godless place ('Her king and her princes are among the nations
where the law is not', ASV). However, it is more probable that the
description of conditions in Zion continues, and the desolation of
the community is emphasised by the absence of the instruction in
divine matters which had been one of the major functions of the
priests (cf. Lev. 11:11; Mal. 2:7). Not all the priests were taken into
exile, but any who remained were debarred from functioning as
priests of the LORD because he no longer recognised the sanctuary

or their ministry. In their blindness the people had claimed that 'the law shall not perish from the priest' (Jer. 18:18), but now they have been deprived even of that fixed reference point.

The same absence of direction and guidance for the population was also evident in that *her prophets too have not found any vision from the LORD.* These prophets are the establishment figures found at the Temple and often associated with the priests there (cf. Jer. 5:31; 6:13; 18:18; Ezek. 7:26). Although they claimed to be spokesmen of the LORD, he had not commissioned them (Jer. 23:21-22) and they derived their messages by copying them from on another (Jer. 23:30). In the aftermath of the collapse of the city, they had nothing to say because the claims of their theology had been falsified by events, and they could not find any word of guidance or encouragement to pass on to others (cf. Ps. 74:9). Those referred to here are not figures such as Jeremiah or Ezekiel who continued to exercise genuine prophetic ministries, though not within the city itself. The Jerusalem prophets are further discussed in 2:14.

❧ 2:10   They are sitting on the ground;
          the elders of daughter Zion are silent.
      They have tossed dust upon their heads;
          they have put on sackcloth.
      The young women of Jerusalem
          have bowed their heads to the ground.

The tenses of the verbs change in the first line. Whereas the kings and rulers had been removed from the city, and the remaining priests and prophets had nothing to say, *the elders of daughter Zion* (cf. 1:6) are still present in the city. Perhaps they may be able to offer advice to the residents of Zion in their distress. But no, the elders (cf. 1:19) share the same lot as the city as a whole (cf. 1:1): *they are sitting on the ground,* mourning, overwhelmed, disheartened as the ongoing burden of conditions after the fall of the city proves too much for them (cf. 1:19). They *are silent*, because overpowered by sorrow they have no counsel to offer others (cf. Ezek. 7:26). Like the population as a whole they have engaged in mourning rites, tossing dust on their heads (cf. Josh. 7:6; 1 Sam. 4:12; 2 Sam. 1:2; 15:32), possibly an acting out of the sentence of Gen. 3. *Sackcloth* was a coarse material often worn next to the skin as a sign of mourning or penitence (cf. Gen. 37:34; 2 Sam. 1:11; 3:31; 13:31). Crushed by events, the elders cannot articulate any way forward for the community.

Another much younger group is mentioned to emphasise how completely dejection has gripped the city. *The young women of Jerusalem* echoes the description of 1:4. They too share in the grief of the elders, and have *bowed their heads to the ground.* This gesture is not attested elsewhere in the Old Testament, but the context clearly associates it with mourning. It might be simply that their gaze is downwards, or it may be that they are lying on the ground in the dust. The day of the outpouring of the LORD's anger saps even the resilience of youth.

Reflection

• The prevalence of anger as a response to situations is indicated both in Hebrew and in English by the number of terms which exist to describe it. In the Bible more is said about divine wrath than about human anger. God's anger shows that he cares about situations. His impositions are not petulant or irrational outbursts, but proceed from his holiness as he asserts his right to determine what sort of behaviour is to be tolerated in the world that he has created and over which he rules. Divine anger is a sign that the universe is not ultimately irrational, but moral, guided and accountable.

• Divine wrath against sin is an inescapable feature of this world in which we live. 'God is a righteous judge and a God who reacts with indignation every day' (Ps. 7:11). Even so, it must be recognised that divine wrath is not of the essence of God in the way in which his love or holiness is. God's wrath is the response of his holiness to the sin of a rebellious creation. Without sin there would be no wrath, but there has always been God's love. Consequently Scripture affirms 'God is love', but never 'God is wrath'. The imposition of judgement is something that is 'strange' and 'alien' to him (Isa. 28:21). It is one of the vital aspects of his self-revelation that he is 'slow to anger' (Exod. 34:6), and so it is the case that 'his anger is for a moment, his favour for a lifetime' (Ps. 30:5). That he longs to be gracious and is eager to show compassion does not, however, compromise the truth that he is a God of justice (Isa. 30:18).

• The basic principle of accountability extends to God's people. The LORD is not passive when they act in defiance of his covenant stipulations. Indeed, in such circumstances his anger does not cancel his love, but coexists with it and is in fact an expression of his love. 'You only have I known [sovereignly recognised as having special status before me] of all the families of the earth; therefore I will punish you for all your iniquities' (Amos 3:2). However, this divine chastisement, though real and severe, has for its aim the reclamation of his people from their rebellion and their reinstatement in his favour. The determination of his electing love works through the problems caused by their defection to purify them from sin and to reinstate them as those in whom he delights.

• The reality of divine wrath is not to be dismissed as outmoded Old Testament teaching. Since it reflects vital, unchanging aspects of God's nature, it remains of fundamental significance both in respect of his Fatherly punishment of his people's sin (cf. Heb. 12:5-11) and as regards the eternal fate of those who reject the Gospel. 'Whoever believes in the Son has eternal life, but whoever does not obey the Son will not life, but God's wrath remains on him' (John 3:36).[68]

• Even though God had given covenant promises to Israel, that did not exempt them from experiencing his judgement on their sin — indeed it ensured it as a breach of covenant obligation. Similarly, the new Israel of God drawn from Jew and Gentile is not spared divinely imposed punishment upon sin. While there is the promise of security and perpetuity, namely that 'on this rock I will build my church and the gates of Hades will not prevail against it' (Matt. 16:18), that should not engender an attitude of carelessness in any Christian church. 'Remember therefore from where you have fallen, and repent and do the works you did at first; if not, I will come to you and remove your lampstand from its place, unless you repent' (Rev. 2:5).

---

68. For further discussion regarding the wrath of God, see Seth Erlandsson, 'The Wrath of YHWH', *Tyndale Bulletin* 23 (1973): 111–116, and R. V. G. Tasker, *The Biblical Doctrine of the Wrath of God* (London: Tyndale Press, 1951).

- Whereas the mode of divine punishment was fitted to the polity of Old Testament times in which the national and religious life people of God were united in one entity, in New Testament times the way in which God acts is conditioned by the societal and religious structures which now prevail. If a church denies the inspiration of God's word and arrogates to itself the right to sit in judgement on Scripture, then its message becomes skewed because it is tampering with God's word and is no longer openly stating the truth (cf. 2 Cor. 4:2). Divine abandonment of such a church is evident in the ineffectiveness of its proclamation because it no longer enjoys the blessing of the Holy Spirit to give it true impact.

- The divinely mandated destruction of the Temple and the abandonment of the prescribed worship ceremonies there indicates very clearly the priority accorded to heart commitment in God's estimation. Privileges inherited from the past and even the reality of former usefulness in God's service must continue to be accompanied by faithfulness and devotion. 'I desire steadfast love and not sacrifice, the knowledge of God rather than burnt offerings' (Hos. 6:6; cf. Matt. 9:13).

B. Distressed at Jerusalem's Plight (2:11-17)

Up to this point the poet has remained relatively detached and unemotional as he described the harrowing scenes before him — and his descriptions are all the more effective for that. But he cannot continue that neutral tone any longer. Whereas in chapter 1 the impassioned voice of Zion had broken into his comments, here it is the poet himself who is unable to maintain his composure, and reveals his emotional involvement in what he is witnessing (2:11). It is particularly the suffering of the young that has impacted on him (2:12). The fate of the devastated city is traced back to the inadequacy of the ministry of the prophets in its midst (2:14). Because of their failure the city had lost its splendour and become the butt of its enemies' sarcasm and mockery (2:15-16). However, all the suffering and derision arose from the determination of the LORD himself that this should come upon them (2:17).

(1) The Heart-Wrenching Tragedy (2:11-12)

ר 2:11 My eyes have failed with tears;
            my stomach is in turmoil.
         My heart has been poured out on the ground
            because of the breaking of the daughter of my
               people,
         when young children and infants faint
            in the streets of the city.

The suddenness with which the verse begins causes uncertainty as
to who the speaker is. The intensity of the sentiments expressed
might suggests that it is Zion, but the mention of 'the daughter of
my people' (2:11) and later the address to Jerusalem and Zion
(2:13) show that it is the voice of the poet himself which we hear.
He no longer hides behind the mask of inscrutability he has
maintained so far, and reveals that what he has witnessed has
affected him as much as it has affected Zion herself. *My eyes have
failed with tears* implies that, like Zion, the poet's crying has so
blinded his vision that he cannot see clearly (cf. 1:16). Further than
that, so intense has been his grief, that he lacks the physical capacity to continue lamenting. *My stomach is in turmoil*[69] repeats the
term used of Zion's experience in 1:20, and so underlines the
poet's empathy with Zion in her predicament. He is part of it, and
knows what it is like.

My heart is literally 'my liver', a metaphorical reference to the
seat of the affections, which cannot be taken directly into English.
Whereas *on the ground* links with the description of the young
women in 2:10, *has been poured out* repeats the verb of 2:4, and
applies it to the poet's own experience. 'I am poured out like water'
(Ps. 22:14) depicts a physically and emotionally draining ordeal
which has resulted in utter loss of strength. The poet here records
that he too has been dealt an shattering blow by the catastrophe
which has occurred and by its agonising consequences which are
evident on every side. *Because of the breaking of the daughter of
my people* uses language reminiscent of the language of Jeremiah

---

69. The poalal verb *ḥŏmarmārû* probably has a stative force and hence the
translation of the perfect form by a present tense.

who employs 'breaking', a physical wound or fracture, as a metaphor for the destruction of the city (cf. Jer. 4:6, 20; 6:1, 14; 8:11, 21; 48:3; 50:22; 51:54) and also 'the daughter of my people' (cf. Jer. 4:11; 6:14, 26; 8:11, 19, 21, 22; 9:1, 7; 14:17) as an affectionate form of address similar to 'my dear people'. Notice that both terms occur together in Jeremiah 6:14; 8:11, 21. If this is not Jeremiah himself speaking, then it is someone who was familiar with his prophecies and was deliberately echoing them here to show that what had befallen Jerusalem fulfilled the warnings she had received. There was no need in Lamentations to analyse the dimensions of Zion's failure; it was sufficient to endorse in this way what had been clearly spelled out earlier.

But the impact of the covenant curse on Jerusalem was not confined to the adult population (cf. Deut. 28:41, 50, 53-57). The poignancy of Jerusalem's circumstances was particularly evident in the suffering of *young children*, those still dependent on their parents to feed them, and *infants*, those still being nursed at the breast (which in the east might continue to the age of three or more). Their dreadful anguish caused them to *faint*, to swoon with exhaustion because the famine had totally drained them of physical vitality. It is not death that is described, but without any relief that is what will come. This scene of hardship and imminent demise is not located in the seclusion of their homes, but starkly *in the streets of the city*, 'the broad places', not just those between buildings forming alleyways, but also the larger plazas and squares in the town. Where once there had been scenes of life, commercial and political activity, now there are scenes of destitution, precursors of the grave. Those found in the streets would have included those whose houses had been destroyed and those who had camped there having mistakenly fled into the city for refuge before the siege began as well as those who had left their homes to search for food. This was in fulfilment of the warnings conveyed by Jeremiah that the outpouring of the LORD's anger would affect even the children in the street (Jer. 6:11; 9:21).

ל 2:12 They keep saying to their mothers,
     'Where is the corn and wine?'
   as they faint like someone wounded
     in the streets of the city,

as their life is poured out
on their mothers' bosom.

This verse runs on from 2:11 and is a graphic particularisation of
its third line. The young children are not alone in the squares and
marketplaces of the city. Their mothers are there too, as is emphasised by the repetition of 'mothers' bracketing this verse. But the
focus is still on the needs of the children. Mention of *corn* rather
than 'bread' suggests that the children's question is focused on
whether there are supplies of any sort to be found, rather than
immediately consumable items.[70] Supplies should have been available in the bazaars of the city, but no stalls have been set up in the
ruins. Wine would usually have been brought into the city for sale
in the markets — but there is no food or drink to be had.

In the absence of supplies the children *faint*, and the comparison
used points out that this is a deadly condition. Though the verb
comes from the same root as in 2:11, the stem is modified to
indicate that here it is the feelings of the children which are being
described. They are aware that their life strength is ebbing away
just as *someone wounded* with a mortal, but not immediately fatal,
blow languishes in weakness as his strength drains from him. How
often must that have been witnessed in the fighting during the
siege! Their mothers who had taken them with them as they sought
supplies are thus left nursing them *as their life is poured out* — a
touching scene with the children's questions intensifying the grief
of the mothers as their offspring die in their arms. Note the repetition of the verb 'pour out' here and in 2:11, which verbally links
the poet's emotional exhaustion to the prolonged terminal suffering
of the children.

(2) Probing the Extent of Zion's Calamity (2:13-17)

נ 2:13   What evidence can I present to you?
            To what can I compare you, daughter Jerusalem?

---

70. Adele Berlin suggests that the unusual combination 'corn and wine'
refers to commodities which can be stored and that the question as a whole
looks not for new supplies of these items, but for any remnants of stored-up
food which may have been overlooked so far (*Lamentations* [Louisville: West-
minster/John Knox, 2002], 72).

> To what can I liken you that I may comfort you,
>   O virgin daughter Zion?
> For your breaking is great as the sea;
>   who can heal you?

The poet for the first time directly addresses the city. This and the following verse are connected by the desire to comfort Zion, but nothing the poet has to say or teach can reverse the injury done by the false prophets. Despite his identification with the city's agony, the rhetorical questions the poet poses only serve to emphasise his inability to provide answers. The opening question is somewhat obscure, 'What will I act as a witness ˻for˺ you?' Though prophetic testimony was often comprised of warning and correction, a different construction is used here and the sense may be positive (Job 29:11; cf. Mal. 2:14). In the light of the rest of the line, it seems probable that, when the poet addresses Zion, he responds to her earlier challenge to see if there was any suffering like her suffering (1:12), and asks what evidence he can bring before Jerusalem or what analogy he might draw to set her situation in perspective. For a third time mention is made of the need for an adequate comparison, *to what can I liken you?* The vocative *daughter Jerusalem* (literally, 'the daughter, Jerusalem', possibly with an emphatic use of the article) indicates the poet's attachment to the city and his identification with it in its suffering.

Zion's need throughout has been for *comfort*, but the refrain throughout chapter 1 emphasised that such comfort was not forthcoming (cf. 1:2). The poet is trying to provide solace by identifying a place that has undergone an experience similar to that of Zion. If there had been any other instance of survival after such a catastrophe, then that might provide a glimmer of hope for Jerusalem, a precedent which might have moulded her thinking. But the implied answer to the questions is that no adequate comparison can be found. The addition of *virgin* to the address *daughter Zion* serves to emphasise the extent of the suffering. 'Virgin' refers to a young woman of marriageable age, one who is viewed as healthy and strong (cf. 1:15) — yet here she has been struck a crippling blow! Zion as the focus of divine revelation and presence is suffering in a unique way because her vitality has been sapped by the withdrawal of the LORD who had previously blessed her.

To the ancient Israelites *the sea* stood for what was inconceivably immense, agitated and threatening. The poet cannot visualise any suitably comforting comparison for Zion's situation, and has to admit that her *breaking*/'injury' (cf. 2:11) is incomparable. The thought may be that the injury done to her is as great as that which the fury of the sea might inflict, but the repeated and relentless action of the sea may well focus on the unbounded nature of Zion's affliction. *Who can heal you?* does not at first sight present any solution to the problem posed by the wound experienced by Zion. But then, did not Zion confess that the LORD was greater than any force or set of circumstances to be found in the created realm? 'You rule the raging of the sea; when its waves rise you still them' (Ps. 89:9). 'Mightier than the sound of many waters, mightier than the waves of the sea, the LORD on high is mighty' (Ps. 90:4). Here is the crux of the matter. These forces had been unleashed against Zion by the deliberate act of the LORD. Even as she is driven to see that the LORD who imposed this blow is the only one able to control it or take it away, there still remains the question of why he should remove what he has justly imposed.

ב 2:14 Your prophets have envisioned for you
          emptiness and deception;
       and they have not exposed your iniquity
          so as to restore your fortunes.
       But they have envisioned for you oracles
          of emptiness and seduction.

The next four verses intensify the bleak situation of Zion. The poet probes why her situation had developed in the way it had. She had been deceived, and that had led her deeper into her rebellion against God.

Your prophets (cf. 2:9) ought to have been the ones to apply the LORD's spiritual and moral standards to the current situation of the community. Instead they had become so aligned with the prevailing attitudes and so tolerant of misbehaviour that they failed to evaluate it properly. It would be wrong to suppose that these men were inherently immoral or wilful liars. However, they subscribed to the consensus interpretation of God's word, which was taken to give Zion an unconditional assurance of inviolability (cf. 'they have been healing the wound of my people slightly, saying, 'Peace,

peace' — and there is no peace', Jer. 6:14). Their complacency was reinforced by the community's willingness to sacrifice and engage in outward acts of devotion to the LORD. Consequently, the need for inward allegiance and for moral living in accordance with the covenant played no part in the prophets' message.

These peace-prophets had *envisioned for you emptiness and deception.* They had told the people what they wanted to hear, not just to be rewarded by them, but also because they genuinely believed their oracles to be true. Nevertheless setting out the time-honoured dogmas of the Jerusalem establishment was worthless because it did not correspond to what Yahweh was saying to the people. It was 'empty' in the sense that it lacked genuine revelatory content from God. Furthermore it was a deceptive sham. *Deception* may also be understood as 'whitewash', a coating of ground lime applied to a wall to make it smooth and white. This description of the prophetic message is elaborated further in Ezekiel 13:11-14. The Jerusalem peace-prophets were engaged in a religious cover-up of the very grave underlying situation in the land.

Consequently, *they have not exposed your iniquity.* This is the central statement of the verse, framed by similar initial and final lines. There is a wordplay here on the two senses of the root 'to expose' (cf. 1:3). Lack of prophetic exposure had led to the exposure of the exile, the destruction of the city, and the intense suffering of those who remained.

The key task of the genuine prophet was not making detached pronouncements regarding the future, but drawing the link between the present conduct of the people and the LORD's verdict on it. Blessing was contingent on obedience; the curses of the broken covenant would come on the disobedient (cf. Isa. 1:19-20). As the LORD's covenant spokesmen, the prophets had the task of uncovering deviations from the norms of the covenant (cf. Mic. 3:8), especially where the people were unaware of the aberrant nature of their conduct. This called for divine endowment of understanding and resolution.

'Iniquity' (cf. 4:6; 5:7) covers the act that twists away from the standards of the LORD's statutes, the guilt that consequently attached to persons who acted in this way, and the penalty that the LORD would impose. The people had not had their wrongdoing and its consequences clearly set before them. If the prophets had done so, then the result would have been *to restore your fortunes*.[71] Repenting of their sins and returning to the LORD would have led to his acceptance of the people and forgiveness of their sins.

But the Jerusalem prophets had not the theological perceptivity to see how the standards of behaviour and the thought patterns of the community were at variance with the covenant demands of the LORD (cf. 4:13). Furthermore they were unaware that the notions which came into their own minds were not direct revelation from God. Jeremiah had unsparingly declared the divine verdict on their ministry. 'They strengthen the hand of evildoers so that they do not return, each from his wickedness. All of them have become to me like Sodom, and her inhabitants like Gomorrah' (Jer. 23:14). They prophesied 'visions of their own minds' (Jer. 23:16) and 'the deceit of their own hearts' (Jer. 23:26). So their oracles were *emptiness*, repeating the term of line 1, and *seduction,* which has the implication that they were alluring and beguiling. The people heard what they wanted to hear as they stubbornly followed their own inclinations and received a prophetic word of reassurance that it would be well with them (cf. Jer. 23:17). *Oracles* is a technical term for a prophetic word. It probably has the sense of a 'burden', being frequently used of a doom-laden pronouncement against foreign nations (cf. Isa. 13:1; Nahum 1:1). The peace-prophets were encouraging the citizens of Jerusalem that their prosperity would be ensured while divine doom would come upon their oppressors (cf. Jer. 28:2-4).

ᗞ 2:15 They have clapped their hands at you,
    all who passed along the way.
They have whistled and shaken their heads
    at daughter Jerusalem:
'Is this the city which was called
    the perfection of beauty,
    the joy of all the earth?'

71. The meaning of the phrase ləhāšîb šəbîtēk (kethibh)/šəbûtēk (qere) is disputed. It is unlikely that the noun, however it is spelled, is to be linked to the root šābâ, 'to take captive', but has instead the sense of restoring fortunes by bringing a situation back to what it had once been (cf. Jer. 33:7; *HALOT* 4:1385-87.)

In 2:15-16 the poet reminds Zion of the reaction of others to her predicament. *All who passed along the way* are the same group of travellers as Zion appealed to in 1:12. Their response to her situation does not seem to be one of mockery, but of uncomprehending surprise and consternation. *They have clapped their hands* is not a gesture of applause, but of horror. *They have whistled*/'hissed' indicates a sharp sibilant sound used to express fright and shock (rather than derision) at the ruins which faced them as they travelled past Jerusalem (cf. 'they will be astonished and will whistle/hiss', 1 Kgs 9:8; also Jer. 19:8; 49:17; 50:13). They have *shaken their heads* (cf. 1:8) is a gesture often employed in derision (e.g. 2 Kgs. 19:21; Ps. 22:7), but here it might well be one of bewilderment that this fate had come upon such a renowned city. No sympathy or assistance is to be expected from such a group.

Jerusalem's eminence was well known to travellers in the region, and they wondered at her changed circumstances. *Daughter Jerusalem* perhaps looks at the city less in a religious setting, and more as a political and economic entity, than 'daughter Zion'. Formerly she had been called *the perfection of beauty* (a different term from that in 2:1; cf. Ps. 50:2). To the outward eye this was a matter of situation and architecture, but Zion's beauty was deeper than that. As Psalm 48 makes clear, her beauty was a reflection of the presence of her divine King within the city of God. Even passers-by would have seen the magnificence of the city in terms of the blessing of her God, and therefore its woebegone state is all the more a reason for astonishment. There is an implied puzzlement as to why God had allowed this fate to come upon his city which had been *the joy of all the earth*. 'Earth' may also be rendered 'land', in which case the focus would be on Judah's religious rejoicing in all that the capital city meant for her. But the use of the term in Psalm 48:2 supports the idea of 'earth' here. The claims made on behalf of Jerusalem were that there would be universal joy when the nations would also come to recognise the significance of what has been revealed in Jerusalem (cf. Isa. 2:1-4), but the sack of the city leaves the nations asking what had become of such presumptuous assertions. The verse ends with a tricolon (a line consisting of three members), a poetic feature whose drawn-out nature reflects the ongoing perplexity of those who speak.

ﭏ 2:16 All your enemies have opened wide
their mouth against you.
They have whistled and gnashed their teeth;
they said, 'We have swallowed ⌐her⌐!
Yes, this is the day for which we longed!
We have found ⌐it⌐; we have seen ⌐it⌐!'

As well as the reaction of passers-by who were not intrinsically hostile, another factor which intensified Zion's distress was the exultation of her enemies. They had **opened their mouth against you**, an action which may be related to taunting her or to preparing to consume her (cf. Ps. 22:13). **They have whistled**/'hissed' is again an expression of astonishment at the extent of the catastrophe which had befallen the city (cf. 2:15), but on the lips of her enemies it is not difficult to detect a note of malicious glee. To **gnash the teeth** was a gesture employed to express emotions wider than those of anger or frustration. It may involve mockery (Ps. 35:16) or threat (Ps. 37:12). Both seem to be present here. The enemy behaves like a wild animal grinding its teeth (cf. Ps. 124:6) and ready to consume its prey. Indeed, it has gone beyond anticipation. **They said, 'We have swallowed her!'** For 'swallow' see on 2:2. The enemy armies have devoured Jerusalem just as completely as a marauding predator would. This may have involved more than the forces of Babylon, because there were neighbouring peoples who were hostile against Judah and would make use of her weakened situation to their own advantage (cf. 4:21).

Jerusalem's downfall as the realisation of a long cherished goal probably refers to neighbouring nations rather than to Babylon, for whom Judah was a minor irritant. As the Assyrian empire collapsed in terminal decline, Judah's influence in the region had been reasserted under Josiah (cf. 2 Kgs. 23:19-20; 2 Chron. 34:33). There can also be little doubt about the antipathy harboured by the Ammonites, Moabites and Edomites so that they **longed** for a change of fortunes. Their impatient and tense anticipation bursts into intense glee when the unexpected actually comes true. **Yes**/'certainly' conveys their exultation at what has occurred. **We have found; we have seen!** With immense satisfaction they exclaim that they had finally found what they had been looking for; it had come true before their eyes.

There is a reversal here in the order of the alphabetic acrostic because the first letter of the initial word of 2:17 usually precedes that of 2:16. Such an inversion had not occurred in chapter 1,[72] but it is found with the same letters in chapters 3 and 4. It may have been a poetic device signifying disorder. However, there is some evidence that, though what became the accepted order of the Hebrew alphabet is already attested at Ugarit over a millennium earlier, there were divergent practices at this point.[73]

ע 2:17 The LORD has done what he planned;
        he has fulfilled his word
    which he commanded from long ago;
        he has thrown down and has not shown pity,
    and he has made the enemy rejoice over you —
        he has exalted the horn of your foes.[74]

It is implausible that these words continue the enemy's speech; rather the direct address of the poet to Zion is now resumed. Judah's pain goes beyond the deficiencies of her prophets (2:14), the bewilderment of strangers (2:15) and the exultation of her enemies (2:16). There is a more profound level still to her experience because none of these things would have occurred had it not been for the LORD's attitude towards her. Her downfall was not the result of divine inadvertence, but the consequence of his deliberate action. *The LORD has done what he planned.* This may be compared with what is said about Babylon: 'The LORD has both devised and done what he spoke concerning the inhabitants of

---

72. Reversal of these two letters in chapter 1 also is in fact attested in one Qumran manuscript, 4QLam[a]. For a description and evaluation of this manuscript which contains most of chapter 1 of the book, see Hillers, *Lamentations*, 39–48.

73. An ostracon dated to around 1200 B.C. from ʾIzbet Sartah contains an alphabet with the order *pê ʿayin*, but the writing is unskilled and has many mistakes. (It also goes from left to right!) There are later alphabets from Kuntillet ʿAjrud in the southern Negev, dated to around 800 B.C., with the order *pê ʿayin*.

74. There are differences of viewpoint as to the metrical structure of this verse: for instance, the ESV favours three bicola but the NIV two tricola (cf. the discussion on the structure of 1:1). The approach adopted here and in the ESV reflects the Massoretic accents, but both understandings are plausible.

Babylon' (Jer. 51:12). His action against his own rebellious people had been well thought out; indeed, it had been announced centuries beforehand through Moses (Lev. 26:14-39; Deut. 28:15-68). *He has fulfilled his word which he commanded from long ago*/'days of old', where 'from' possibly points to the ongoing prophetic republication of the demands of the Mosaic covenant. The term 'fulfil' here is derived from the language of weaving to describe cutting off a piece of finished fabric. So the LORD has worked out the intricate pattern of his dealings with his people and brought it not just to an end, but to a consummate conclusion — of devastating judgement.

It was ultimately the LORD who had *thrown down* (cf. 2:2) the city using the enemy as his instruments of demolition. He *had not shown pity* (cf. 2:2). When he imposed his penalty, it was without hesitation or reserve. The repetition of these terms forms an inclusion with the beginning of this long section of the poem, and prepares the way for a change of perspective in the concluding verses.

All that had come upon the people was the doing of the LORD. *He has made the enemy rejoice over you*. The invitation is to have insight which penetrates behind the present humiliating fact of the ascendancy of the enemy and their jubilation. This could not have happened had not the LORD been in control. Since it is his imposition, there remains the possibility of its removal, though for the present *he has exalted the horn of your foes.* His judgement had entailed cutting off the horns of Israel (cf. 2:3) and raising high the horn of their adversaries. That too was ultimately his achievement, not that of their foes. So it was in his power to reverse it. It did not improve the prevailing harsh conditions, but their eyes could be lifted up, if only momentarily, to embrace a future hope.

Reflection

- The suffering of the young and of the helpless is a particularly distressing aspect of major catastrophes. It is not surprising then that there have been those who have wondered at the righteousness of the LORD's action in punishing Zion in such a way that it would inevitably bring suffering on the 'innocent'. Such an approach to the matter fails to do justice to the constitution of humanity which has been structured by God into groups where there is interpersonal and intergenerational solidarity. In contradistinction to the divine appraisal 'it was good' over other aspects of creation, there was the verdict, 'It is not good that the man should be alone' (Gen. 2:18). God took direct action to remove this deficiency, and it is on that basis that humanity is organised in families, communities and nations. Within that structure the actions of an individual have repercussions for the good or ill of others. There should be no complaint about this because it is on the basis of such solidarity that salvation is extended to fallen mankind (Rom. 5:17). Equally, however, it imposes responsibility on each member of society for the impact of their actions on the well-being of the group. It is a misconception to attribute 'innocent' suffering to divine abusive violence. The suffering was the product of the intransigence of the community despite the repeated warnings God issued to them. Their thoughtless disregard for the good of those who would be affected by their wrong-doing has precipitated the current crisis. Even so, the fact of that the young are drawn into suffering of the whole community constitutes a valid plea for divine compassion.

• There were varying degrees of guilt regarding the crisis into which the people were plunged. The religious leadership of the community had failed to live up to the requirements of their office, and this was especially true of the prophets whose duty was to apply God's word in the current setting (2:14). Their guilt was greater, but being misled by those who should have provided spiritual guidance did not remove responsibility from the people as a whole. As Jeremiah observed, 'A horrible and appalling thing has happened in the land: the prophets prophesy by falsehood, and the priests rule by their hand, and my people love ⌐it⌐ so. But what will you do at the end of it?' (Jer. 5:30-31). They acquiesced in the empty and deceitful visions, and did not try the prophets by the standards of God's word to assess their status (cf. 1 Thess. 5:20-21; 1 John 4:1). In an age when many false prophets are destined to arise with the skill and signs to deceive if it were possible the elect (cf. Matt. 25:4-5, 11, 24), we ought to emulate the church in Ephesus by testing those who falsely call themselves apostles and so seeking to expose their imposture (Rev. 2:2). Though even in this, we must remember that Satan himself is adept at citing words from Scripture (cf. Matt. 4:1-11).

• The key thought of the chapter, divine determination and control of events, is to be found in 2:17. Amid the uncertainties of life and the weakness of our own perception, there is the abiding guarantee of the declared word of God. 'The word of our God will stand for ever' (Isa. 40:8). He is the one who alone can say, 'My counsel will stand, and I will do all my purpose … Surely I have spoken, surely I will bring it about; I have formed it, surely I will do it' (Isa. 46:10-11). His word is particularly the terms of his covenant, both those of blessing and those of cursing (cf. Lev. 26:3-45; Deut. 28:1-68). While the curse on disobedience may not be evaded or its warnings disregarded with impunity, encouragement is to be derived from the word of blessing which is now guaranteed to all who commit themselves to Christ Jesus. 'All the promises of God find their Yes in him' (2 Cor. 1:20; cf. Heb. 13:8).

C. Zion's Plea (2:18-22)

The concluding verses of the chapter contain two sections. First, the poet appeals to Zion to pray to the Lord because of the dire circumstances affecting her, and particularly her children (2:18-19). Then, as if partially recovering from a state of exhaustion, Zion breaks her silence and expresses her perplexity as to what she has suffered (2:20-22). She does not make any specific request, but merely asks that the LORD consider what he has done.

(1) Plead for the Sake of Your Children (2:18-19)

צ 2:18 Their heart has cried out to the Lord:
               'O wall of daughter Zion!'
          Let tears run down like a torrent
               by day and by night!
          Do not give yourself any respite;
               do not let your eyes stop!

There is an abrupt transition here in that there is no immediately evident referent for 'their' in *their heart*. Grammatically the nearest antecedent is 'your foes' at the end of the previous verse, but that does not yield any sense. Emendation is often resorted to, particularly changing the verb to an imperative 'cry out!' and so aligning it with subsequent imperatives addressed to Zion (cf. NRSV, NLT). Early versions do not, however, support such any alteration. There are two ways of understanding the Hebrew as it stands. It may refer to the people as a whole (cf. NIV), or it may refer to the pleas of the children of Zion, resuming the thought of 2:12 and adding prayer to God to their entreaties to their mothers.[75] Of the two options, the former, more general reference seems less forced. The fact that the population have already voiced their needs to the Lord forms the basis for the following imperatives with which the poet urges them to continue doing so with unremitting fervour.

Somewhat surprisingly the verb 'cry out' occurs only here in Lamentations. It denotes a loud call, generally uttered in a situation of emotional tension, frequently as a cry for help in distress (e.g. Exod. 3:7; Judg. 10:12). Such a loud cry requires physical strength, and possibly here the fact that it is their hearts which are said to cry out indicates the extent to which the deprivation experienced in the famine has weakened the inhabitants of the city. Views differ as to how the remainder of the first line should be integrated into the rest of the verse. It may be read as a poetic personification of the wall of the city (cf. Isa. 14:31) or as a vocative which by synecdoche refers to Zion as a whole. Further, the vocative may denote the one addressed by the preceding imperative form (if that emendation is read) or it may be taken with the following line. However, it seems best to take the phrase as the poet's presentation of the substance of

---

75. Renkema argues for 'their' being identified as Zion's children on the basis of the concentric structure of 2:18-19 so that the 'their' of 2:18a is explicated by the corresponding use of 'your young children' (2:19c). The force of this argument depends on how well established such concentric structures are in Lamentations and on how conclusively a concentric analysis of 2:18-19 is grounded. Renkema points to the recurrence of 'their heart' (2:18a) and 'the life of your young children' (2:19) as the most obvious inclusion in the context. While an intriguing aspect of the poet's technique, such concentricity does not seem to provide a firm basis for further exegetical argument (Renkema, *Lamentations*, 306–9.)

the cry[76] in which the Lord is addressed as **wall of daughter Zion.**
He is the one they look to to provide protection for the city (cf.
'wall of fire', Zech. 2:5), even though the literal wall now lies in
ruins (2:8).

On the basis of the observed response of the people, there follows a series of urgent exhortations not to give over in pleading
with the Lord to help them. Certainly their leaders and surrounding
nations will not provide assistance and, even though the Lord has
acted with hostility towards them, he remains the only feasible
source of aid. Even so, such supplication has to be sincere. **Let
tears stream down like a torrent day and night!** (cf. Jer. 14:17). A
torrent or wadi was a stream which flowed only in winter when,
replenished by the rain, it would rush forcefully down its channel,
taking all before it. Though Zion's tears have been extensive (cf.
1:2, 16), there must be no diminution in the urgency with which she
expresses herself.

Do not give yourself any respite calls on her not to give over in
her efforts. 'Give' and 'yourself' are feminine forms referring to
Zion. **Do not let your eyes stop.** 'Eyes' is literally 'daughter of your
eye', a reference to the pupil of the eye as sensitive and highly
valued (cf. Ps. 17:8; Zech. 2:8), but even so it must not be spared.
So dire is the situation there can be no excuse for not exhausting
every faculty they possess in presenting their need before God.

ק 2:19 Arise, call out in the night,
            at the beginning of the night watches!
       Pour out your heart like water
            before the face of the Lord!
       Lift up your hands to him
            for the life of your young children
       who are fainting with famine
            at the head of every street.

In this verse (as in 1:7) the three line structure is varied by the
inclusion of an additional line. Such stylistic change does not
indicate a need for emendation, but is employed as an elegance,

---

76. A parallel to the present passage is afforded by 2 Kgs. 2:12 where the
verb 'cry out' is followed by words of disconnected exclamation.

possibly here to emphasise a key stanza.[77] The need for day and night weeping as Zion implores the Lord is further elaborated on as she is told to *arise* from her bed and *call out in the night*, shattering its stillness with her piercing cries.[78] This is to be done *at the beginning of the night watches,* possibly the start of the first of three watches into which the night was divided (though there is little evidence to support that view apart from this passage), or else at the start of each of them (cf. the idiom 'the head/beginning of the middle watch', Judg. 7:19). The need for such action is so pressing that it must take precedence over every normal activity, including sleep.

Pour out (cf. 2:4, 11, 12) *your heart* reflects genuine and uninhibited entreaty and not merely a formal religious exercise (cf. Ps. 62:8). The expression may reflect the divine complaint against Israel recorded by Hosea, 'They do not cry out to me from the heart; rather they wail upon their beds' (Hos. 7:14). There is no need to find here a reference to an otherwise unrecorded ritual in which water was poured out before the Lord; rather *like water* reflects the copiousness of the entreaty of their heart in which all their emotion, desires and thoughts are expressed *before the Lord* as they direct their prayer to him. Their expressions of grief are not to be self-centred outpourings to relieve their own emotions, but consciously directed prayers presented with unremitting intensity before the Lord alone.

Lift up your hands refers particularly to the palms of the hands, and is a gesture associated with prayers of entreaty (cf. Pss. 63:4; 141:2). This intercession is to be for *the life of your young children*, who are described here, as in 2:11, 12, as *fainting* through lack of sustenance, emaciated by the ravages of the famine. Their

---

77. 'The bicolon 2:19d is to be considered as an occasional expansion in the poem. Such expansions often occur and the phenomenon of expansion is usual in Hebrew poetry. Perhaps such expansions (contractions are also possible) do not match Western ideas about symmetry or regularity, but for what reasons must we assume that Hebrew poets were guided by our modern ideas?' (Renkema, 'Literary Structure,' 318).

78. Again Hillers (*Lamentations*, 27, footnote 30) notes the poetic impact of the sequence of clause initial second person feminine verb forms. This reinforces the need for action on the part of daughter Zion.

life-threatening plight is intensified by the fact that their suffering is not in the privacy of their own homes, but out in the open, subject to public gaze, *at the head of every street*, that is, 'on every street corner' as we would express it (cf. 2:11, 12).

(2) The Prayer of Daughter Zion (2:20-22)

In the final speech of the chapter, Zion rouses herself from her weakness and exhaustion, and pleads with the LORD, the God of covenant mercies. Taking her cue from the poet's exhortation, she points particularly to how the children of the city have been affected by the catastrophe and, without making any explicit request, she presents their affliction as that which should induce God to extend mercy.

ר 2:20 See, O LORD, and observe!
   With whom have you dealt in this way?
   Shall women eat their offspring,
      the young children they have cared for?
   Shall there be slaughtered in the sanctuary of the
      Lord
      priest and prophet?

See and observe resumes the plea that had been used in 1:11 (cf. also 1:9, 20; 5:1). Although no response had been forthcoming to her earlier entreaties, in the light of the poet's exhortations Zion once more implores God to pay her the attention she considers her suffering deserves. Since her hope is that the facts of the situation will induce God to respond appropriately, it is unlikely that the tone of the following questions is one of indignant reproach. Zion is appealing for compassion, and it may be that the underlying argument is based on a perception that, though the LORD had imposed this sentence on the city, there were many aspects of the enemy's behaviour which went beyond what he had mandated (cf. Isa. 10:5-12; 47:5-9; Hab. 2:6-20).

The first question, *With whom have you dealt in this way?*, may be interpreted as a claim for special treatment because of Zion's covenant status, but that seems unlikely because it was acknowledged violation of her covenant responsibilities which had led to the existing calamity. More plausibly, it may be understood as an expression of the severity of Zion's sufferings in that God had imposed on no other nation such punishment as had come on Zion (cf. 2:13; see also the NIV rendering here). Furthermore, a good case can be made that even the initial question has the treatment of the young in view. The verb to 'deal with'/'afflict' (cf. 1:22) is spelled very similarly to the word for 'young child'.[79] The question then voices puzzlement that it should be in the LORD's purpose to have the young suffer in the way that had happened at the hands of the enemy.

The second question elaborates on the horror and perplexity which underlay the first: is this what things have come to? *Shall women eat their offspring, the young children they have cared for?* The term for 'offspring' is literally 'fruit' or 'crops', though it is often used figuratively for descendants. Here, however, there may well be an additional factor. Rather than eating fruit gathered from plants, the reference is now to a grotesque, cannibalistic meal. This was no frenzied exaggeration: it could hardly have been urged as a plea before the LORD if it was mere fiction. Indeed, there is abundant evidence that among the atrocities of siege warfare desperate mothers violated every bond of human love and ate the corpses of their dead children upon whom they had once lavished their affection (cf. Lev. 26:29; Deut. 28:53; 2 Kgs. 6:28; Jer. 19:9; Ezek. 5:10). 'Cared for' is a word of unusual occurrence. It may refer to the health and beauty of the child, or to the way the mother has handled it with affection.[80] But now these adored children have perished. The covenant curse had come upon Jerusalem as the fruit of her rebellion, and at the same time she had been deprived of a future she had looked forward to.

The next question, *Shall there be slaughtered in the sanctuary*

79. The verb ʿôlaltā (from ʿālal, 'to deal with') echoes ʿōlălê (from ʿôlēl, 'child, young one').

80. Although there are modern authors who support the view that the verb means 'to bring forth healthy children' (*HALOT* 2:378), the older view is still cogent: 'to care for, cherish', perhaps particularly 'to hug' or 'to play with'. Perhaps there is an implicit challenge: why had the LORD not cared for them in a similar way? Dobbs-Allsopp notes a further possibility in the similarity in sound between ṭippūḥîm, 'cared for', and tappûḥîm, 'apples', extending the metaphor of the first colon (*Lamentations*, 15).

of the Lord priest and prophet?, raises matters of key significance
for the relationship between Zion and the Lord. The prophets
mentioned with the priests would be those whose ministry was
conducted at the sanctuary, and are the same group spoken of
earlier (2:14). The loss of such central authority figures (cf.
2:6, 9) constituted evidence not only of the disintegration of society and
the community, but of the annulment of the covenant bond. The
enormity of these outrages would have been intensified by their
location in the sacred precincts. That the Lord had permitted such
affronts in his dwelling place on earth signalled the extent of his
estrangement. He had abandoned the people and the institutions he
had given them.

Such slaughter was probably unusual for the Babylonians. Their
superstitions led them as far as they could to avoid giving offence
to any deity by interfering with sacred practices and cultic personnel, but in the case of Jerusalem the sanctity of the Temple and the
claims made for it had fuelled repeated insurrection, and political
considerations made it imperative to eradicate such a site of
possible future trouble.

ﬠ 2:21   There are lying[81] on the ground in the streets
              boys and old men.
           My young women and my young men
              have fallen by the sword.
           You have slaughtered them in the day of your
              anger;
              you have butchered them — you have not
              shown pity.

Much of what is said in this verse recapitulates previous descriptions, probably to indicate the vehemence with which Zion urged
her situation on the Lord. There are three stark presentations of the
violent deaths occasioned by the merciless treatment of the city's
captors. Some of the killings were probably by way of vengeance
on a city which had resisted them for so long; others may have been
intended to intimidate the population or to extort from them any
wealth they still possessed. But as a result Jerusalem was subject to

---

81. A perfect with present consequences: 'have lain down' (wounded and
dead) and so 'are lying'.

a bloodbath that engulfed all in the population whether *boys and old men,* two singular terms used collectively. Zion also complains that her *young women and young men,* who would have formed the community of the future (cf. 1:18), have been summarily dispatched by the sword. It was not just famine that had deadly work to do in the city.

But the most ominous aspect of the situation is that more than the enemy was active: *You have slaughtered them in the day of your anger.* It is acknowledged that the LORD was acting judicially in imposing his sentence on their sin (cf. 1:2, 12). Jerusalem had no doubt regarding the LORD's supervening control of events. *You have butchered them — you have not shown pity.* 'Butchered' is the verb used for killing livestock for consumption as food, but in respect of people it conveys the idea of brutality. The LORD's lack of pity has already been mentioned in 2:2, 17, but here the complaint is probably intensified in that it relates not to property or the situation in general, but to the massacre of people, especially the young. Surely this dire situation will induce some measure of compassion from on high?

ת 2:22 You called as on a day of festival
      my terrors from all around,
   and there was not on the day of the anger of the
      LORD
   any escapee or survivor.
   Those to whom I gave birth and whom I reared
      my enemy has destroyed.

It was the LORD who *called*[82] crowds to gather in and around Jerusalem *as on a day of festival* (cf. 2:7). But the positive note is immediately reversed: these crowds were not there for religious festivities. The LORD's summons had instituted a grotesque parody

---

82. The force of the imperfect verb *tiqrāʾ* needs to be considered. The following verb, 'there was not', clearly refers to the past, and that makes a future, 'you will call', improbable here. Possibly the imperfect is used of repeated action in the past ('you kept calling'), a feature which might have been suggested by the recurrent nature of the festivals. However, most translators and commentators have a past translation, probably on the basis that the imperfect is used here to provide the required opening letter for the line.

of Israel's sacred assemblies. *My terrors* are the enemy invaders who have come *from all around* to feast on Jerusalem and its citizens. This theme seems to be particularly drawn from Jeremiah's prophecy (Jer. 6:25; 20:3, 10; 46:5; 49:29).

This massing against Jerusalem was such that *on the day of the anger of the LORD* (cf. 2:21)[83] there was not *anyone who escaped or survived.* This cannot be maintained with absolute literality in that there were survivors among those taken into exile as well as among those who remained in the land and the others who escaped to surrounding nations, including Egypt. The point being made is that the time for repentance and avoidance of this outpouring of anger had long since passed, and the dire consequences of the outpouring of divine justice could not be evaded.

Zion is not questioning the LORD's right to intervene or the justice of his verdict. She is expressing her despair and hopelessness at the ongoing impact on the community of the LORD's action. *Those to whom I gave birth and whom I reared my enemy has destroyed.* The rare verb 'I gave birth' has also been understood as 'I spread out my hands to hold', the action of a mother in caring for an infant. The use of the singular 'my enemy' here may point to the underlying thought that it is the LORD himself who is the enemy in view so that Jerusalem is appealing to the LORD against the LORD's own hostile action against her.[84] But the final word is 'destroyed'/'brought to an end'/'finished off'. Without relief from on high there is no future for the community. All is bleak and forlorn.

Reflection

• 'Who can heal you?' (2:13) now receives an answer when the poet directs Zion to plead with the LORD. However, there is the need for earnest and unremitting endeavour in this regard. 'They do not cry out to me with their heart' (Hos. 7:14). In crisis situations there is no option but to entreat God even at times which would otherwise be legitimately given over to sleep (cf. Pss. 22:2; 88:1; Luke 18:7). Indeed, in such circumstances Asaph said of God, 'You hold my eyelids open' (Ps. 77:4).

---

83. The use of the third person LORD in direct address to him is permissible in Hebrew idiom (cf. 3:66), especially in what is virtually a technical term.
84. Renkema, *Lamentations*, 330.

- Zion does not plead past mercies or former achievements. She focuses on the mercy and pity of God. The horrific circumstances of the city call for urgent remedies from the only possible source of help, so that she responds to the invitation, 'Call upon me in the day of trouble' (Ps. 50:15). 'The LORD will act for his people and on his servants he will have compassion when he sees that their power is gone and there is none ⌊left⌋, bond or free' (Deut. 32:36).

Lamentations 3

OUTLINE

A. The Agony of Suffering (3:1-24)

  (1) The Darkness of Affliction (3:1-18)
  (2) The Dawning of a New Day (3:19-24)

B. Moving Out Of Darkness (3:25-39)

  (1) The LORD's Goodness (3:25-27)
  (2) Living with Catastrophe (3:28-30)
  (3) The Lord's Compassion (3:31-33)
  (4) Divine Disapproval (3:34-36)
  (5) The Sovereignty of the Lord (3:37-39)

C. Self-Examination and Complaint (3:40-48)

D. Prayer Based on Past Experience (3:49-66)

  (1) Anticipated Relief (3:49-51)
  (2) Past Persecution (3:52-54)
  (3) Past Deliverance (3:55-57)
  (4) Judge My Cause (3:58-63)
  (5) Give What They Deserve (3:64-66)

The more complex literary structure of chapter 3 draws attention to its thematic centrality in the book as a whole. While its basic form is still that of an alphabetic acrostic, this device is now employed in a more intricate and artistically demanding fashion in which each letter of the alphabet is used at the beginning of three successive lines of the poem. This technique is similar to that found in Psalm 119 where each letter is repeated eight times, arranging the psalm into 22 distinct stanzas. The same format of 22 stanzas occurs here, though with three lines/verses per stanza. Since each line in chapter 3 is numbered as a verse, its 66 verses do not represent an overall increase in length from chapters 1 and 2 where the verses typically consist of three poetic lines.

However, although the acrostic structure of the poem is clear, analysis of its content is a matter of some perplexity. The initial technique deployed by literary structure analysis (see *Introduction: C. Literary Structure: Concentric Analysis*) is to identify a thematic kernel at the centre of the poem, but it is admitted that the central stanzas of the poem (3:31-33, 34-36) are unable to bear the weight that this would impose on them. Instead, Renkema proposes that the mid-point of the poem functions to divide its overall structure into two parallel parts at the centre of each of which the key thematic foci of the poem are to be located. So in 3:17 he identifies in the words, 'My soul has scorned peace; I have forgotten what happiness is', the poem's message of suffering, and in 3:50 there is the complementary reaction of waiting in perplexity for divine intervention, 'until he looks down and sees, the LORD from heaven'.[85] However, while this analysis has considerable merit in that it points to major themes of the book and also displays the careful construction of the poem, it does not seem to do sufficient justice to 3:22-24 which many have felt present the essential theological insight of the book.

On balance, therefore, it is preferable to analyse the chapter by observing where changes occur in the viewpoint from which the material is presented. Indeed, the significance of the identity of the

---

85. 'In the neighbourhood of vss. 33 and 34, one cannot find such an accumulation of words as was the case in Lam. 1 and 2. The connection between the ר-strophe and the ע-strophe seems to be stronger' (Renkema, 'Literary Structure,' 321, 333).

speaker in the poem is highlighted in 3:1. No longer does the poet portray himself as an observer of Jerusalem's trauma, nor does he permit us to hear personified Zion as she expresses her grief and perplexity. Instead it is emphasised that there is here a new perspective: a male figure looks inwardly and speaks of his personal suffering (3:1-18). But the speaker's experience of abandonment and bitterness is not left there. While one can hardly speak of his problems being resolved, he does introduce a counterbalancing perspective of prayer and hope (3:19-24). On this basis he sets out various lessons regarding how one should attempt to live through times of affliction by viewing one's life in the light of the LORD's character and purpose (3:25-39). The poet then moves from human experience in general to the specific situation of his own community in Zion and sets out a collective prayer of approach to God in penitence, seeking relief from the ongoing calamity which was afflicting them (3:40-48). As the intensity of Zion's ordeal and grief once more impacts on him, the poet reverts to personal reflection in the remainder of the chapter. He tells of his present grief (3:49-51), but also in a renewed note of faith and trust he recalls his own experience of suffering (3:52-54) and of the LORD's answer to his prayers (3:55-63). He ends by looking forward to the resolution of his present situation through divine intervention (3:64-66).

A. The Agony of Suffering (3:1-24)

The best known passage in Lamentations is undoubtedly the resounding affirmation of faith to be found in 3:22-24. However, to read these words in isolation from their context is to diminish the victory of faith embodied in their utterance. They should not be divorced from the preceding bleak picture of desolation and dejection (3:1-18). There the speaker does not simply record past experiences from which he has emerged and which have been superseded by the joy of morning (cf. Ps. 30:5). The suffering and the circumstances which gave rise to his inner darkness continue to afflict him (cf. 3:3, 20), but now alongside them he is aware of true ground for hope in the character of the LORD, and he sets out his personal experience so that it may become a paradigm for those around him.

But who is this speaker? A variety of answers has been given, including a defeated soldier[86] and Jehoiachin, the young king imprisoned in Babylon (see *Introduction: A. Historical Setting*, page 10). Traditionally Jeremiah was identified as the individual whose life story was being reflected here. Certainly there are aspects of what is said that fit in with what we know of Jeremiah's life, but they are not sufficiently distinctive to constitute a watertight case. This poem, like the others in the book, is written in the anonymous style which is characteristic of Hebrew poetry and which dominates the poetic compositions of Psalms. The poet does not wish to focus his readers' attention on the specifics of his own case, but rather to invite them to generalise from his experience to their own. That is what occurs here also. We cannot rule out the possibility that this poem originated with Jeremiah, but it is presented in such a way as to conceal its origins. Our response should not be to seek to uncover the author, but rather to learn from his message.

More recently there has been a tendency to identify 'the man' of 3:1 not as a specific historical individual, but as a collective figure. We have already been introduced to virgin daughter Zion, who embodies in one artistically presented individual ('persona') the experience of the community as a whole. However, the relationship between 'the man' and the community is not at the same level. Assuming that 'I' has the same reference throughout the poem, the speaker identifies Jerusalem as 'my city' in 3:51, a verse which shows that he has witnessed and experienced all that has befallen her. But he is not simply saying that the community's suffering is to be equated with his own, and that therefore he is a representation of the community. The speaker is a real, historical individual, not a poetic construct. Both have been subjected to intense suffering and grief, but the speaker has experienced more than the anguish of his situation. Despite his ordeal he has regained a measure of hope. His words in this section do not, therefore, constitute the grounds for a plea to God to intervene, but rather an exhortation to his fellows to learn from what he has undergone. They had much in common; perhaps that could be extended to include renewed hope in God.

86. William F. Lanahan, 'The Speaking Voice in the Book of Lamentations,' *Journal of Biblical Literature* 93 (1974): 45.

(1) The Darkness of Affliction (3:1-18)

The initial presentation is of the poet's forlorn and desolating experience of anguish in which hope is completely banished. In many respects the sentiments expressed reflect those of the darkest portion in the Psalter, Psalm 88. The poet is not conscious of any intimacy with the LORD, whose name is not even uttered, but at the same time he cannot escape from the all-pervasive and constricting control God has over his life.

א 3:1   I am the man ⌐who⌐ has seen affliction
             under the rod of his wrath.

א 3:2   He has driven me and made ⌐me⌐ walk
             ⌐in⌐ darkness and not light.

א 3:3   Surely against me he repeatedly turns
             his hand all the day.

It is indeed striking that rather than simply setting down what he has to say, as is customary in Old Testament presentations, the speaker takes time to introduce himself. *I* without such an introduction would be heard as a continuation of the preceding speech of daughter Zion, whereas it is now a male figure who speaks and refers to himself as *the man*. This is not the ordinary term for a male (*'îš*) but a rarer word (*geber*) which describes a man at the peak of his physical power when he is most competent to direct and secure his affairs. Indeed, there are passages where the term is employed with positive, spiritual significance. 'Blessed is the man (*geber*) who has set his trust in the LORD' (Ps. 40:4; cf. also Pss. 34:8; 37:23-24; 94:12).[87] That appears to be its significance here. Despite being one whose trust is in the LORD, the speaker is one who ***has seen affliction under the rod of his wrath*** (cf. Ps. 88:4-7). This metaphorical description of his affliction (cf. 1:3, 7, 9) because of divine wrath (cf. 2:2) is therefore comparable to that of Zion; indeed it has been part of it. Physically, he has suffered the ravages of famine; spiritually, a loss of vitality because his hope in God languished.

Here again the translation of perfect verb forms influences our understanding of the poem (see *Introduction: F. Translation*).

---

87. See entry on *gābhar* by H. Kosmala in *TDOT* 2:378-381.

These forms view actions as complete entities, and are not directly related to the temporal modifications of the verb in English tenses. Using an English present perfect, 'has seen', attempts to encapsulate two aspects of what the poet has undergone: his suffering is not some recently occurring phenomenon, nor is it completed in the past. He does not say, 'I am the man who saw affliction', nor yet, 'I am the man who sees affliction', though both are true. He claims that he 'has seen' it and that it continues as an ongoing part of his experience (cf. 3:3, 20).

'Rod' may refer to a sceptre, a symbol of royal office (Ps. 45:6; Zech. 10:1), or an implement with which an individual is punished (Prov. 13:24; 26:3). Here both are combined. Although the LORD is not directly named, 'his' points back to 2:22, and indirectly affirms that the LORD is the source of what has befallen him. In the situation of Jerusalem's capture by the Babylonians, the LORD had brought the aggressor against his people, just as an earlier generation had experienced the LORD's wrath through attack by Assyria, 'the rod of my anger' (Isa. 10:5).

Driven refers to the direction and control of animals (cf. Gen. 31:18; Exod. 3:1; 1 Sam. 30:20; and especially, 'O Shepherd of Israel, you who drive/ lead Joseph like a flock', Ps. 80:1).[88] *Made ... walk*/'led' is also used of the LORD's regulating the path of his people (cf. Deut. 8:2; Isa. 42:16; 48:21), but here the LORD is no longer the shepherd who provides abundant green pastures for his people and who leads them beside still waters (Ps. 23:2). Rather his wrath had brought about a reversal of their circumstances, and as a member of the community the poet had shared their destiny. Divine control had forced him into total *darkness* from which the *light* of God's favour and blessing is absent (cf. Amos 5:18). This points to circumstances of oppression and bondage (cf. Isa. 8:22), associated with spiritual bewilderment that such a change should have occurred in the LORD's attitude.

The imagery behind 3:3 seems to be that of a charioteer in hot pursuit of a fugitive. No matter how much the hapless victim turns and twists to escape, his pursuer takes corresponding action to keep

---

88. Though the verse begins with *ʾôtî*, 'me', this is probably because of conformity to the acrostic pattern rather than an indication of any special emphasis being placed on 'me' at this point.

up with him. *All the day* he is hunted relentlessly. *His hand* echoes earlier negative references to the hand of the LORD acting with hostility against Jerusalem (1:14; 2:18). It is significant that the two Hebrew verbs in this verse are imperfects (cf. 3:1), indicating an open-ended, ongoing situation. The poet emphatically confirms that he still does not know complete relief from the activities of his divine antagonist.

ב 3:4   He has made my flesh and my skin waste away;
        he has broken my bones.

ב 3:5   He has built against me and surrounded me
        with bitterness and hardship.

ב 3:6   In dark places he has made me dwell,
        like the dead of long ago.

In this stanza the speaker considers how emaciated his body has become through the impact of famine, probably as a result of the siege of Jerusalem and its aftermath (cf. 1:11). Although the language employed is traditional (cf. Pss. 32:3-4; 38:3-4; Isa. 38:13), that does not imply that the experienced described is any the less real or hurtful. But famine is not an impersonal or random force; it is inflicted by the LORD. *He has broken my bones* is a metaphorical expression based on the experience of an individual whose body had been drained of the strength needed to stand upright and be active (cf. Ps. 51:8; Isa. 38:13). So in his inner being the poet has been utterly shattered by the circumstances he is having to endure.

Furthermore his environment has been turned into one of hostility. *He has built against me* suggests the activity of an enemy erecting siege works about a city so that it is *surrounded* (cf. Pss. 17:9; 22:16; 88:17). Similarly the speaker felt himself hemmed in by God with circumstances of *bitterness and hardship*. 'Bitterness' refers to an unidentified wild plant which was unpleasant to the taste and poisonous (cf. 3:19; Deut. 32:33; Ps. 69:21). The term is used metaphorically for extreme adversity. 'Hardship' described the rigours of Israel's wilderness travels (Exod. 18:8; Num. 20:14). That had been the outworking of divine judgement, and now the poet too was trapped in a similarly harsh environment, with seemingly no end in sight.

Dark places refers to more than imprisonment in dungeons that are hidden from the light; it also includes the grave (cf. Ps. 88:6, 18). David's experience of the oppression of the enemy had been expressed in virtually identical terms, 'He has made me dwell in dark places, like the dead of long ago' (Ps. 143:3). So severely afflicted is the speaker and so isolated from others that he was virtually living in the grave *like the dead of long ago*. Those recently departed are mourned by others and their absence is keenly felt, but the speaker thought of himself as one who was no longer cared for or remembered (cf. 1:2).

ל 3:7   He has walled up round about me so that I cannot get out;
        he has made my chain heavy.

ל 3:8   Even though I cry out and plead for help,
        he has shut out my prayer.

ל 3:9   He has walled up my ways with hewn stone;
        he has made my paths crooked.

The imagery of a prison (3:5) or a grave (3:6) is further developed to emphasise the confinement and restriction of the poet's situation. The LORD has acted against him to *wall up* (3:7, 9) any possible way of escape. A wall may give security from external threat ('to give us a wall/protection in Judah and Jerusalem,' Ezra 9:9), or it may prevent the movement of those enclosed within it. It is the latter thought that dominates here because the LORD has hemmed the speaker in. For *about*, compare Psalms 3:3; 139:11. No escape is possible: *I cannot get out* (cf. Ps. 88:8). Furthermore his divine jailer has also shackled him with a heavy *chain*, literally 'my bronze', perhaps a single chain about the neck, or more probably a collective reference to all the chains used to impede the movement of the prisoner. When the LORD imposes maximum security conditions, then it is futile for mere humans to attempt to get away. At a physical level this refers to the siege of Jerusalem; at a spiritual level it was a feeling of spiritual bondage, an inability to escape from an oppressive sense of restriction — to banish the silence and to overcome the breakdown in communication by conversing with God.

Even emphasises the spiritual nature of this confinement. Although he does not directly mention God, it is clear that the speaker has tried to bring his situation before the LORD by crying out to him in prayer and pleading for help, but the LORD is a jailer who refuses to listen to his entreaty: *he shuts out my prayer*. The cell door has been so tightly sealed that no sound can penetrate in either direction. The LORD is resolute in rebuffing any supplication for mercy (cf. 3:44), a theme found elsewhere in Scripture (cf. Job 19:7; 30:20; Isa. 59:2).

Hewn stone is carefully chiselled material. Its use implies that what is constructed from it is no temporary obstruction, but a permanent, expertly crafted, and consequently solid barrier which will successfully resist any attempt to remove it. Every route which suggests itself to the poet to alleviate or reverse his circumstances has been divinely blocked (Job 3:23; Hos. 2:6). The description *he has made my paths crooked* suggests that life has become an inescapable maze. Nothing is straightforward anymore. Whichever way he turns, the speaker is thwarted in his attempts to find relief or to escape.

ד 3:10 He is a bear lying in wait for me,
            a lion in hiding.

ד 3:11 He has turned aside my ways and torn me to pieces;
            he has made me desolate.

ד 3:12 He has bent his bow and set me
            as a target for his arrow.

The portrayal of the LORD's hostility and obstructiveness is intensified as he is pictured as a wild animal (3:10-11) and then as an enemy archer (3:12-13). It is no longer a matter of preventing the speaker from going where he wants, but of actively and aggressively pursuing him. Both *bear* and *lion* were familiar animals at this period, and the threat they posed to human life was well known (for the bear, cf. 2 Sam. 17:8; Prov. 17:12; for the lion, Jer. 4:7; 49:19; 50:44; for both together, 1 Sam. 17:34-36; Prov. 28:15; Hos. 13:8; Amos 5:19). They are used figuratively for an individual's enemies. Hosea had relayed the LORD's threats, 'I will be like a lion to Ephraim, and like a young lion to the house of Judah' (Hos. 5:14). The first threat had come true in the past for the northern kingdom when Samaria had been captured and its people deported; it was the second which had recently been realised in the fall of

Jerusalem. The LORD had been waiting for his people to return to him, but when in their perversity they did not, his waiting became in effect an ambush from which he sprang like a beast of prey to consume them.

The exact significance of the first part of 3:11 is disputed. *He has turned aside my ways* probably conveys the idea that, aware of a presence like that of a wild animal on the route he would take, the speaker has tried, and continues to try, to escape — but to no avail. He *has torn me to pieces* shows that the animal has caught him and savagely mauled him — but the description stops short of death. However, the poet has been rendered *desolate* (cf. 1:4, 16), physically ruined and psychologically a wreck.

The imagery then changes to that of an archer, possibly a huntsman, but more probably a soldier (cf. 2:4). He has used his foot to bend his bow so that it may be strung ready for action. Indeed, the archer has chosen his target and taken aim.

ד 3:13 He has caused the arrows of his quiver
        to enter into my inners.

ה 3:14 I have become the laughing-stock of all my people,
        the theme of their mocking-song all the day.

ה 3:15 He has made me consume abundantly of bitter herbs;
        he has filled me with wormwood.

Although the acrostic structure of the poem requires the start of a new stanza at this point, thematically there is continuity as the arrows of the divine archer of 3:12 reach their target and penetrate *into my inners*, literally 'my kidneys'. 'Kidneys' is found as a metaphor for the inner life of an individual, including both thought and emotion (cf. Ps. 73:21; Jer. 12:2; 17:10). While 'arrows' may be a figurative usage for disease and illness (cf. Job 34:6; Ps. 91:5), the LORD's blows are not just physical; the speaker has been traumatised psychologically and spiritually — and the wounds have not yet healed.

What is more, the poet has become an object of ridicule, but whose? This is a textual problem of long-standing. The Hebrew text reads *of all my people*, but even the Massoretes who preserved the ancient text found this awkward. Why would his fellow countrymen treat him as a *laughing-stock*? This objection is particularly cogent in view of the fact that they were enduring the same fate. Consequently, an ancient correction, which is followed by about fifty medieval Hebrew manuscripts, reads 'all peoples', that is, foreigners, and this is adopted by a number of English translations, being seen as a fulfilment of Deuteronomy 28:37.[89] However, the strongly-attested Hebrew text may be taken as describing not the people's scoffing at the suffering of the speaker, but at his continued faith in the LORD.[90] Throughout he has ascribed all that has come upon him to divine activity, and so he is treated with ridicule by the very covenant people who should have most readily understood and adopted his point of view. But the people have been demoralised by their experience of suffering. The devastation which came upon Jerusalem had falsified their superficial theology, and in their misery they dismiss, if not the LORD himself, then any interpretation of events which ascribes sovereignty and control to him — even a presentation of it as inherently negative as the one which the poet supplies. The popular reaction to the speaker intensified his feeling of rejection as he finds himself dismissed not only by the LORD but by his compatriots also. For *theme of their mocking-song*, see on 3:63.

While *he has made me consume abundantly* might easily depict a situation of satisfaction and contentment, that is not so here. *Bitter herbs* as used in the Passover meal (Exod. 12:8; Num. 9:11) were what was on the LORD's menu for the besieged city. Unpleasant to consume in any quantity, they would be left to the last even in the severest famine. Along with them they had to drink *wormwood*, traditionally identified as the sap of a bitter-tasting shrub. If that is correct, then this commodity is the same as absinthe, which can be consumed in small quantities. But here the situation is that of being *filled*/'made to drink to saturation' with

---

89. While the Massoretic Text reads *ʿammî*, 'my people', the Massoretes themselves were suspicious of this. In some medieval Hebrew manuscripts (supported by the Syriac Peshitta) *ʿammîm*, 'peoples', is found, and this is reflected also in the RSV and ESV. However, the majority of Hebrew manuscripts follow the Massoretic Text (supported by the LXX and the Vulgate), and this reading is adopted by AV, NASB, NIV, NRSV, NLT. The evidence for reading 'my people' is decidedly superior. 'Peoples' is an easier reading, wrongly adopted to give a more readily understood sense to the text.

90. See Renkema, *Lamentations*, 370.

the liquid — perhaps leading to poisoning and serious illness (cf. Job 9:18). Quite possibly such measures were resorted to because of the intensity of the famine. The total picture is one of severe suffering imposed in judgement (cf. Jer. 9:15; 23:15).

❦ 3:16 He has made my teeth grind on gravel;
         he has made me cower in ashes.

❦ 3:17 My soul has rejected peace;
         I have forgotten what happiness is.

❦ 3:18 So I have said, 'My grandeur has perished,
         and ⌜also⌝ my hope from the LORD.'

In the extreme circumstances of the besieged and ruined city, food and shelter have been hard to find. *He has made my teeth grind on gravel* is not a picture of someone being forced to eat gravel, but rather of someone desperately scavenging for any source of food and picking up small stones from the ground along with previously discarded scraps or roots from plants as they scrabble on the ground. *He has made me cower in ashes*. The scene is one in which an individual is found in the city rubbish dumps, either looking for food, or else living there because his own accommodation has been destroyed. It is a picture of utter destitution. Also the similarity in sound between 'ashes' (*ʾēper*) and 'dust' (*ʾāpār*), the latter term being one associated with dying (cf. Gen. 3:19; Ps. 90:3), casts a deathly pallor over the episode, hinting that the speaker is close to expiring. This too he recognises as the direct imposition of the LORD.

In 3:17 there is a transition from a description of the nature of the suffering being endured to the speaker's despairing reaction to his dire situation. *My soul* points to the life force of the individual, all that constitutes him a living being and infuses him, particularly inwardly, with vigour. But he is no longer a picture of vitality. Instead he has to record that *my soul has rejected peace*, literally, 'from peace', is an awkward expression which is difficult to explain. A variety of translations are possible. 'You have rejected my soul from peace' (cf. AV, NKJV) understands the subject of the verb to be God himself. However, direct address to God is improbable at this point in the thematic development of the poem. Another approach is to emend the verb to a passive form, 'My soul has been rejected from peace' (cf. NASB, NIV, NRSV, ESV).[91] In this case 'peace' (*šālôm*) would be taken in its widest sense of all that was conducive to the well-being and fulfilment of the speaker. However, it is preferable to retain the Massoretic text, and to understand 'peace' as here relating particularly to inward calm and equilibrium (cf. 'no peace in my bones', Ps. 38:3). The poet is not saying that such inner harmony is undesirable but that, in the light of his outward circumstances and the internal despair he feels, it is unattainable. He cannot be at rest with himself since he knows he is the target of divine hostility, and so he is unable to keep up a pretence that all is well.

The thought of the second part of 3:17 parallels that of the initial colon. *I have forgotten what happiness is.* 'Happiness'/'good' refers to what makes life pleasant and desirable. Objectively it may point to the blessings bestowed by the covenant King upon his people, but here the focus is more on subjective appropriation of those benefits, including the privilege and satisfaction involved in worshipping God (cf. 'the goodness of your house', Ps. 65:4). So the forgetting which is in view is not a lapse of memory regarding the existence of God's gifts and the enjoyment derived from them;

---

91. The qal imperfect *wattiznaḥ* may be a third person feminine singular form with 'my soul' (a feminine noun) as its subject, or second person masculine singular with 'you' (= Yahweh) as subject. If the latter, then the translation would be, 'you have rejected my soul away from peace'/'you have excluded my soul from peace' (cf. AV). However, this would result in direct address to the LORD, which has been deliberately avoided in the context. Reflecting sensitivity to this factor and also to the prevalent use of the verb with a divine subject (cf. 2:7; 3:31), the LXX reads a masculine verb, 'he has deprived my soul of peace'. The Vulgate understands the verb as a niphal form, *wattizzānaḥ*: 'my soul has been rejected from peace', and this is followed by many translators. However, both the LXX and the Vulgate seem to be attempts to translate the Massoretic text, and so point to its originality. While the verb *zānaḥ* in the qal does not occur elsewhere with the preposition *min*, 'from', it is not attested at all in the niphal. One way of retaining the Massoretic text and dealing with its awkwardness is to take the letter *mêm* not as the preposition *min* before the following noun, but as an enclitic *mem* to be read at the end of the preceding verb, yielding 'My soul rejected peace' (cf. Hillers, *Lamentations*, 114; Bruce K. Waltke and Michael P. O'Connor, *An Introduction to Biblical Hebrew Syntax* [Winona Lake, Indiana: Eisenbrauns, 1990], §9.8).

the speaker is not suffering from amnesia. Quite the contrary, it is his memory of past privileges which intensifies his present distress. The root of the word 'forgotten' is of relatively rare occurrence, one striking instance being in the phrase 'the land of forgetfulness' (Ps. 88:12) to describe the state of the dead. They are not presented as those who have no memories; rather they have nothing but memories and are frustrated by being unable to participate in the divinely bestowed good they remember they once enjoyed.

In 3:18 we arrive at the bleakest vista in the entire poem, and yet, surprisingly, it is here that the first glimmer of light appears. The poet continues to set out his ongoing reaction to his situation. *I have said* may well refer to inward speech: 'I have thought'. The verb form does not locate this exclusively in the past; it expresses his total response to his circumstances. *My grandeur* comes from a noun (*nēṣaḥ*) which combines two ideas not ordinarily associated in English in one term: perpetuity and grandeur/splendour. While it is possible to find here a reference to the speaker's inability to endure (cf. ESV) or, possibly, to his future destiny, it is perhaps more probable that what is in view is his loss of all that gave him special status before the LORD. Surveying what has afflicted him he can arrive at only one conclusion: the special relationship is over, and so too is *my hope from the LORD.* Because the LORD had inflicted this suffering on the speaker and had refused to respond to his entreaties, he could only conclude that there was no longer any objective basis on which to entertain positive expectations for the future. The LORD had withdrawn himself and his promises. Life in its deepest and most meaningful form had come to an end.

And yet, at the nadir of his spiritual pilgrimage, something has happened. The poet has been forced to abandon his self-imposed avoidance of the divine name. He has talked throughout about God, but only as 'he' — a distant, faceless, implacable foe. The speaker has not denied the existence of God, but his language has reflected his spiritual estrangement from him. Here, however, as the poet explores the depths of his misery, he has been compelled to use the name Yahweh (or Jehovah), the covenant name of God. He is the living reality who intrudes into the downward spiral of gloom and despair. Awareness of what is entailed by the name of the LORD continues to be heightened in the speaker's consciousness, and to provide much needed light to counter his heartache and dejection.

(2) The Dawning of a New Day (3:19-24)

It is remarkable that, while thematic analysis of Lamentations clearly identifies its centre as being found in 3:22-24, there is no consensus as to where a new unit in the poem is best identified as beginning, with 3:19, 3:21 and 3:22 each having advocates. Justification for a change in outlook beginning at 3:19 depends on the way in which the initial verb of that verse is translated. Reading it as a prayer indicates that the poet's introverted chain of thought now starts to be oriented towards the LORD (3:19), with recognition of the bitterness of his own experience (3:20), but also a new resolve to consider his circumstances in the light of what is known about the LORD (3:20-24). Despite the emptiness and despair which had engulfed the poet, he recognises that another side to the matter is to be found in the nature and dealings of the LORD himself. The very fact that the community has survived to any extent at all is itself an indication of the LORD's mercy (3:22) and of his faithfulness (3:23). These characteristics open up the possibility that, alongside the vexation of rejection and pain, there may be hope for unmerited intervention from the God who has not changed (3:24).

❧ 3:19 Remember my affliction and my homelessness,
             the wormwood and the bitter herbs!

❧ 3:20 My soul continually remembers ⌞them⌟
             and is bowed down within me.

❧ 3:21 This I will recall to my heart;
             therefore I will hope.

Doubt about the correct translation of the first word in 3:19 makes it difficult to trace with certainty the development of the poet's thought at this juncture. The initial verb may be either an imperative or an infinitive in form. While in the Septuagint it is translated as 'I remember' (cf. NIV), this probably does not reflect a different original text, but is rather a dynamic rendering of an infinitive. 'The thought of ...' (NLT, NRSV) identifies the verb as an infinitive, and similarly understands the poet to be recording how calling to mind his afflictions and homelessness continues to be a bitter experience for him.

However, the verb is probably a singular imperative ***Remember***, which, addressed to the LORD, follows on naturally from the mention of his name at the end of the preceding verse. The speaker is intensely aware of his personal agony, and sets out his hopelessness as a reason for divine intervention. He has never doubted that God exists. What has overwhelmed him is the problem of reconciling his present situation with a positive view of God's attitude towards him. Perhaps the extent of his misery will induce divine compassion. The plea to remember is not directed simply at a recall of facts, but bringing them before one's mind with a view to taking appropriate action. For *affliction* see on 3:1. *Homelessness* is the singular form of 'wanderings' (cf. 1:7), but referring here to an individual an emphasis on lack of an abode seems more appropriate.[92] *The wormwood and the bitter herbs* looks back to the harsh diet the LORD had appointed for the speaker (3:15).

My soul (cf. 3:17) refers to the inward reaction of the speaker to the insistent pressure of his situation. Not a moment goes by but that he is aware of all that it is his lot to endure. Since there is nothing he can do to alleviate his misery, he is overwhelmed by depression as his soul *is bowed down within me*. A related verb form conveys the thought of dejection in Psalm 42 (Pss. 42:5, 6, 11; 43:5). Because the LORD himself has brought this upon the poet, he alone is able to do something about it. Perhaps divine pity will be aroused by the burden imposed on this bent and suffering figure.

In such a setting where waves of self-pity again threaten to engulf the speaker, the faith which had roused him to call on the LORD spurs him on to think through the implications of his act of prayer. If the LORD can be brought into the picture, then his situation should not be conceived as one of unrelieved doom and gloom. *I will recall* reflects a conscious decision to bring back into his thinking (*heart* here reflects the cognitive aspect of his inner being, not merely an emotional response) what had previously enlightened his spiritual life. He will resume his attitude of faith and reliance on the LORD by giving *this*, that is, the considerations which he will subsequently set out, a controlling perspective in his life. By acting in this way (*therefore*, cf. 3:24) he is confident that

---

92. The RSV again (cf. 1:7) changed the mention of 'wandering'/ 'homelessness' (*mərûdî*) into one of 'bitterness' (*mərôrî*), but this alteration is unnecessary and dropped in the NRSV.

his outlook will be changed: *I will hope*. The verb comes from the same root as the noun 'hope' in 3:19, but here the thought is positive. It describes not a fanciful or passing desire for future good fortune, but a well-grounded and enduring anticipation of blessing. This hope is derived from faith grasping the revelation God has given of his own character and of his power to transform even the bleakest of situations. This is the Scriptural remedy for those who find themselves in the depths spiritually. 'O Israel, hope in the LORD, for with the LORD there is steadfast love, and abundantly there is redemption with him; and he is the one who will redeem Israel from all his iniquities' (Ps. 130:7-8). This hope is oriented towards the LORD, and its motivation is developed further in the following verses of the poem (3:22-33).

נ 3:22   The LORD's acts of steadfast love — for we have
              not been brought to an end,
         for his compassions have not ceased.

נ 3:23   They are new every morning;
         great is your faithfulness.

נ 3:24   'The LORD is my portion,' says my soul,
              'therefore I will hope in him.'

There is an awkward beginning to 3:22,[93] and it has been speculated that occurs because the poet is quoting an otherwise unknown hymnic composition which was part of the religious heritage of his day.[94] Evidence to substantiate that view does not exist, but what is certain is that the poet no longer shrinks from using the name of the LORD, and that his confidence swells as he focuses on God, not on self. This is the route to genuine hope.

---

93. The translation of this line is difficult. Following the Syriac Peshitta and the Targum, the ESV renders it as, 'The steadfast love of the LORD never ceases', and in a footnote suggests that the Massoretic text may mean, 'Because of the steadfast love of the LORD, we are not cut off.' This is virtually the same as the rendering adopted by the NIV, 'Because of the LORD's great love we are not consumed', where 'because of' is a translator's supplement.

94. Cf. Knut M. Heim, 'The Personification of Jerusalem and the Drama of Her Bereavement in Lamentations,' in *Zion, City of Our God* (ed. Richard S. Hess and Gordon J. Wenham; Grand Rapids: Eerdmans, 1999), 157.

The initial exclamation of the poet, *the LORD's acts of steadfast love*, introduces a key term in the theological thinking of the Old Testament, *ḥesed*. Unfortunately it is difficult to find an adequate English rendering for this word. As well as 'steadfast love', translators have resorted to 'covenant love', 'lovingkindness', or 'constant love'. *Ḥesed* denotes the quality of the relationship between two parties as being one of goodwill and mutual concern by which a favourable inner disposition reveals itself in practical acts of assistance and support for the other party. This frame of mind and its complementary actions are not one-off displays of kindness, but constitute an enduring bond of fidelity. The *ḥesed* relationship may be initiated by the action of one party, but it inherently requires a reciprocal response. This reaction may be formally structured in a covenant which sets out the terms of the relationship between the two parties, and in such circumstances *ḥesed* is specifically 'covenant love'.

As regards the situation after the fall of Jerusalem, the question naturally arises as to whether it is possible for the poet to appeal here to the *covenant* love of the LORD. Had not the sin of the people and the outpouring of the LORD's wrath upon them annulled the covenant relationship? Was this not a divorce between the LORD and his people? Certainly there are texts which speak in absolute terms ('they violated/nullified/suspended my covenant', Jer. 31:32), and which would suggest that hope for the future had to rest on a totally new relationship initiated once again by the sovereign impulse of divine love. However, there is another, early strand to the revelation of the covenant which shows that matters were not as simple as that. In Deuteronomy 28 and 29 there are enumerated in considerable detail the 'extraordinary afflictions, afflictions severe and lasting, and sickness grievous and lasting' (Deut. 28:59) which would come as the curse of the covenant on the people when they disobeyed the LORD's commandments. He would act against them in 'anger and fury and great wrath, and cast them into another land' (Deut. 29:28), but there is then surprisingly set out the possibility of restoration if, when they have been subjected to the LORD's judgemental wrath, they come to their spiritual senses in repentance (Deut. 30:1-10). It is one of the basic perspectives of modern critical thought that such a passage as Deuteronomy 30 is a subsequent rationalisation of what in fact happened in the era after the Exile. But if Deuteronomy is truly a Mosaic production, then what we have in fact is a fundamental insight into the nature of the covenant bond. It is initiated by the LORD's sovereign choice but his commitment is enduring. Though his partners in the covenant renege on their pledges and are subject to the LORD's wrath, the nature of the relationship thereafter depends on the LORD's attitude. Since the people's sin has not caught him by surprise, his level of commitment to the relationship has not been affected by the judgement he has had to bring on them. Indeed that penalty is a measure of his fidelity in upholding the covenant. It is to this aspect of the situation that the poet turns in this exclamation regarding the *ḥesed* of the LORD.

In fact the term *ḥesed* is used here in the plural to intensify the character of God's love (cf. 'great love', NIV) or, more probably, to point to the abundant instances of the LORD's covenant love which are brought under review and used as a basis for future hope.[95] In particular, with an eye to the lesson he wishes to teach, the poet singles out the fact that *we have not been brought to an end.* 'We' here obviously refers to the people.[96] If their rebellion had signalled the abrogation of all that the covenant involved, then the LORD's anger would have ensured that there would be no survivors. The very fact that there is a remnant, albeit one that is barely clinging on to existence, provides a reason for supposing that the LORD's dealings with them have not terminated. While it would be wrong to characterise this insight as abounding hope, it is folly to dismiss it as no hope at all.

The situation is traced further back to the fact that *his compassions have not ceased.* 'Compassions', which occurs only here in Lamentations, is always a plural form, which like the preceding 'acts of steadfast love' indicates the abounding nature of the emotion expressed. The term is formed from a word for the womb, and so it is has overtones of the intensity of a mother's love for her child. 'Can a woman forget her nursing child so as not to show compassion to the son of her womb? Surely these may forget, but I

95. See Waltke and O'Connor, *Syntax*, §7.4.2.
96. If is often argued that 'we' is intrusive in this first person singular context, and the verb is emended to 'they have not been ended', but this is not necessary.

am not one who will forget you' (Isa. 49:15). God's compassion towards his children does not come to an end no matter how severely he acts against their sin (cf. Ps. 103:15).

The antecedent of *they are new* is 'acts of steadfast love', rather than 'compassions' which describes a constant, prevailing attitude. But *every morning* the poet discerns tokens of divine lovingkindness in the provision, however sparse, which enables the people to survive. Each day presents a new struggle for which there is no surplus from the previous day's supplies. Moreover, 'new' presents a note of surprising, unanticipated provision. It is not a matter of presumption, but grateful recognition of the unforeseen ways in which the goodness and wisdom of God are displayed time and again when he imparts resources to cope with the challenges of life.

The four Hebrew words of 3:23 conclude with the realisation *great is your faithfulness.* 'Your' shows the poet has become so conscious of the divine that he naturally addresses the LORD rather than speaks about him. 'Faithfulness' relates to the LORD's being true to his word of promise. It describes behaviour that is reliable and consistent, never deviating from the norm whatever the occasion, and it and related terms are frequently used alongside *ḥesed* to point to the committed nature of God's love (cf. Pss. 36:5; 89:1, 2, 24, 33; 98:3; 100:5; 'abounding in steadfast love and faithfulness', Exod. 34:6). Though the focus is undoubtedly on the LORD, one cannot help but wonder if there is not a sideways glance at the behaviour of the other covenant partner for whom faithfulness had been an ideal rarely achieved (Deut. 32:20; Ps. 78:37; Hos. 4:1). 'Great' may indicate the extensiveness of the LORD's action which is such that it embraces situations of all sorts with an undeviating commitment.

To these grand truths regarding the LORD the poet responds by setting out his personal appropriation of them by *my soul*, his being at its very core (cf. 3:17). He confesses, *The LORD is my portion.* 'Portion' relates to the land which was allotted by the LORD to each Israelite as his inheritance. The Levites, however, were not allocated territory in the way the other tribes were. To Aaron the LORD had said, 'I am your portion and inheritance in the midst of the Israelites' (Num. 18:20), which in practical terms meant that the priests survived by receiving a portion of the offerings made at the sanctuary by the other tribes. This image for enjoying a particularly close relationship with the LORD and depending on divine provision for survival became a metaphor for a truly God-centred life which was able to survive in times of difficulty and crisis (cf. Pss. 16:5; 73:26; 142:5).

Therefore I will hope in him. This repetition of the concluding thought of 3:21 is significantly expanded by the addition of 'in him', which makes clear where the foundation of the poet's hope lies. Only the character and commitment of the LORD provide a reliable basis for looking forward positively. And it is looking forward that is in view, for there is no claim that the poet's immediate circumstances have altered. 'Who hopes for what he sees?' (Rom. 8:24). What has changed is the speaker's outlook. The anguish and the physical deprivation remain, but now he confidently awaits a time when wounded relationships will be fully healed and enjoyment of divine favour restored. A glimpse of the tranquillity to be realised has already touched his heart.

Reflection

• The impact of suffering is aggravated when the believer is no longer aware of the closeness of God, and prayer to him meets with no evident response (3:7-8). Not all prayers are indeed answered. Those who persist in indulging in disobedience and clinging to iniquity have no right to expect that God will hear them (cf. Prov. 28:9; Ps. 66:18). On other occasions God does answer prayer, but not in the way or at the time we expect.

• Here the poet makes no mention of personal sin, only of divinely imposed catastrophe. Apparently he has been caught up in the judgement of the nation as a whole, and through that experience his faith is being tried by God. The perspective of the Old Testament does not endorse the view either that material well-being and prosperity indicate acceptance with God, or that suffering necessarily springs from divine rejection. The psalmist can sincerely write, 'It ⌐is⌐ good for me that I was afflicted, that I might learn your statutes' (Ps. 119:71; cf. Hab. 3:17-18) but, even so, that meditation is on past experience, recalled and subsequently evaluated. 'All discipline at the time seems to be not pleasant but painful' (Heb. 12:11), and it is the spiritual dimension of that pain which the poet is concerned to set out.

- The spiritual dynamic which is set out here is to be found also in the refrain of Psalms 42 and 43. 'Why are you bowed down, my soul? And ˪why˩ are you upset within me? Hope in God, for I will yet praise him, my salvation and my God' (Ps. 42:5). 'Bowed down' denotes present spiritual perplexity which can only be quieted by considering the certainty and completeness of God's provision. 'My salvation' is 'the salvation of my face', that which brings a smile of relief to the sorrowful countenance. Knowledge of that salvation has been made much more evident in New Testament times through 'the light of the knowledge of the glory of God in the face of Jesus Christ' which is able to sustain through situations of affliction and perplexity in the life of the believer in anticipation of what is yet to come (cf. 2 Cor. 4:6-18).

- The heart of the message of Lamentations is to be found in 3:22-24, which is based on the key disclosure of the LORD regarding his character as expressed in Exodus 34:6-7. Here there is set up a link between the steadfast love and faithfulness of the LORD and an expectation of forgiveness: 'keeping steadfast love to the thousandth ˪generation˩, forgiving iniquity and transgression and sin, but who will by no means clear the guilty' (Exod. 34:7). The same thought is again expressed in Numbers 14:18, and again it is in a context where the people have sinned. While not excluding the possibility of divine visitation in punishment, Moses pleads for the pardon of Israel's iniquity on the basis of the LORD's self-revelation of his character. This theology informs the pleas of several prophetic passages (Hos. 14:1-3; Joel 2:12-14; Mic. 7:18-20). The LORD is known for pardoning iniquity and passing over transgression. There is therefore every reason to expect an end to the outpouring of his wrath, and the enduring character of the LORD is a sure source of hope.

- The word 'portion' (3:24) is used in two ways to express the relationship between God and his people. On the one hand it is the case that 'the LORD's portion is his people' (Deut. 33:9) for he has separated them off as 'my treasured/personal possession among all peoples' so that they may fulfil the special role he has allotted them (cf. Exod. 19:5-6; Tit. 2:14). On the other hand, the LORD is the portion or possession which has been gifted to his people (cf. 'the LORD is the assigned share of my portion and my cup', Ps. 16:5). Astonishingly he himself is the 'very great reward' of his people (Gen. 15:1). This gift guarantees security to all those who are his because the LORD is then 'the rock of my heart and my portion for ever' (Ps. 73:26) and a refuge in the troubles of life (Ps. 142:5). Consequently, in recognition of the LORD's place in their lives they dedicate themselves to keeping his words (Ps. 119:57).

B. Moving Out Of Darkness (3:25-39)

There is no need to suppose that the voice of a different speaker is heard at this point. It is rather the case that the poet, having given personal testimony regarding his struggles with the tensions of his own experience, uses it as a basis for generalising about how the suffering community should live in times of divine displeasure without abandoning their faith. In doing this he employs a didactic style which in many respects reflects the language of Old Testament wisdom literature.

The keynote of his advice is to keep the nature of God in mind, especially his inherent goodness (3:25-27) and justice (3:34-36). That will enable patient resignation under the yoke of his chastisement (3:28-30). Past experience has shown that God does not persist in rejecting his people. Indeed, it is inherent in the character of God that he is ultimately not a God of wrath but of mercy, and so the future should be viewed in the anticipation of his compassion and steadfast love (3:31-33). The human forces which the LORD uses in carrying out his purposes may act unjustly, but the Lord does not approve of their wrongdoing and oppression (3:34-36). The Lord is the one who is in sovereign control of all events, and it is incongruous for an individual to complain about the way he is being treated, particularly in the light of the offences he has committed against God (3:37-39).

(1) The LORD's Goodness (3:25-27)

ᴜ 3:25 The LORD is good to those waiting for him,
           to the soul that seeks him.

ט 3:26 ⌊He is⌋ good. ⌊Let there be⌋ waiting and silence
for the salvation of the LORD.
ט 3:27 ⌊He is⌋ good to the man when he bears
a yoke in his youth.

Each verse in this stanza begins with 'good', a word with a wide
range of meaning, encompassing practical and material good,
abstract good such as beauty, and moral good. But whatever form
goodness takes it has to be traced back to its source in God. Instead
of first person singular references, here impersonal third person
forms occur to set out general norms. Also the very short lines of
this stanza give additional emphasis to the initial threefold occurrence of 'good'.

To say *the LORD is good* is to trace how his inner disposition
becomes evident in what he does, and in the quality of the relationship he maintains with his people. 'You are good and keep
doing good' (Ps. 119:68), and so the call for praise echoed through
the assemblies of Israel, 'Give thanks to the LORD, for he is good'
(Ps. 136:1). Specifically as the covenant King of Israel, the LORD
provided for his people a 'good land' as their inheritance (Deut.
4:21-22) and, when he would bless them, it was by opening up his
'good storehouse' to meet their needs (Deut. 28:12). Indeed, the
essence of covenant blessing was 'life and good' (Deut. 30:15).

Not all share in the blessings of his covenant goodness, and
there is a doubly expressed qualification of those to whom his
bounty extends. *Those waiting for him* are characterised by an attitude of intense anticipation, just as Jerusalem's enemies had earlier
awaited her downfall (2:16).[97] There is no indication that the
LORD's intervention to relieve their situation is going to come soon,
but they do not give over in their expectation. *The soul*/'individual'
that seeks him describes one who is eager to have a positive
spiritual relationship with God, which will result in knowing his
will and aligning one's life with it. Since the Temple had been

---

97. The plural translation 'those waiting' follows the qere *qōwāyw*, a plural
participle with a third person singular pronominal suffix. The kethibh could
possibly be read as *qōwēw*, an abbreviated form of *qōwēhū*, a singular
participle, 'the one waiting for him', but this is improbable even though the
parallel expression is singular.

destroyed, seeking God could no longer be effected through the institutions of organised religion, but an appropriate spiritual rapport with him had always been available without such liturgical assistance.

A second aspect of what is *good* is set out in 3:26, but the syntax of the first three words is unclear: 'good and-waiting and-silence'. This is generally taken to indicate a favourable evaluation of the conduct of those who wait in silence: 'It is good that one should wait quietly'. However, especially in the light of the third line, there may well be an initial elliptical acclamation, '⌐He is⌐ good', referring back to Yahweh, and indicating that reliance on what he is should motivate one to adopt an appropriate attitude.[98] *Waiting* is not derived from the same root as the word in 3:25, but it conveys a generally similar meaning of future expectation, though perhaps with less intensity than the former term. It is the qualification *and silence* which is the significant additional feature in this verse. This is not the stunned silence of the dumbfounded (2:10), but the respectful reverence of those who guard their speech recognising that what has come upon them is from the LORD. 'I kept silent; I would not open my mouth because it is you who did this' (Ps. 39:9). Nevertheless, there is also a positive aspect: *for the salvation of the LORD.* He is the one who has the power to intervene in unprecedented ways to rescue his people from every dire situation and provide them with deliverance.

For a third time the poet reverts to the theme of goodness. While the introductory words are generally translated, 'It is good for a man that he bears the yoke in his youth', it is not evident that yoke-bearing in one's younger days does necessarily impart spiritual blessing. To obviate this difficulty the Targum rendered the reference as being not to the yoke of Yahweh's penalty imposed on sin (cf. 1:14), but the yoke of the obligation to obey the commandments. However, in the context of Lamentations it is surely a yoke of suffering under foreign domination that is in view. It would then seem preferable to take *good* as referring to Yahweh's disposition towards *the man,* the one with spiritual commitment (*geber*; cf. 3:1) when the circumstances in his life are such that *he bears a*

---

98. This analysis of the text is derived from Renkema, *Lamentations*, 394–99, whether further argumentation in its favour is to be found.

yoke of suffering, even at a time when his strength is not yet fully mature, *in his youth.* This is then a tribute to the fact that the LORD sustains those who trust in him.

(2) Living with Catastrophe (3:28-30)

❛ 3:28 Let him sit alone and be silent
               when he has laid ⌊it⌋ upon him.
❛ 3:29 Let him put his mouth in the dust —
               perhaps there is hope.
❛ 3:30 Let him give his cheek to the one who strikes;
               let him be filled with reviling.

The individual who is described in this stanza continues to be the man (*geber*) of 3:27, who has to bear the burden of a yoke of suffering imposed on him by the LORD. He is not to adopt an attitude of restless complaint and bitterness, but rather one of self-composure, waiting for the resolution of his situation from the LORD. This constitutes in effect an exhortation to the poet's audience to emulate such humble behaviour, of which three related aspects are described.

Sit alone recalls the opening description of Jerusalem (1:1), and is deliberately employed here to indicate that the burden to be endured is identical with the catastrophe which has come upon the city. The affliction is not superficial or momentary, but severe and lasting. A right attitude avoids complaint and is *silent* (from the same root as 'silence' in 3:26). This is not intended in quite the same way as that of the elders of 2:10, but refers to accepting without murmuring the rigours and calamity of the situation. *When* indicates the same set of circumstances as in 3:27. *He has laid ⌊it⌋ on him* points to the divine imposition of 'it' = the yoke. The verb is quite rare, and seems to connote the infliction of punishment (cf. 2 Sam. 24:12), not as an arbitrary penalty but rather as one that accords with God's sovereign and righteous will. Here what is imposed reflects the verdict on the corporate rebellion of the nation. Since the individual sufferer may not have personally contributed to the guilt of the situation in which he has got caught up, the LORD will in such circumstances preserve his life and let him have it as booty taken from the battle (cf. Jer. 39:18; 45:5).

As the burden laid on the sufferer saps his strength, he sinks to the ground. ***Let him put his mouth in the dust*** denotes becoming prostrate on the ground before someone. This might be the forced posture of a captive before his captor, but it could also be a voluntary act of submission to a superior (cf. Ps. 72:9; Mic. 7:17). The reason advanced for acquiescing in the LORD's rule and provision is ***perhaps there is hope.*** 'Hope' is derived from the same root as the term 'waiting' in 3:25, and points to grounds for anticipating divine intervention to effect a reversal of the misfortune of the people. However, it is far from a confident hope which is being described. 'Perhaps' indicates the outlook of a faltering faith that is no longer sure of what is to be expected. It is still the sentiment of one who is looking to the LORD, but there is reverent hesitation regarding how his purposes are going to work out for his people — in the immediate future at any rate. No individual can demand that God sanction a particular way forwards; what will happen is a gift from the God who is sovereign and free.

The sufferer is further enjoined not to resist the blows that are imposed by the instruments of the LORD's chastisement of his people. ***Let him give his cheek to the one who strikes.*** Such a blow to the face is an act of utter disrespect, but it is to be endured because the superior position of the one who strikes has been accorded to him by the LORD and is part of the way in which he is working out his purposes (cf. Isa. 50:6). ***Reviling*** refers not only to cutting remarks made by others to indicate the low esteem in which they hold an individual (cf. Ps. 22:7; Mic. 6:16; Zeph. 2:8), but also to the subjective impact of those remarks, the feelings of shame and being humiliated. This has to be acquiesced in to the full because it is what the LORD has imposed on his people.

(3) The Lord's Compassion (3:31-33)

ב 3:31 For the Lord will not reject
                for ever;
ב 3:32 for, if he brings grief, he will have compassion
                according to the abundance of his steadfast love;
ב 3:33 for he does not willingly afflict
                or grieve to the children of men.

The same word, *for*, introduces each verse of this stanza, and points to the Lord's character and the way in which he works as providing reasons why the lowly posture of 3:28-30 should be accepted by those caught up in the catastrophe. It is argued that the experience will not be permanent. *Reject* has already been used in connection with the Lord's scornful dismissal of the altar and the whole system of worship as practised in Judah (2:7). Now it is employed absolutely in respect of all aspects of the life of the nation, but the thought presented is that the Lord (*'ădōnāy*, cf. 1:14) will not do so *for ever.* Rejection might be reversed (cf. Ps. 60:10-12), though there was always an awareness that a change in outlook could not be taken for granted (cf. Ps. 74:1), and that it might take a long time to happen. Still there was a perception that simply because God is who he is, 'he will not keep his anger for ever' (Ps. 103:9).

This understanding of the nature and *modus operandi* of the Lord is further explained in 3:32. There will be times when he *brings grief* (cf. 1:5, 12) through just imposition of penalty, but even so his relationship with his people is such that *he will have compassion*, feeling for them even in their misery and seeking to alleviate their distress (cf. 3:22). This is an exercise of his good will, that is, of his love. Though it will result in repentance of the people, it is not conditioned by it, but is ultimately attributable only to his sovereign inclination. *According to the abundance of his steadfast love*[99] (cf. 3:22) reaches back to the LORD's commitment to the relationship he has instituted, and to the fact that he will not let anything frustrate the accomplishment of his purposes, not even the perversity and transgression of his own people. There is an abundance to his love which contrasts with the abundance of their sin (cf. 1:5).

The matter is probed even further, and goes beyond the covenant relationship the LORD has instituted in the flow of human history. It relates to what he is in himself. *He does not willingly afflict or grieve the children/*'sons' *of men.* To 'afflict' is to impose suffering which leads to distress (cf. 1:3), and 'grieve' is a

---

99. The kethibh of the Massoretic Text has a singular form *ḥasdô*, 'his steadfast love', whereas the qere has a plural form *ḥăsādāyw*, 'his acts of steadfast love', probably by attraction to the form found in 3:22.

verb form related to 'bring grief' (3:32).[100] 'Willingly' is literally
'from his heart'. At a human level the heart is used metaphorically
for the inner thought life of the individual (cf. 3:21). By analogy
what is being said here is that deep within himself God takes no
delight in punishing those who stray from his way. That is not what
he wishes to see (cf. Ezek. 18:23, 32); his aim is not a negative outcome, imposing grief and pain. It is true that judgement has come
forth from him, and there can be no denying its necessity or its
righteousness. Nonetheless judgement will not be permitted to be
the last word on the destiny of the LORD's people because in the
ultimate analysis wrath is not of the essence of the character of
God.[101]

(4) Divine Disapproval (3:34-36)

ל 3:34 To crush under his foot
            all the prisoners of the land,

ל 3:35 to divert justice from a man
            in the presence of the Most High,

ל 3:36 to suppress an individual in connection with his
            grievance —
            ⌊of these⌋ the Lord has not approved.

These three verses have to be taken together as a threefold description of behaviour which meets with the disapproval of the Lord.
But whose behaviour is presented here? It is possible to read this
stanza as expressing why God had acted so severely against the
people. Because they had mistreated others in this way, they had
brought the Lord's punishment on themselves. At this juncture,
however, it is more probable that the poet is focusing not on the
circumstances which led to the fall of Jerusalem but on the present
distress caused to its inhabitants by the occupation forces who were
ruthlessly oppressing the inhabitants of Jerusalem, indeed *of the*

---

100. This may be an instance where the piel of *yāgâ* (I) is used in 3:33 in the
sense 'to bring into a state of grief and emotional torment', whereas the more
common hiphil form (found in 3:32) conveys the more active idea of causing
them to feel grief and anguish.

101. See the reflection earlier on 2:1-10 (page 95).

land as a whole.[102] **Prisoners** then does not just refer to those who were confined in special buildings; their whole land had become a prison camp where they were compelled to labour on their enemies' behalf and experienced exploitation and persecution. It is this behaviour which incurs the censure of God.

Man is again *geber*, probably used in its particular sense of one has enjoyed a close relationship with God (cf. 3:1, 27). Those who had remained faithful were experiencing doubts because of the perceived injustice of the treatment being meted out to them. **To divert justice** is to act in such a way that an individual is deprived of a proper legal hearing to establish what is rightfully his (cf. Isa. 10:2; 29:21; Amos 5:12). It would seem that the marginalised in the community were especially liable to such abuse (cf. Exod. 23:6), but now such oppressive behaviour was being extended to the whole population because of the power of the adversary before whom they were defeated and defenceless (cf. 1:9; 2:12). **In the presence of the Most High** signals the disappointment and sense of betrayal that is evident. The title 'Most High' points to the sovereignty and majesty of the LORD as creator and possessor of heaven and earth (cf. Gen. 14:19, 22). He therefore has inalienable jurisdiction over all the earth (cf. Pss. 83:18; 97:9), and that usually constitutes a basis for his people being able to find refuge in him (cf. Ps. 91:1, 9). Yet this injustice is occurring right before him. He cannot claim he does not know about it; it has violated the fundamental structures of justice in his kingdom; and yet he has not intervened to help.

The complaint underlying 3:36 is expressed in a more general fashion in that **an individual** (*ʾādām*) is any person, regardless of their particular relationship to the Lord. **Grievance** may be used narrowly of a legal process ('lawsuit'), but if the background here is the action of the enemy, then they had little regard for due process and the term is being used more widely of any complaint against the behaviour of the occupying forces. They were acting ruthlessly, according no rights to those who had been maltreated.

---

102. While the Hebrew term *ʾereṣ* can also mean 'earth', it is improbable that in this context the emphasis is on universal injustice. It is true that the standard of behaviour of which the Lord approves is universal, but the focus is on the application of this standard in the particular circumstances of Judah.

Suppress refers to treating someone in a crooked and distorted fashion.

The concluding clause, 'The Lord has not seen', is often treated as an implied question, 'Has not the Lord seen?', with the implication that those who have perpetrated such injustice are marked men because the Lord will shortly react to this injustice. Another possibility is to take this stanza as expressing the complaint of the people, 'the Lord has not seen' all that the enemy is doing, for if he had seen it, he would obviously have acted to relieve the people.[103] However, on the basis of a thematic analysis of the chapter in which the poet is at this point urging his contemporaries to adopt an approach similar to his own in coping with the anxieties of their situation, it is preferable to take the words as countering the implicit objection of the people by reminding them of the justice of God, in the same way as he had earlier reminded them of his goodness. 'See' would then be used as equivalent of 'view with approval' (cf. Hab. 1:13). There should be no doubt about the fact that *the Lord has not approved* the conduct of which they complain, even though he has given them over into the hands of the enemies.

(5) The Sovereignty of the Lord (3:37-39)

נ 3:37 Whoever spoke and it came to be
           ⌊when⌋ the Lord has not commanded it?
נ 3:38 Is it not from the mouth of the Most High
           that bad and good come?
נ 3:39 Why should an individual who is alive complain,
           a man, about the punishment of his sin?

The final stanza of this section of the poem consists of three rhetorical questions, which are used to make strong assertions

---

103. Renkema adopts this understanding on the basis of his analysis that the second poem in this chapter has started at 3:34 and that here there is a reversion to the theme of complaint against the LORD (*Lamentations*, 415). Calvin too, having reviewed various interpretative options for this verse, argued similarly: 'I therefore think that the reference is to the impious words of those who complain that God is not moved by any compassion' (John Calvin, *Commentaries on the Book of the Prophet Jeremiah and the Lamentations* 5:424).

regarding the situation of Zion. In 3:37, **whoever** conveys a note of surprise that it should be thought that anything has happened in defiance of the will of the sovereign Lord (*ʾădōnāy*, cf. 1:14). The argument is based on the fact of creation in which God **spoke and** the created realm **came to be.**[104] There is a clear echo here of the words of Psalm 33: 'He spoke and it came to be; he commanded and it stood ˻in place˼' (Ps. 33:9). There must be no misconception about the reality of the Creator's continuing control — even over the suffering which has come upon his people. **Commanded** does not imply that there was a direct divine mandate for the oppression and atrocities of the enemy. It refers rather to a divine decree which uses and overrules the wicked acts of mankind to achieve God's purpose. 'The secret things belong to the LORD our God' (Deut. 29:29), and it is pointless to pry into them. 'How unsearchable are his judgements and inscrutable his ways!' (Rom. 11:33). That, however, should enhance rather than undermine our perception of the control he continues to exercise.

Although there is no explicit interrogative in 3:38, its position between two rhetorical questions argues for it also being rendered as one. **Bad** is an intensive plural form, 'calamities'/'evils', that is, all manner of such things. Both 'bad' and 'good' have the article. This may be a generic use indicating the whole class of experiences which may be so classified, in which case the combination of bad and good[105] is a merism, an expression of totality by naming the extremes of a spectrum. More probably, however, the article has a demonstrative force: 'those evils we are experiencing, and that good we long for'. If so, there would be the same element of hope implicit in the statement as is to be found in similar assertions in the Old Testament. '˻I am the one˼ who forms light and creates darkness, who makes peace and creates evil; I am Yahweh who makes all these' (Isa. 45:7). 'If evil/disaster exists in a city, has not the LORD done ˻it˼?' (Amos 3:6). Because of the character of God

---

104. 'And it came to be' (*wattehî*) is a feminine verb form which is probably to be explained by the feminine being used in a neuter sense to distinguish this phrase with its absolute use of the verb from the common formula 'and it came to pass that' (*wayhî*).

105. The ESV sequence 'good and bad' perpetuates that of the RSV (found also in GNB, NASB, NRSV), but this reversal of the Hebrew order is without textual basis.

who exercises supreme control over events, it is possible to hope that he will in his mercy reverse the judgement he has imposed.

The *individual* (*ʾādām*; cf. 3:36) is further specified in 3:39 as *a man* (*geber*; cf. 3:1, 27). This is the complaint of those who still considered themselves to be in a special relationship with the Lord, but they were murmuring and grumbling (cf. Num. 11:1) because they felt themselves hard done by either on account of the severity of the treatment they were receiving or through a sense that the fault in the matter was not really theirs, being rather a consequence of the circumstances they inherited. However, it is strongly pointed out that the individuals who were reacting in this way were *alive* (cf. 3:22), and so they were overlooking the fact that they were survivors. That in itself was a sign of the LORD's favour towards them, not merely a prolongation of agony (cf. 4:9).

Besides they ought to acknowledge that more could be said about what had befallen the people than that God had decreed it should happen. Sin has not figured largely in the speaker's thinking up to this point, but he has to introduce it into his discourse to vindicate God against the allegation that he was one who tortured others for his own gratification. Although the second part of the verse may be translated (carrying the sense of the verb over from the first part), 'a man complain about his sin', it is generally accepted that the word 'sin' here is used in an extended fashion to refer to the punishment entailed by sin.[106] Searching for the origin of the catastrophe is not at an end when one contemplates the control and justice of God. What had precipitated the calamity was the existence of sin within the human heart, and therefore matters will not be advanced by the people indulging themselves in murmuring against God. Each must probe within and examine his own responsibility for what has occurred. The existential link between *my* suffering and *my* sin has to be acknowledged so that there may be recovered a right perception regarding who God is, who I am, and how I may return to him.

_____

106. There is a variant reading in the MT, with a qere of *ḥăṭāʾāwy*, 'his sins', and a kethibh, *ḥeṭʾô*, 'his sin'. The latter is to be preferred if the extended sense of the term is understood.

Reflection

- The poet speaks on behalf of those who have themselves been embroiled in this catastrophic outpouring of divine wrath, and who feel acutely the resultant pain, misery and bewilderment. He does not urge them to adopt a stoical attitude towards their suffering: that, because they can do nothing to remove it, their response should be to adopt a pose of indifference. Rather, the poet provides the community with a means to articulate their pain, and also to adopt a right perspective on it because of what they affirm regarding the character of God. Their lives are not determined by some cold, impersonal fate; they are in the hands of the living God, who is good. How much more confidently should we now be able to assess our experience in the light of Christ's redemptive suffering, for 'our light, temporary suffering is producing for us an eternal weight of glory far beyond any comparison' (2 Cor. 4:17). And that is equally true when unjust suffering is endured 'mindful of God' (1 Pet. 2:19).

- Israel's praise was motivated by recognition of the fact that the LORD is good (cf. Ezra 3:11; Pss. 100:5; 106:1; 107:1; 118:1, 29; 135:3; 136:1), but what was implied by that confession? As with so much of God's character as revealed in the Old Testament, the fundamental perspective is established in the narrative of God's dealings with Moses at Sinai. To Moses' request that God show him his glory, the LORD responded that he would make his 'goodness' pass before him (Exod. 33:18-19), and that revelation was encapsulated in the many facets of the name of God proclaimed in Exodus 34:6-7. Goodness is intrinsic to the divine glory ('None is good but God alone', Mark 10:18), and he leaves that stamp of his moral excellence and purity on all that pertains to his creation and kingdom. This decisively separates what is of God from the evil introduced by Satan into the created realm which had been pronounced 'very good' (Gen. 1:31). When faith relies on the intrinsic goodness of God it has a secure basis for hope.

- The occurrences of 'perhaps' (3:29) in the Old Testament are significant in that they are connected with the possibility of acceptance by an offended God (cf. Exod. 32:30; Amos 5:15; Zeph. 2:3; cf. 'who knows?', Joel 2:14; Jonah 3:9). This

describes a reverent acquiescence in the fact that there are
unrevealed aspects of God's plan (cf. Deut. 29:29). To attempt
to intrude into these areas is presumptuous folly. True faith is
content to wait in confidence, not that its particular aspirations
or hopes—conditioned as they are by human finitude—will be
realised, but that God will act to do all things well.

- The compassion of God (3:32) is an aspect of his love which
focuses particularly on the depth and tenderness of his feelings
towards his people when they are in need. This reflects the disposition of his heart towards them (cf. 'willingly', 3:33). The
bond which exists between the LORD and his people is, on his
part, one of intense affection, and it survives even in the face of
their sin. Regarding the prospect of handing Ephraim, the northern kingdom, over to punishment, the LORD exclaimed, 'My
heart recoils within me; my compassion grows warm and
tender' (Hos. 11:8). Even after they were exiled from their land,
the LORD testified about Ephraim, 'My heart yearns for him; I
will surely have compassion on him' (Jer. 31:20). It had long
been predicted that divine compassion was the only hope for
Israel when they were afflicted because of their rebellion against
the LORD. 'You will return to the LORD your God and obey his
voice, for the LORD your God is a compassionate God' (Deut.
4:30-31). This readiness to replace judgement with grace is
reflected in the attitude of the father towards his returning son in
Jesus' parable (Luke 15:20).

C. Self-Examination and Complaint (3:40-48)

The introduction of material written using the first person plural
clearly marks 3:40 as the start of a new section of the poem, but the
theme carries over from the previous section where, on the basis of
his own experience, the poet had set out in general terms his recom-
mendations regarding the way back from catastrophe into renewed
enjoyment of fellowship with God. His presentation now becomes
more immediate and personal as in 3:40-42 he associates himself
with his contemporaries and urges that they all engage in self-
examination and prayer. When they address God, they again
become acutely aware of the extent to which he has broken off his
relationship with them (3:43-45) and of how they are suffering as a

result (3:46-47). Contemplating the pain of his people leads the poet to break down in tears (3:48).

ב 3:40 Let us search and examine our ways,
            and let us return to the LORD.

ב 3:41 Let us lift up our heart as well as ⌐our⌐ hands
            to God in the heavens:

ב 3:42 'As for us, we have rebelled and been defiant;
            as for you, you have not forgiven.'

There can be little doubt that when the poet addressed the community they all had discerned that the disaster which had befallen them had come from God and that the continuing situation in the land was a consequence of his disfavour. There was no need for further analysis as regards that. What was lacking was a recognition of personal responsibility for the events which had occurred. *Let us search and examine our ways* is an exhortation to conduct a thorough-going investigation into their own action and the inner disposition which motivated it. The speaker recognises that such an examination was necessary before they could approach God. Once they had admitted their own deficiencies and the extent to which they had contributed to the present situation, then they would have a right frame of mind to *return to the LORD* (cf. 5:21). Here the covenant name of God is used for the first time since 3:26, as is fitting for the personal nature of what is envisaged.

The poet then emphasises the need for the community to have a religious praxis that goes beyond formal, outward engagement with God. While lifting up their hands in prayer (cf. 2:19) is an appropriate gesture, *as well as*[107] points to the need for an harmonious combination with true heart orientation towards him (cf. Hos. 7:14). They must genuinely seek contact with *God* (*'ēl*), the one who alone is divine. This term occurs frequently in Job and Psalms, but only here in Lamentations. Indeed, the related term for God (*'ĕlōhîm*), which occurs much more frequently in Scripture, is not used at all in this book. They must approach him with due reverence because he is exalted *in the heavens*.

---

107. 'As well as our hands' is literally 'to hands', but the preposition *'el* is evidently used in the sense 'together with', which it has also in Lev. 18:18.

The prayer of 3:42 is the poet's expression of what the people should say; it is not a record of what they in fact said. It is structured around the two sides of the covenant relationship, *as for us ... as for you*. The people are to confess their guilt. *We have rebelled* points to actions taken that were wittingly contrary to the ruler's known commands (cf. the noun 'rebellion' in 1:5). This is sin at its most serious. *Been defiant* points to both attitudes and conduct which resist the implications of the LORD's authority (cf. 1:18, 20). The two verbs probably constitute a hendiadys, together describing a single action of obstinately going in other ways and by other paths.

At one level then it was not surprising that the LORD had not *forgiven*, that is, set aside the guilt of the people. Since their conduct had been heinous, they had no grounds for pleading for pardon. But in fact they had never had such grounds. Divine forgiveness is an act of grace, and it is a fundamental perception of faith that the LORD is the one with whom forgiveness is to be found (cf. Ps. 130:4). So there is a measure of puzzlement, verging on complaint, that the continuing state of the people demonstrates that the LORD has not been merciful as his revealed nature and past action had led them to expect. Unlike the complaints of 3:1-18, however, this is addressed not to others, but to the LORD himself. There is an implicit plea that he return to his characteristic behaviour and forgive the offences of those who have rebelled against him.

ם 3:43 You have covered with anger and pursued us;
            you have slaughtered and not shown pity.
ם 3:44 You have covered yourself with a cloud
            so that no prayer should pass through.
ם 3:45 You have made us rubbish and refuse
            in the midst of the peoples.

It is unclear if this continues the prayer of 3:42 or is a separate address of the speaker to God, though the latter is more probable. If so, the poet moves from exhorting his audience to addressing the LORD about his unabated anger towards the people's sin. The Hebrew does not quite make clear in 3:43 who or what the LORD has *covered with anger*: is it himself or the people? While the former may be suggested by 3:44 where the verb is repeated with the additional word *yourself*, it is more probable that *us* is to be understood with both verbs in 3:43. The LORD who had been expected to be the protector of his people, covering them from the hostile actions of their enemies in the day of battle (cf. Ps. 140:7), has now enclosed them with the outpouring of his wrath so that they quail beneath repeated blows. He has *pursued* (cf. 1:3) them unremittingly just as an enemy would in his attempts to catch and overwhelm them (cf. Pss. 119:150; 143:3). Indeed, he had *slaughtered* (cf. 2:4, 21) *and not shown pity* (cf. 2:2, 17, 21) in that the penalty which his people had anticipated would fall on hostile nations had been visited upon them for their transgression.

There was also another barrier interposed between the LORD and the people. In Old Testament theophanies, when the LORD visibly presenced himself with Israel, a frequent accompaniment was dark clouds which veiled his glory (cf. Exod. 19:9; Num. 12:5; Ps. 97:2). But this cloud no longer signals the privilege the people enjoyed in having such a divine manifestation in their midst. Now, as a further consequence of their rebellion, the cloud has been turned into an impenetrable barrier *so that no prayer should pass through.* The one who hears prayer (Ps. 65:2) is no longer disposed to listen to their petitions (cf. Ps. 80:4). Notice the difference in the experience from 3:8, where the speaker felt his prayer never left the earth. Here it reaches heaven, only to find a 'Not available' notice on the door. God would not heed their entreaties, and all they were left aware of was their exposure to his wrath.

The two pejorative terms, *rubbish and refuse,* express the way surrounding nations contemptuously dismiss Jerusalem as they survey the wreckage of the city. The ruins contain nothing to excite their admiration or draw them into the service of the LORD. 'Rubbish' refers to something that is scraped off a pot, and 'refuse' what is rejected for use (cf. 1 Cor. 4:13 for a similar thought, though the words Paul uses are not those found in the Septuagint translation of this verse).

ב 3:46 All our enemies have opened
        their mouths wide against us.
ב 3:47 Panic and pitfall have come on us,
        this devastation and destruction.

** פ** 3:48 My eye runs down with rivers of water
                because of the destruction of the daughter of
                my people.

It is not always clear where transitions occur in the remainder of the chapter.[108] Certainly they are not located only at the close of stanzas. Here, for instance, there is a notable switch from plural to singular between 3:47 and 3:48. It would seem that the poet sets out the community's dire straits before reverting in 3:48 to describing his reaction to the catastrophe which has overtaken the people.

There is a resemblance between 3:46 and 2:16 (*open wide the mouth* occurs in both places), though here those who are exposed to mockery are the poet and the people on whose behalf he is speaking rather than the personified presentation of daughter Jerusalem. Essentially, of course, those referred to are the same.

The word pair, *panic and pitfall* (*paḥad wāpaḥat*), involves both alliteration and assonance. 'Panic' suggests a terror-stricken reaction to a sudden threat (cf. Prov. 1:26; 3:25), which may be divinely initiated (cf. Isa. 33:14; Mic. 7:17). 'Pitfall' indicates a concealed trap into which a panicked animal would unwittingly be forced. Both terms occur together in Isaiah 24:17 and Jeremiah 48:43. A similar word-play is involved in *this devastation and destruction* (*haššē't wǝhaššāber*). The first noun occurs only here, but the root from which it is derived points to the ruination of cities and fields (cf. Isa. 6:11). *This* attempts to bring out the particularising force of the definite article which is attached to each noun. The focus is on the specific outrages committed against Jerusalem.

As he sets out the woes which have overwhelmed his nation, the poet again cannot remain unmoved (cf. 2:11). In this he shares the grief of the city as a whole (cf. 1:16; 2:18), which rendered it speechless. He too has no words to add to his prayer, but his tears continue his entreaty for divine mercy. *Rivers* refers to canals or irrigation channels specifically dug to permit the flow of water. Here the metaphor brings out the intensity of the poet's grief at the *destruction*, the 'breaking' of the people (cf. 2:11). For *daughter of my people*, see on 2:11 also.

---

108. For the reversal of the letters *pê* and *'ayin* in 3:46-48 and 3:49-51, see on 2:16.

It is noteworthy that the speaker moves back from embracing the community with him in the sweep of his thought to the more isolated stance of personal reflection, which is maintained to the end of the poem. Though 3:48 is similar to 2:11 in exposing the intensity of the poet's emotional reaction, what is said here is not mere repetition, nor is variety to be introduced by supposing that it is another voice which is heard here. In the first part of chapter 3 the poet's grief had principally arisen from his personal suffering; now it is derived from the distress and anguish of the community. In chapter 2 he had spoken to Zion of his empathy with her in her agony; here he takes on the role of pleading her case before God.

Reflection

- Self-examination as to where we stand in relation to God is a vital spiritual exercise (cf. Luke 21:34; 2 Cor. 13:5). Just as a doctor does not perform a surgical operation without first carrying out a physical examination to establish the precise nature of a patient's malady, so action to correct spiritual ailments requires prior identification of what is wrong. We are prone to rest content with hearing God's word and failing to practice what he enjoins, just like the unmindful person of whom James wrote, who after seeing himself in a mirror forgot what he looked like (Jas. 1:22-24).

- Such spiritual self-examination is primarily a personal exercise (cf. 1 Cor. 11:28), but it must not stop there. We are each responsible for how we live as families, communities and church fellowships, and these other aspects of our existence must also be tested to ensure that they conform to God's requirements.

- The Old Testament idiom for repentance is to 'return' to the LORD (3:40). It seems to be related to perception of life as a path along which one walks (cf. Ps. 17:5; Prov. 2:20; Isa. 2:3). Repentance begins with recognition that one is lost, having chosen to follow a wrong path, and it also involves sorrow for having behaved in that way. But neither knowledge that one is off the correct road nor regret over ill-considered decisions in the past constitutes 'return'. There must also be a rejection of the false way and a determination to follow the path that truly leads to God; otherwise a person might just through spiritual inertia continue sorrowfully on his previous path merely to see where it takes him. Only when an individual's will has been renewed and empowered by God is it truly able to return by decisively abandoning the wrong path and walking obediently on the correct route.

- The relationship between repentance and forgiveness is a vexed one. Is God obligated to forgive if one repents? In Jeremiah 14–15 the prophet turned this question over before God. He had confessed the sin of the people and the fact that the LORD alone was sovereign (Jer. 14:19), but the LORD's response is that the intercession of others would not suffice to avert the doom of a people who had persistently rejected him (Jer. 15:1-6). Confession by others is not enough. Even so, a spirit of true repentance is ultimately a gift of God (cf. Acts 5:31; 2 Tim. 2:25) and, when an individual returns to the LORD, there is guaranteed acceptance (John 6:37).

D. Prayer Based on Past Experience (3:49-66)

The poet is again plunged into sorrow, but there has been a movement away from the unremitting desolation of his experience in 3:1-18. Now he anticipates a terminus for his grief (3:50), and he argues for this on the ground of the LORD's past interposition on his behalf. Formerly he had been hard pressed by his enemies (3:52-54), but the LORD had intervened in response to his prayer (3:55-57). This constituted a precedent which yielded a secure basis for expecting a similar response in the future. Certainly the LORD was well aware of all that was being suffered (3:58-59). At this point there is a change in perspective, signalled by the plea, 'Judge my cause' (3:59), and the poet, as one involved in the suffering of the nation, implores the LORD to act on the basis of his knowledge (3:60-63) and impose on their adversaries their just deserts (3:64-66). In this way the poet and the community will gain relief from their cruelty and abuse. The perspective of the concluding stanza demonstrates that the poet is not just giving thanks for past deliverance. While he had previously benefited from divine intervention, he is not yet out of deep waters, but now he can speak as one who is confident that the LORD will act.

The contents of this section again raise the matter of a possible connection with Jeremiah. He too had expressed great grief over the anguish of his people. 'I myself will weep because of your pride, and cry bitterly, and my eyes will run down with tears, for the flock of the LORD has been taken captive' (Jer. 13:17; cf. Jer. 9:1; 14:17). Also the experience of 3:53 in the pit (*bôr*) resembles the prophet's imprisonment in a cistern (*bôr*, Jer. 38:6). There are, however, discrepancies if this is taken as a literal description. Unlike the situation of 3:54, Jeremiah's cistern had no water in it (Jer. 38:6), and also there is no record of Jeremiah being stoned (cf. 3:53b). There are therefore no satisfactory grounds for associating this passage directly with the prophet's personal history. The language is metaphorical, drawing on several standard descriptions of distress and peril.[109]

It is more difficult, however, to establish the precise sequence of events behind 3:52-63, and how they may be related to the poet's ordeal described in 3:1-18. It may well be the same experience, described first in terms of the direct action of God, and subsequently in terms of the activities of the human agents through whom he worked, but there are difficulties connected with any reconstruction.

(1) Anticipated Relief (3:49-51)

ע 3:49 My eye will flow and not stop —
              there will be no interruption —
ע 3:50 until he looks down and sees,
              the LORD from heaven.
ע 3:51 My eye has brought me deep pain
              because of all the daughters of my city.

109. Though Keil accepts that the Jeremianic authorship of Lamentations is as well established as any ancient tradition can be, he acknowledges that the language of this section has to be understood as metaphorical. 'The figurative character of the whole account thus shows itself in the very fact that the separate portions of it are taken from reminiscences of passages in the Psalms, whose figurative character is universally acknowledged' (Keil, *Jeremiah, Lamentations*, 425).

The description of the poet's grief continues from the previous stanza, with *my eye* providing an obvious verbal link back to the central word of 3:48. The poet himself responds to the exhortation which he had given Zion in 2:18, but here the emphasis is on the duration rather than the intensity of sorrow. *My eye will flow* employs the metaphor of a stream of liquid which does *not stop*. Though the word *interruption*/'remission' occurs only here, its meaning is clear, being derived from a root indicating 'to grow weary or feeble', and so it is used to show that there will be no let up in his grieving over the conditions he sees around him.

The poet's reaction, however, does not just function as a release for pent-up emotion; it also constitutes a plea for divine relief. *Until he looks down and sees* calls not just for divine awareness, but for divine action (cf. Ps. 102:19; Isa. 63:15). The delayed identification of the subject as *the LORD from heaven* (cf. 3:41) serves to reinforce the focus on him as the source of help. Yahweh, the God of the covenant, is on his heavenly throne, and it is only as he condescends to take notice of the dire situation in his realms below that there can be any amelioration of Zion's plight. Therefore the poet will be unremitting in his efforts to induce the LORD to respond to the plea for relief embodied in his tears.

The repetition of *my eye* (3:49, 51) has the effect of framing the enclosed verse and emphasising its thematic importance. Again the poet brings out the hurt that the present situation is causing him (for 'bring deep pain'/'inflict', cf. 1:12). As he views it, it strikes to the very heart of his being: *me* is 'my soul'/'my inmost self' (cf. 3:17, 20) and the poet literally says, 'My eye has dealt severely with my soul'.

Mention here of *all the daughters of my city* is frequently assumed to be an intrusion requiring adjustment in some way or other, but there are various ways of understanding the phrase. Least likely is that the plural is another way of expressing a reference to 'daughter Zion' (1:6). More probably 'daughters' points to the grief of the women of Jerusalem as one feature of the situation which intensified the poet's grief. While, however, this suffering is described elsewhere in the book (2:10, 12; 4:2, 10; 5:11), there does not seem to be anything to motivate singling them out for mention at this juncture. So it is quite possible that 'daughters' is

here an instance of the Hebrew idiom for the villages and settlements surrounding a major city (cf. Num. 21:25; Neh. 11:25, 30).
As the poet surveyed the territory outside Jerusalem, this increased
the pain he felt at the havoc which had occurred throughout the
nation and at the continuing misery experienced there.

(2) Past Persecution (3:52-54)

צ 3:52 They hunted me like a bird,
              those who were my enemies without cause.
צ 3:53 They silenced my life in the pit
              and threw stones on me.
צ 3:54 Water flowed over my head;
              I said, 'I am cut off.'

The theme of the poet's reflection had already moved from Jerusalem to its surrounding villages, and in this stanza he looks back in
time to relate events that had occurred in his own life. Though he
expresses himself in conventional terms shared with the laments of
the Psalter (cf. Pss. 11:1; 124:7; 140:5), that does not make his
experience any the less real. The familiar imagery constituted a
bridge whereby his audience could identify with his experience as
he tells them, 'I too have suffered. I know what it is like.' He will
go on in the next stanza to use the empathy thus established as the
basis for urging on them the example of his prayer.

The people had been hunted by their enemies (3:46-47), and so
too had the speaker. In the ancient world fowlers used many techniques to catch wild birds, and here the poet envisages himself as the
object of their activities as they seek to flush him from his cover
and force him to fly in panic into their nets, or else as they shoot at
him with bow and arrow.[110]

That these actions were taken by *those who were my enemies
without cause* raises the question of their identity. The reference
might be to the Babylonian forces as they came against Jerusalem,
but then 'without cause' might seem to imply that the speaker was

110. The alliteration in the first three words of 3:52, *ṣôd ṣādûnî kaṣṣippôr*,
with its repeated *ṣ* sounds suggests that they are 'trapping and enwrapping the
line just as the enemies hunt and entrap the poet' (Dobbs-Allsopp, *Lamentations*, 17).

going back on his involvement in the rebellion mentioned in the communal confession of 3:42. If that understanding is valid, the incident the poet is referring to may instead have been one involving other parties, whether from within or without the community. However, the most compelling interpretation is that what is in view is the randomness with which the occupation forces took action against the inhabitants of the land — in this case unjustly accusing the poet and threatening his life.

The imagery changes in 3:53 to one of deprivation of resources. *The pit* was an underground reservoir for storing water, with smooth plaster sides and an overall bulbous shape which made escape through the narrow neck impossible. To be confined in this way was a lingering death sentence (cf. Jer. 38:9; for the metaphor, cf. Pss. 40:2; 143:7). The precise force of the verb rendered *silenced* is uncertain. It may indicate taking severe action against someone even to the extent of bringing about their death, though in this passage it is frequently translated as 'to toss' or 'to fling' (e.g. in NLT, NRSV, ESV), apparently on contextual grounds. *Stones* is a singular form which could refer to a large stone used to cover the entrance to a cistern but, in view of the accompanying verb 'to shoot' or 'to throw', it is probably a collective use of the noun to describe missiles tossed at the unfortunate person confined in the pit.

Water flowed over my head pictures the pit as having more than a muddy sediment at its bottom. Whatever water might have been in it initially, it would fill up with rain from the channels which drained into it. So it was not just a place of imprisonment; it was an execution chamber and the speaker was in peril of his life. It was therefore unsurprising that as he contemplated his circumstances he could only conclude, *I am cut off.* There was no hope for him surviving the situation (cf. Pss. 69:2; 124:2).

(3) Past Deliverance (3:55-57)

The translation of the perfect verb forms in this stanza is much debated as there is no consensus regarding the experience being described. 'I called' (3:55) may be taken as a present perfect, 'I have called and still do', and there is evidence elsewhere of this verb having such a present sense (cf. Pss. 17:6; 88:9; 119:145, 146;

130:1). Possibly the form may be an instance of a performative perfect, 'I do hereby call', in which the speech act is conceived of as completed in its utterance. This then leaves 'you heard' (3:56) and subsequent perfect verb forms. They have been understood as perfects of certainty, setting out 'the full assurance from which the request comes',[111] 'You shall hear my voice.' Recent commentators are more attracted by an interpretation involving the use of a precative perfect (a perfect of entreaty, which falls somewhat short of a command but is closest to an English imperative), 'Hear my voice', and also 'Draw near ... say' (3:57), and similarly in the next stanza. Such an proposal is grammatically feasible, and it does have several interpretative advantages, but ultimately one wonders why, if that had been the poet's intention, he did not signal it more clearly by using imperative forms for at least some of the verbs.[112] Although the approach is not without difficulties of its own, the following comments are based on taking the perfect verb forms as describing a sequence of events which has already occurred, and which the poet is using as a paradigm for the community.

פ 3:55 I called on your name, O LORD,
            from the very bottom of the pit.

פ 3:56 You heard my voice, 'Do not close your ear
            to my gasping cry, to my plea for help!'

פ 3:57 You drew near when I called on you;
            you said, 'Do not be afraid!'

The LORD is presented in other passages as drawing close to those who call on him from the depths (cf. Pss. 30:2-3; 40:1-3; Jonah 2:2) and in this way saving them from imminent death. In his distress

---

111. Cf. C. F. Keil, *Jeremiah, Lamentations*, 427.

112. For further explanation of the terminology used in connection with the verb forms, see Waltke and O'Connor, *Syntax*: for performative, see §30.5.1d; for perfect of certainty, §30.5.1e; for precative perfect, §30.5.4c, d. Particular note should be taken of the advice in this last section that a precative perfect will be found alternating with an imperfect or imperative which indicates the sense in which the perfect is to be understood. The employment here of precative perfects is advocated by Iain W. Provan, 'Past, Present and Future in Lamentations III 52–66: The Case for a Precative Perfect Re-Examined,' *Vetus Testamentum* 41 (1991): 164–75, and *Lamentations* (New Century Bible; London: Marshall Pickering, 1991), 105–6.

the poet drew on these examples of faith and followed their approach. For *the very bottom of the pit*, compare Psalm 88:6. Possibly the very bottom/lowest part has overtones of Sheol (cf. Deut. 32:22; Ps. 86:13). There could be no doubt about the dire nature of the experience.

You heard my voice relates how in the poet's desperate circumstances the LORD no longer wrapped himself in a cloud (cf. 3:44), but responded to his entreaty. Although the following words may be read as a separate prayer,[113] it is more natural to take them as the content of the plea. *Do not close your ear* asks not only for acknowledgement that his petition has been heard, but for action in response to it. The second part of 3:56 consists of two words in Hebrew. It is difficult to establish the sense of the term translated *gasping cry*. It comes from a root which refers to a broad expanse, and hence is used metaphorically for entry into such a place from a situation of constriction (cf. Exod. 8:11; Ps. 66:12). But this does not easily fit in here, and in the light of the following word it may well indicate a cry for relief. *My plea for help* is from the same root as 'plead for help' (3:8). This word was used of the Israelites' petition in Exodus 2:23, and the divine response became the basis of many subsequent prayers (cf. Pss. 18:6; 34:15; 145:19).[114]

The poet then (3:57) relates that God had drawn near to him (cf. Ps. 69:18), making him aware of his presence and supporting him (cf. Ps. 145:18). In this case help is extended by use of the words of encouragement, *Do not be afraid!*, which served to quell the poet's anxieties and to assure him that divine assistance was at hand. Though God does not here address a new revelatory word to Zion in her agony, this statement does qualify the view that the voice of the LORD is not heard at all in Lamentations. Indeed, it is probable that the poet is not claiming that he himself had received direct revelation, but rather that, through the Spirit, the LORD had made

---

113. Those who favour taking the perfects as precative read this as a separate plea using a jussive form, 'Hear my voice! Do not close your ear!' The presence of a jussive facilitates understanding the surrounding perfects as precative. See footnote 112.

114. There is a tendency to assume that 'cry for help' is a gloss added to the text by a later scribe to explain the uncommon form 'gasping cry'. The LXX has only one term, though the Vulgate has two.

words of inscripturated truth come real in his experience (cf. Deut. 1:29-30; Josh. 1:9; Judg. 6:23; Ps. 27:1; Isa. 41:10). As the promises of Scripture had previously spoken into the poet's anxious situation, so they could now similarly speak to his contemporaries in their need.

(4) Judge My Cause (3:58-63)

ר 3:58 You pled my case, O Lord;
           you redeemed my life.
ר 3:59 You saw, O LORD, the wrong done me;
           judge my cause.
ר 3:60 You have seen all their vengeance,
           all their scheming against me.

Again there is difficulty in establishing whether the verbs portray past definitive action which continues to impact the present, or a desire for future action (see section 3 above). As past action, *you pled my case* shows how God had extended assistance to the poet. Both 'pled' and 'case' come from a root which describes a dispute or grievance whether of a formal or of an informal nature. The expression is more literally, 'You contended the contentions of my soul.' It may well be that a legal setting is envisaged here, and the sovereign Lord (*'ădōnāy*, cf. 1:14) is acting not as judge, but as advocate, of the speaker's cause. 'My case'/'the case of my soul' shows that the matters in dispute were of the deepest personal concern to the poet, because his well-being, indeed his life, was at stake in these pleadings.

The Lord's intervention was successful. *You redeemed my life* employs a well-known Scriptural metaphor which describes action on behalf of another on the basis of an acknowledged relationship (cf. Lev. 25:25-34, 47-55; Ruth 2:20; Isa. 43:1-7). God is the one 'who redeems your life from the pit' (Ps. 103:4), and the speaker found it to be the case that the Lord intervened in his oppressive circumstances to deliver him. If we try to envisage the actual situation lying behind these words, it may well be that the speaker is giving thanks for divinely-granted efficacy to the pleas uttered on his behalf before some tribunal of the occupation powers which resulted in him being released from the pit into which he had been thrown (3:53). It does not imply that the difficulties facing the city as a whole had been resolved.

You saw, O LORD, the wrong done me explicitly claims the covenant relationship involved in the divine name Yahweh. In the past the LORD had seen, that is, observed with a view to taking appropriate action what was being imposed on the speaker. 'The wrong done me' is closely related to the word for 'iniquity', with the underlying metaphor being of something twisted away from what is straight and true (cf. 2:14). Those oppressing him had acted unjustly and therefore he claims that the covenant King should intervene on his behalf: *judge my cause.* The repeated use of the root *šāpaṭ* might be brought out by a paraphrase such as, 'Exercise justice with respect to my justice'. This does not necessarily require a legal verdict, but calls for the imposition of a just and fair order in society, and particularly here with respect to the speaker. This is what a king was expected to achieve.

The use of the imperative in 'judge my cause' poses the greatest challenge to a past reading of this passage because it speaks of a situation in which intervention is still needed. It would seem that the poet is beginning to merge the circumstances of his own history with the application to be derived from it for the present difficulties of the community which still has to face enemies (cf. 3:64-66).

In 3:60 the speaker again draws attention to God's awareness of what has been taking place: *You have seen all their vengeance.* Is he still referring to those he has described as his enemies in 3:52? Perhaps there is an indication of who is involved in the designation of their behaviour as 'vengeance', that is, action taken in response to a wrong perceived to have been done against one. Now in 3:52 the poet claims that the hostility of his enemies was 'without cause'. This makes it more likely that, having focussed on the current situation in the immediately preceding words of 3:59, the poet's thoughts continue in that vein.[115] The vengeance in view was that sought by the Babylonians at the level of the nation as a whole.

---

115. It is in view of the perceived change of focus at this point that I have translated this and subsequent perfect verbs in 3:61-62 as present perfects, indicating past action which continues to occur and to have present consequences (cf. 3:55).

Judah had rebelled against Babylon, and Nebuchadnezzar had sought redress for the damage done to his rights as their overlord. Furthermore, in the months following the fall of the city, Gedaliah, the Babylonian appointed governor of Judah, had been assassinated (Jer. 41, especially v. 18), and there were no doubt reprisals for that action. Additionally, within the serried ranks of the imperial army, there were many national contingents who harboured long-standing grudges and enmities against Judah. This was particularly true of the Edomites who were maliciously intent on deriving satisfaction and advantage from Jerusalem's downfall (cf. 4:21; Ps. 137:7; Ezek. 25:12-17; Obad. 11, 13-16).[116]

All their scheming against me does not imply that the poet was the target of their plans in a way not shared by his fellow-citizens. While the calculation and contrivance involved in 'scheming' need not be with ill-intent, the term is frequently used of activity designed to take improper advantage of another (cf. Pss. 10:2; 21:11; 56:5). In their ruined and helpless condition the people were unable to protect themselves from the attacks of their enemies — and the LORD was aware of this.

ע 3:61 You have heard, O LORD, their reproach,
        all their scheming against me—
ע 3:62 the lips of those who have risen against me
        and their whispers against me all the day.
ע 3:63 Consider their sitting and their rising;
        I am the theme of their mocking-song.

The poet gives more details regarding the way in which he has been ill-treated by those who have conquered his nation, and he makes clear that the abuse still continues. He does this so as to draw the LORD's attention to what is going on, and in this way he tenders a yet another plea for divine intervention. *You have heard* adds to the notion of divine vision of the injustices being perpetrated in

116. Mintz also argues that a change of focus begins at this stage in the poem. Though the poem had begun with the speaker as an 'individuated' individual speaking out of the loneliness of his suffering and eventually charting the way he broke free from it, here the same individual has so identified himself with the community that he has truly become a personification of it (Mintz, 'Rhetoric,' 15).

Jerusalem (cf. 3:60) that of divine audition of what is being said *against me.* The poet pleads that the covenant King react to his adversaries' wrongful and spiteful speech. *Reproach* refers to the scornful abuse to which the occupying forces subject him and his fellows, contemptuously insulting them and mocking their situation and their God (cf. Pss. 44:16; 74:10; 89:51).

Again referring to *their scheming* (cf. 3:60), the poet graphically talks about *the lips of those who rose against me.* 'Lips' here stands for what is spoken by means of them, but which speakers are in view here? 'Those who rose against me' may be a general term for enemies (cf. Pss. 3:2; 44:5; 74:23), but why should they whisper? The enemy armies had engaged in loud triumph (cf. 2:7). Possibly this refers to groups like the Edomites who kept up a relentless campaign of character assassination and propaganda against the inhabitants of Jerusalem designed to influence the attitude of the occupying power to those who remained.

There is again a call for divine scrutiny of the prevailing situation: *Consider* (cf. 1:11). *Their sitting and their rising* (cf. Ps. 139:2) is a merism naming two opposite activities to describe every aspect of their conduct. As the LORD probes the misconduct that permeates every aspect of his adversaries' behaviour, the speaker is sure that he will be stirred up to react against them and that his response will be intensified by the fact that, when they pick up their stringed instruments to play, *I am the theme of their mocking-song.* Their taunts are not merely the derisive comments of the heathen, but words that they utter against one who is identified with the LORD (cf. 3:14). It is not casual abuse, uttered on a single occasion, but persistent verbal attack felt all the more keenly because embodied in the lyrics of a song.

(5) Give What They Deserve (3:64-66)

ת 3:64 You will bring back on them what they deserve, O
           LORD,
           according to the work of their hands.
ת 3:65 You will give them anguish of heart;
           your curse will be on them.
ת 3:66 You will pursue in anger and eradicate them
           from under the LORD's heavens.

Each of the concluding three verses begins with a verb which predicts what the LORD will do, or requests that he will act in this way ('May you bring back … give … pursue').[117] Either rendering shows the situation is ultimately capable of resolution only by divine action. *What they deserve* describes recompense that is in proportion to their previous behaviour either by way of reward or penalty (cf. Ps. 28:4). *According to the work of their hands* leaves no doubt that the poet expects divine judgement to fall on his oppressors for their actions as well as their hurtful words. Jeremiah had used the same root when he declared against Babylon, 'The LORD is a God of recompense; he shall fully repay' (Jer. 51:56), and in this there is enunciated a basic belief of Israel regarding divine imposition of justice (cf. Deut. 32:35).[118] Although the adversary had been divinely mandated to act against Judah and Jerusalem, their vengeful atrocities went beyond what the LORD wished done. Just intervention is needed to redress the situation (cf. Isa. 10:24-27; 17:14).

It is unclear precisely what penalty the poet envisaged as appropriate. The noun rendered *anguish* occurs only here, and its meaning is debated. Many associated it with a root meaning 'to shelter' or 'to cover' (e.g. 'put a veil over their hearts', NIV), while more recently others have suggested 'shamelessness' or 'insanity'. It is unlikely that a veiled or unresponsive heart is intended here — that would have meant a perpetuation of the situation of Jerusalem. A connection with a root meaning 'to afflict' (cf. 1:4, 12; 3:32, 33) is more probable, with the thought as a whole being similar to that

---

117. The three verbs are imperfects which refer to actions that are incomplete, generally those in the future or continuing from the present into the future. The imperfect may also be used to express a wish, particularly in the context of a prayer. Translations vary in the rendering they adopt: a future (RSV, ESV); an imperative (AV, NIV, NRSV).

118. The petitions of the concluding verses of this chapter do not provide any direct evidence regarding authorship. While Jeremiah promoted a policy of not resisting Babylon because it was the LORD's chosen instrument for punishing his people, that did not mean he exempted Babylon from divine scrutiny and judgement as Jer. 25:12 and 50–51 clearly show. There is therefore no tension between the sentiment of this portion of the poem and the known attitude of Jeremiah to constitute an argument for differing authorship.

expressed by Jerusalem, 'Let them be as I am' (1:21).[119] In this way
your curse will be on them. But of what does this curse consist? As
the enemy, being foreigners, were not parties to the covenant, the
curse in view is not specifically that imposed for covenant violation. But conscience testifies to God's standards, and so all are
therefore liable to divine scrutiny and judgement (cf. Amos 1–2).

It is anticipated that the LORD will be consistent in his execution
of justice. *You will pursue* relates to action taken to assert the
standards of divine justice by apprehending and punishing those
who have violated them. This had already happened to Judah in the
context of covenantal infringement (cf. 3:42). The enemy can
expect nothing else for their gross misbehaviour than that they too
will experience the judicial *anger* of the Lord.

Eradicate refers to the extermination of a group of people.
Moses had told Israel that the LORD would give the nations of
Canaan over before them, throwing them into great confusion until
they were eradicated (cf. Deut. 7:23). A similar removal of their
heathen conquerors and their abominations is here envisaged. However, it is no longer confined to removal from the land, but *from
under the LORD's heavens,*[120] totally wiping out all the LORD's
enemies.

Reflection

*   Importunate pleading will not give over in presenting God with
    its demands for action 'until he looks down and sees' (3:50).
    Especially those who express concern for the future of God's
    people are to be unremitting in bringing the matter before the
    LORD (cf. Isa. 62:6-7). Such persistence is commended by

---

119. Derivation of the noun *māginnâ* from *yāgâ* (I), 'to grieve, afflict'
(rather than *nāgan*, 'to shelter, cover') is reflected in 'sorrow' (AV) and
'anguish' (NRSV).

120. The rendering 'from under your heavens, O LORD' reflects the reading
of the Syriac Peshitta, which is adopted by some translations (e.g. RSV, ESV
citing the support of the LXX and Vulgate with respect to the use of a vocative) and also by commentators who feel uncomfortable that the LORD is mentioned in the third person in direct address to him. Such a grammatical change
is not, however, strange in Hebrew, especially when, as here, 'the LORD's
heavens' is virtually a technical term (cf. 'day of the LORD' in 2:22).

Christ because God will speedily give justice to his elect (Luke 18:1-9).

- 'You said' (3:57) probably refers to the action of the Holy Spirit in bringing before an individual a portion of Scripture and impressing him with the reality of the message it contains. This points to the value of familiarity with God's word. 'In my heart I have hidden/stored up your word' (Ps. 119:11), and in this way there is provided guidance regarding how to live appropriately (cf. Ps. 37:31) and a basis on which the Holy Spirit builds as he bears inner witness to the veracity of the Word which he has inspired (cf. Rom. 8:16). This is an aspect of his ongoing ministry in the life of believers, assuring them of their status as children of God and thus of the availability of divine assistance in whatever circumstances they find themselves.

- Fear is a basic human reaction to the unknown, the uncertain, and the overwhelming, all of which constitute potential dangers. But those who trust in God are instructed not to be crushed by panic-stricken terror because of threats presented by others (cf. Matt.10:28; Phil. 1:28). Instead God repeatedly directs them not to pattern their behaviour after the response of sinful men (cf. Num. 14:9; Isa. 8:12). Such fear is inappropriate on the part of those who have been assured of God's presence with them. 'Do not be afraid, for I am with you' (Gen. 26:24) is the dynamic which God repeatedly uses to bolster the flagging spirits of his people. When they direct their thoughts towards him and what he can do, then they may say with the psalmist, 'The LORD is on my side; I will not be afraid. What can man do to me?' (Ps. 118:6; cf. Deut. 31:6; Ps. 23:4; Heb. 13:6). God's presence and the resources he provides are more than sufficient to offset any challenge presented in life.

Lamentations 4

OUTLINE

A.   Zion's Continuing Torment (4:1-10)

B.   Rejected by the LORD (4:11-16)

C.   Helpless is Man's Aid (4:17-20)

D.   The Destiny of Edom and Zion (4:21-22)

After the somewhat more positive message of chapter 3, Lamentations now reverts to the grim scenario of Zion's suffering and misery. The repeated 'Ah, how!' (4:1, 2) clearly indicates that we are again entering the world of loss and mourning. This, however, is not to be taken as implying that the struggle to reach the measure of faith attained in chapter 3 has so exhausted the poet that he can no longer maintain any optimism. It is rather the case that, if a basically concentric analysis of Lamentations correctly reflects the structure of the book, then the encirclement of chapter 3 by chapters 2 and 4 provides a deliberate reinforcement of the point that the faith of the poet has to be exercised in circumstances where the final resolution of the tragedy of Zion has not yet occurred. Even if the community adopted the viewpoint which the speaker has urged on them, a right relationship with the LORD is not going to be immediately achieved. Unlike the relief provided for Samaria in 2 Kings 7, what was envisaged for Jerusalem was going to be an extended process.

However, concentric structuring of the material is not the only device employed by the poet. At a thematic level there is a measure of progression, so that chapter 4 does not simply reiterate the issues raised in earlier chapters, particularly those associated with the LORD's anger against the city and the impact of famine and suffering on it. In the concluding verses of the chapter (4:21-22), what had been a prayer in 1:22 is now confidently predicted in the presentation of the contrasting destinies of Zion and Edom. For the former, the worst is already behind her; for the latter, it has still to begin. The community in Zion will not be left perpetually posing the question, 'For ever will the Lord cast off and gracious be no more?' (Ps. 77:7, Scottish Metrical version), for the LORD will grant closure to her present distress as he reverses the punishment imposed on her.

Once more the literary structure of the chapter is that of an alphabetic acrostic with each verse beginning with successive letters of the Hebrew alphabet. However, this poem is shorter than those found in chapters 1 and 2 in that each verse is now composed of two, not three, lines. This fits in with the overall *qînâ* structure of Lamentations in which the concluding units fall away in their intensity.

While 4:21-22 are generally recognised as a distinct unit within the poem, other subdivisions are less certain. Renkema argues that the poem should be centrally divided after 4:11, with the two balancing sections containing at their centres a joint portrait of Zion's condition: that the severity of her suffering has been occasioned by the gravity of her sin (4:6); and that her situation is, humanly speaking, one of utter helplessness (4:17).[121] However, it is again the case that many of the features which Renkema adduces to support his position do not convincingly bear the weight he places on them.

A thematic analysis of the chapter may be built up by employing changes in the viewpoint adopted in the poem to delineate the structure of the material. We no longer have 'the man' of chapter 3 presenting his own experience and focusing on his personal involvement in the tragedy. The poet's stance is more that of the observer as in earlier chapters, looking from the outside at a situation which he describes in third person terms. He is not, however, completely detached and unsympathetic as the use of 'the daughter of my people' (4:3, 6, 10) indicates. He brings out the agony of Zion's continuing torment in 4:1-10, particularly by describing reversed circumstances. In 4:11-16 there is a change of stance, and the poet looks back as he probes the reasons for the city's suffering. A switch to first person plural language in 4:17-20 permits us to hear the community speak, though the persona of daughter Zion is not employed here. The people declare how all they had set their hopes on had proved ineffective. There is, however, no hint that God remains as the only possible source of relief, and they do not directly engage with him. Nevertheless the concluding words of the poet (4:21-22) point to eventual divine intervention as the way in which Zion's situation will be resolved.

A. Zion's Continuing Torment (4:1-10)

This section presents a matter-of-fact, third person plural description of the suffering of the survivors in Jerusalem, and reflects a number of features found in 2:9-11, especially in the listing of the groups involved: infants, young children, dignitaries, mothers.

---

121. Renkema's analysis of the structure of the chapter is most fully set out in 'Literary Structure,' 334–46.

Starvation is widespread in the city, and its ravages are not confined to the homes but are openly displayed in the streets (2:11-12; 4:4-5). The destruction of the city (2:9) is matched by 'the destruction of the daughter of my people' (4:10). Repeated contrasts between past and present bring out how greatly the condition of the people has been transformed.

א 4:1 Ah, how the gold is darkened,
⌊how⌋ the pure gold is dull!
Holy stones lie scattered
at the head of every street.

The introductory *Ah, how!* (repeated in 4:2; cf. 1:1; 2:1) refocuses our attention from the faith of the poet to the tragedy of Jerusalem as epitomised by the state of the Temple. The personal misfortunes of the city's inhabitants were being played out against a backdrop of ruins which testified to the departure of the LORD. When he abandoned the city, it became vulnerable before its foes, and as a result it now lies devastated.

The poet uses expressions which are tantalising and somewhat obscure, and only as he develops his theme do his intentions become clearer. *The gold is darkened* refers to the Temple which Solomon had lavishly overlaid with gold (1 Kgs. 6:20-22, 30, 32). Subsequently it had been looted on a number of occasions, but every effort had been to restore the magnificence of the building (cf. 1 Kgs. 14:26; 2 Kgs. 18:16). The description is reinforced by *the pure gold is dull,* where 'gold' is a poetic synonym of the earlier term, possibly referring to gold in a refined state. Two problems are often detected in this line: gold does not tarnish, and laments are usually over people. Indeed, there would hardly have been gold, tarnished or otherwise, left after the city had been plundered. This is rather a poetic description of how the once splendid Temple had become a charred ruin.

Although Zion's children are elsewhere said to lie at the head of every street (2:19), this does not necessarily imply that the children and holy stones are to be equated. *Holy stones* (literally, 'stones of holiness') does not have the article ('stones of the holiness'), and this leaves open the possibility that, rather than the reference being specifically to the stones of Temple, it is to the rubble of the sacred city in general that the poet points. These stones now *lie scattered* (literally, 'are poured out' like liquid from a vessel, cf. 2:4; 4:11), and the repetition of the verb in 4:11 where it refers to the pouring out of Yahweh's wrath may imply that both verses describe the same state of affairs. This scene is one of havoc consequent upon divine judgement.

ב 4:2   The precious children of Zion,
              worth their weight in fine gold,
          ah, how they are regarded as earthenware pots,
              the work of a potter's hands!

The speaker's gaze moves from the buildings of the city to its citizens. *The children*/'sons' *of Zion* are here described as *precious*, possibly in view of their status as chosen by the LORD (cf. Isa. 43:3; Jer. 31:20). The term 'sons' does not imply that only the young are in view (cf. Zech. 9:13). *Worth their weight* refers to the commercial practice of establishing the value of a commodity by setting it in one pan of a pair of scales to balance it against a recognised standard. The inhabitants of Zion had once been regarded as more valuable than *fine gold* (a third term for gold, refined and purified), but the tragedy that is being played out means that they are reckoned as of no more significance than *earthenware pots*. It may be that this expression does not just convey the thought of ordinary items of little value, but points to them as fit only to be discarded on the city rubbish heap once they have been damaged. By whom are the pots that had once been skilfully shaped now rejected? Certainly Zion's conquerors gave no thought to the welfare of the population, but ultimately their destiny has been determined by the fact that they have been discarded by the LORD. The shattered earthenware jar is a symbol of his judgement (cf. Isa. 30:14; Jer. 18:1-6; 19:1-15; 22:28).

ג 4:3   Even jackals offer the breast,
              they nurse their young,
          but the daughter of my people has become cruel,
              like ostriches in the wilderness.

4:3-5 deal with the extent of the tragedy which has come upon Zion, particularly in the famine during and after the siege. *Even* introduces an unexpected comparison. The verb 'to uncover and *offer*' involves a transference of human behaviour to animals. It is a gnomic perfect, expressing a general maxim, for which English ordinarily uses a present tense. The mention of *jackals* fits in with the picture of a ruined city in which scavengers and predators prowl and with the subsequent reference to the wilderness (cf. 5:18).[122] The point being made here is that even such animals follow their natural instincts and *nurse their young.* However, in the wake of the catastrophe that had come upon Jerusalem unnatural behaviour was being displayed. Precisely what was involved depends on the identification of *the daughter of my people* (cf. 2:11). While at first it would seem to be a reference to mothers in Jerusalem who have abandoned their young children, if the construction is properly interpreted as an endearing reference to the people as a whole ('my dear people'), the population in general are accused of having become so affected by the ongoing famine that parents no longer nourish their offspring. They have *become cruel*[123] and their conduct is worse than that of animals (cf. Isa. 1:3; Jer. 8:7).

A further animal comparison is employed in *like ostriches in the wilderness.* Until recent centuries ostriches could be found in the Negev, the wilderness zone to the south of Israel, and they are mentioned in a number of places in the Old Testament, including Leviticus 11:16 and Deuteronomy 14:15 (where the species is categorised as impure). Here the point of the simile seems to be in the behaviour of the bird: at a time of danger it may leave its nest, possibly to divert attention from it; at other times it may abandon its eggs to incubate in the sun. At any rate its conduct was under-stood as heartless and without regard for the well-being of its young. There is an extended reference to this in Job 39:13-18. Such lack of affection had become characteristic of the inhabitants of the city.

---

122. The kethibh *tannîn* may be analysed as a singular form meaning 'sea monster' (cf. LXX, AV), but it is fairly certain that the plural of *tan*, 'jackal', with an Aramaic style ending (cf. 1:4), is intended. The qere advocates reading *tannîm*, 'jackals', with a normal Hebrew plural ending, and this is adopted by the majority of modern versions (cf. *HALOT* 3:1759).

123. 'Cruel' (*'akzār*) is preceded by a *lāmed* whose function is not immedi-ately obvious. It may serve to give emphasis, but there is no certainty about that. It is ignored in translation.

ד 4:4   The tongue of the infant has stuck
            to the roof of its mouth because of thirst.
         Young children asked for bread;
            no one is breaking it for them.

During the siege of the city and for some time thereafter its
inhabitants suffered from thirst and starvation. The poet poignantly
describes how this affected the most vulnerable of the population.
The infant, one not yet weaned — in that culture the period
extended up to three years of age — is dying *because of thirst* and
lack of nourishment. They are so weak that they cannot even
whimper because their dried mouths prevent speech (cf. Job 29:10;
Ps. 137:6; Ezek. 3:26). The *young children*, toddlers who were
some years older (cf. 2:11), are able to verbalise their requests *for
bread*, typically a round loaf, which may stand for food of any sort
(cf. 2:12). But no one has any thing to *break*/'spread out' before
them. Indeed they do not care about the hunger of the young; the
citizens of Jerusalem are so desperate that each accords personal
survival overwhelming priority.

ה 4:5   Those used to eating delicacies
            have become desolate in the streets;
         those brought up in scarlet
            have embraced rubbish tips.

The extent to which the famine has taken hold of the city is emphasised by a pair of stark contrasts with the conditions which
formerly prevailed in Jerusalem. It is probable that the descriptions
still focus on the children of the city (rather than say the nobility).
Great care had formerly been taken of the young, who were thus
used to eating delicacies, the choicest of items which gave pleasure
to whoever consumed them (cf. Gen. 49:20). But fare fit for a
king's table is no longer their lot, for they *have become desolate*
(cf. 1:4, 13; 3:11). Bewildered by the catastrophe which has overtaken the city, they have been left to wander destitute in the streets
and fend for themselves.

   Brought up refers to those being cared for or nursed, again
probably with the children of the city particularly in view. *Scarlet*
was a vivid dye obtained from the shells of scale insects. The cost
of its production made fabric dyed with it expensive, affordable

only for the well-off (cf. Prov. 31:21). The picture here may be of blankets produced in this way to wrap young children. The pressure of life in the besieged, and subsequently ruined, city has led not just to the abandonment of such pampered luxuries, but to gross impoverishment. They *have embraced rubbish tips*, scavenging there for any scraps, and possibly living there too.

❶ 4:6   Indeed, the iniquity of the daughter of my people
              has been greater
          than the sin of Sodom,
          which was overthrown in a moment,
          and hands did not move in her.

This verse is connected to what precedes and comments on the catastrophe.[124] At first sight it seems to explain the scale of the disaster which had come upon Jerusalem by declaring that her conduct had been far more reprehensible than that of the cities of the plain on which the LORD had rained down sulphur and fire. *Sodom* and Gomorrah are frequently identified in the Old Testament as displaying the depths of depravity in their homosexual perversions (cf. Gen. 18–19; Deut. 29:22-28; Isa. 1:9; 13:19; Jer. 2:10-11; 23:14; 49:18; 50:40; Amos 4:11; Zeph. 2:9). On this understanding it is accepted that the treatment accorded Zion is to be explained by the fact that she had sunk lower than Sodom in her corruption (cf. Ezek. 16:46-52). It is not alleged that the people had committed the same transgressions, but that their conduct was more remiss because they had sinned against light when they had in effect repudiated the covenant of the LORD.

The second colon, however, does not focus on the heinous nature of the sin involved, but on the extended character of the penalty inflicted on Jerusalem, and this has led to *iniquity* being taken as referring primarily to the punishment of Zion's iniquity rather than the offence which gave rise to it (cf. 2:14) and *the sin of Sodom* to refer similarly to the judgement imposed on her for her

---

124. The *waw* which begins *wayyigdal* is of course necessary for the acrostic structure, but even so it is not to be dismissed as redundant. It would seem to be an epexegetic use of the *waw* consecutive (cf. Waltke and O'Connor, *Syntax*, §33.2.2), and so is rendered 'indeed'.

wrongdoing (cf. NIV, NRSV).[125] *Overthrown* is used as a technical
term for the fate of Sodom (cf. Deut. 29:23; Jer. 20:16), but that
had occurred *in a moment*, whereas the agony of Jerusalem was
protracted.

The meaning of *hands did not move in her* (or, 'they [an
indefinite subject] did not move hands for her') is unclear. 'Her' is
more probably Sodom than Jerusalem and, if the preposition 'in' is
taken in a hostile sense, 'against', then there is a contrast between
the sudden, direct divine action against Sodom and the prolonged,
indirect action which God had imposed on Jerusalem by means of
hostile forces. Alternatively, 'move' may have the sense of 'writhe'
so that the picture is one of frantic gestures of grief and ineffective
attempts by the inhabitants of the city to relieve their situation.
There had been no time for that to occur in Sodom, whereas Zion's
drawn-out punishment was intensifying her agony.

However, though the emphasis is on the extended nature of
Zion's suffering, the range of reference of the Hebrew terms means
that the penalty is not viewed in isolation from the offence.
Debased conduct, characterised as 'iniquity' (cf. 2:14) and 'sin' (cf.
1:8), has inevitable consequences in the moral governance of the
world. Even though the poet views Zion in affectionate terms as *the
daughter of my people* (cf. 4:3), he has to admit that her behaviour
had been culpably outrageous and so God's reaction was amply
warranted.

❡ 4:7   Her dignitaries were brighter than snow;
              they were whiter than milk.
         Their bodies were redder than coral;
              their appearance was like sapphire.

From the children of the city the spotlight moves to the upper
classes of Jerusalem. Again the impact of the tragedy is presented
by means of contrasting before (4:7) and after (4:8).

Her dignitaries are those of high status and of influence in the
conduct of Jerusalem's affairs. It is probably a wider category than

---

125. 'As to the words, then, they designate punishment as well as sin, the
cause of it. But the reason which follows leads me to consider punishment as
intended, for he says that *Sodom was overthrown as in a moment*' (John
Calvin, *Jeremiah and Lamentations*, 462).

the king and his officials, though it would include them.[126] These noblemen had been splendid in their appearance. Their clothing was more dazzling than sunlight reflected from snow. *Whiter than milk* (cf. Gen. 49:12) presumably repeats the previous thought regarding the gleaming splendour of their garments. 'Whiter' comes from a root that conveys the idea of brilliance, but with overtones of warmth not evident in the comparison with snow.

If the first line describes the clothing of the upper classes, then the focus switches to their bodily health. *Bodies* is literally 'bone'/ 'skeleton', which is used here for their physical appearance. The term *coral* occurs elsewhere in contexts which indicate that it was a precious stone (cf. Job 28:18; Prov. 8:11; 31:10), and some translate it as 'rubies' or 'pearls'. It is the reddish colour characteristic of Mediterranean coral rather than its cost which is the point of the comparison: these men were in the pink of health. *Appearance* or 'form' comes from a root meaning 'to cut, divide', and possibly the reference is to their profile ('the beauty of their form', ESV) or to their hair (NRSV). The latter idea is supported by the mention of *sapphire* or, more probably, the semi-transparent lapis lazuli. This blue material seems to have been employed in ancient art to represent hair.[127] The 'before' picture is one of grandeur and beauty.

נ 4:8   Their appearance has become blacker than soot;
          they are not recognised in the streets.
          Their skin has shrivelled on their bones;
          it has become as dry as wood.

The contrast which has come over Jerusalem's formerly impressive dignitaries is starkly presented. *Their appearance* is no longer stately and imposing. It is unclear whether it is the physical effect of famine which has made their skin *blacker than soot* or whether this results from the emotional impact of their situation as a whole. Dishevelled and dirty in the remains of the burned city, their

---

126. This understanding of the term *nāzîr* is based on its use in Gen. 49:26 and Deut. 33:16 to refer to one 'set apart' and so functioning as a 'leader'. Contextually less probable is a narrower reference to the Nazirites (cf. AV, NKJV), a group who took special vows of abstinence (cf. Num. 6:18-21).

127. Cf. Hillers, *Lamentations*, 140.

appearance has so changed that *they are not recognised in the streets.* They have become virtual strangers in the city they once controlled.

No longer are the dignitaries the picture of health. Their skin has dried out and they have lost their vitality and strength as famine has taken its toll on their physique. They are now just skin and bones.

ט 4:9   Those slain by the sword were better off
             than those slain by famine,
          who waste away, thrust through
             for lack of produce from the fields.

The next contrast is not between the past and present of a single group of people, but between the fate of two groups of the city's inhabitants. A quick death is viewed as preferable to the prolonged agonies of starvation. *Slain* is literally 'pierced through' and is an appropriate description of death by the thrust of a sword. Here the term is used in an extended sense of the effects of famine, and the metaphor is continued in *thrust through* which also describes a quick, stabbing motion. *Waste away* envisages a much slower fate; possibly the idea is of a wound with long term consequences. *Produce from the fields* was denied to the citizens of Jerusalem even after the city had fallen (cf. 1:11), and so they had become progressively weakened through starvation.

י 4:10   The hands of compassionate women
             have boiled their own children;
          they became their food
             during the destruction of the daughter of my
                people.

The horrors that existed in the city climaxed in the behaviour of the mothers of Jerusalem. Formerly they had been *compassionate women*, displaying affectionate concern for their young (cf. 'compassions', 3:22). But no longer do the children of the city die on their mothers' laps. What had been contemplated as a question in 2:20 had become a reality as the womenfolk were driven to hideous, repulsive extremes (cf. 2 Kgs. 6:24-29). It is not said here that they killed their children, but *the hands* which once cared for them *have boiled their own children* so that they may consume them as food, the fulfilment of the covenant curse (Deut. 28:53-57).

It is not the ordinary term for what may be eaten that is here rendered *food*, but one that denotes a diet intended for a sick person. The community had been afflicted to the point of extinction. For *destruction*/'breaking' or 'shattering', see 2:11 and 3:48. *The daughter of my people* (cf. 4:6) contains the only hint of emotional involvement as the poet relates this collapse of all sense of feeling and propriety in the starving city.

Reflection

• Often those who are traumatised and depressed through severe loss go over time and again the events associated with their personal tragedy. The poet here reflects that psychological phenomenon, and he endorses such reflection on memories, sometimes pleasant, but often (as here) very upsetting, as a legitimate basis for coming to terms with grief. It does not effect a complete adjustment to changed circumstances and, if persisted in for too long, it may become a hindrance rather than a help. However, a frank recognition of what has occurred, no matter how painful, is needed to provide a realistic foundation for coping with what lies ahead.

• Whichever interpretation of 4:6 is adopted, the verse reminds us of the greater responsibility which lies upon God's people to live in accordance with his precepts. '⌊As regards⌋ everyone to whom much was given, much will be sought from him, and ⌊as regards him⌋ to whom they entrusted much, they will ask more of him' (Luke 12:48). 'If you know these things, blessed are you if you do them' (John 13:17).

B. Rejected by the LORD (4:11-16)

In 4:11 there occurs the first mention of the LORD in the chapter, as attention is refocused from how the tragedy unfolded to look back and consider where it had all sprung from. A thematic division is also indicated here by the variation in the poet's perspective on the city, which changes from 'my people' (4:3, 6, 10) to the more detached third person pronouns of '*its* foundations' (4:11), and '*its* prophets', '*its* priests' and '*its* midst' (4:13). Over against any merely political interpretation of the catastrophe, it is made clear that the city's destruction was caused by the LORD acting in wrath against it (4:11). Such an astounding shift in God's attitude towards the city he had once signally blessed (4:12) was provoked by the misconduct of her religious leaders (4:13), who were consequently punished (4:14), being disowned by their own people (4:15a) and by foreigners (4:15b).

כ 4:11 The LORD gave full vent to his fury;
            he poured out his fierce anger,
        and he kindled a fire in Zion,
            and it consumed its foundations.

In setting out the divine role in the overthrow of Zion, the poet uses language which echoes that of the description of the day of the LORD's anger in 2:1-8, and there are many words in common: 'fury' (2:4), 'pour out' (2:4), 'anger' (2:1, 3, 6), 'fire' (2:3-4), 'consume' (2:3). *Fury* refers to the heat of the LORD's anger when the covenant King had become so incensed at the infidelity and treachery of his people that he *gave full vent* to his indignation. Though the verb ordinarily means 'to finish, complete', there is no hint here that the consequences of his wrath were exhausted in the onslaught which culminates in the fall of the city.

The following three statements set out a sequence which expands on the initial thought. The LORD 'gave full vent to his fury' when *he poured out his fierce anger.* The focus is not on the emptiness of a vessel which has been drained of its contents, but on the copiousness of what has been spilled out. The LORD has expressed his anger without restraint and has held nothing back of the curses of the broken covenant from rebellious Jerusalem. 'Fierce' (cf. 1:12) conveys the idea of heat, which was literally experienced in the conflagration which *he kindled* and which did not cause merely superficial damage. Mention of *its*[128] *foundations*, those of the city including those of the Temple, indicates the comprehensive impact of the LORD's action against Zion — Zion which he had founded and which he loved (cf. Ps. 87:1-2).

---

128. 'Its' renders a third person feminine pronominal form, referring to Zion. This explains 'her' (NIV), but in this poem Zion is not personified until 4:22, and it seems preferable to treat the feminine as equivalent to a neuter for which Hebrew has no separate form.

ל 4:12 Kings of earth did not believe,
        or any[129] of the inhabitants of the world,
        that foe or enemy could enter
        the gates of Jerusalem.

Despite events such as those recorded in 1 Kings 14:26, 2 Kings 14:13 and 2 Kings 24:10-17, in the century before the fall of Jerusalem it had become a prevalent belief in Judah that the city would never be completely overthrown. This stance derived from the presence of the LORD in the Temple and his commitment to the city (cf. Pss. 46:5; 48:3-6), but taken in isolation it was a distortion of what had been revealed because it separated enjoyment of the blessings of the covenant from obedience to its requirements.

In this verse, however, the focus is on the perception of surrounding nations regarding Jerusalem. They too had witnessed the surprising turn of events when Sennacherib failed to take the city in 701 B.C. (cf. 2 Kgs. 19:35-36). If the emperor of Assyria had met with such a rebuff, they *did not believe* anyone else would succeed. Here 'believe' is not used as a term of religious commitment, but in a secular sense of considering something to be likely or possible. The astounding fact that Jerusalem, which had withstood so much in the past, had now fallen to the Babylonians overturned not only the religious beliefs prevalent in Judah but also the assessment of other nations and their rulers, who could not escape noting and pondering the impact of the LORD's judgement.

מ 4:13 ⌐This happened⌐ because of the sins of its prophets,
        the iniquities of its priests,
        who shed in its midst
        the blood of the righteous.

The matter of Zion's culpability is probed, and it is the religious leadership of the community who are held to be responsible for the tragedy which occurred.[130] Zion's *prophets* have been mentioned

---

129. 'Or any' (*wəkōl*) is literally 'and all'. The qere and the LXX do not have the conjunction 'and', but this does not affect the meaning of the passage.

130. There is no linguistic link with the preceding verse, but the flow of the argument requires a supplement such as 'this happened'. Less probably, one might treat the whole of 4:13 as a prepositional phrase which should be linked to 4:14 to complete the sense (cf. Hillers, *Lamentations*, 141).

already in 2:14 where they were criticised for not exposing her iniquity and for clouding the perception of the people with deceptive oracles regarding the future. Such *sins* undermined the integrity of the land and led to its downfall.

In 2:20 *the priests* had been mentioned as suffering along with the peace-prophets, but their role had not been explored. Now their joint responsibility in precipitating the calamity is made clear. In the prophetic books of the Old Testament the misconduct of the priests is identified in various ways. Particularly scathing is Isaiah's indictment of their drunken debauchery (Isa. 28:7-8), and their ungodly and venal conduct is also exposed (Jer. 6:13; 23:11; Ezek. 22:26; Mic. 3:11). They were part of the Jerusalem establishment and were not prepared to do or say anything that would upset the prevailing consensus which accorded them social status and which was so much to their economic benefit. Their unwillingness to promote and to adhere to the standards of the covenant is summed up by the term *iniquities* (cf. 2:14).

However, there is also a more specific allegation made: prophets and priests *shed in its midst the blood of the righteous*. Possibly this signifies sins of omission, implying that prophets and priests alike have the death of innocents on their consciences because they had failed in their duty to give them adequate warning regarding the LORD's disapproval of their conduct. But the Scriptural record shows that sins of commission were also involved (cf. Jer. 6:13; 8:10; 23:11-14; Ezek. 22:25-31; Hos. 5:1-2; 6:7-11). In the decades before the city fell, the religious establishment sought to suppress any voices that critiqued the situation in Jerusalem. For instance, we see prophets and priests united in pressing charges against Jeremiah for alerting the people to the impending judgement of God on them (Jer. 26:11). Jeremiah warned the priests and the prophets that if they succeeded in having him put to death they would bring innocent blood upon themselves and upon the city (Jer. 26:15). Though Jeremiah was able to escape, the prophet Uriah, who bore similar testimony to Jeremiah, did not (Jer. 26:20-23). It had been a dangerous time for those prepared to speak out for maintenance of covenant standards of truth and conduct. Even so, what is mentioned here shows that there had been righteous individuals in the community who had maintained a stand against the conduct and policies prevalent in the city.

ב 4:14 They wandered ⌐like the⌐ blind in the streets;
          they were defiled with blood
          so that no one was able to touch
          their garments.

Many aspects of the scene described in 4:14-16 are obscure. The
immediate antecedent of 'they wandered' is the righteous of the
previous verse, but if their blood has been shed it becomes difficult
to envisage them wandering the streets, and the subsequent picture
is even more confused. There are two possible approaches to identifying the subject of the verb. It might be the people as a whole,
viewed as suffering from the lack of guidance given to the
community by its spiritual leaders and so undergoing the judgement
of the day of the LORD (cf. 'I will bring distress to the people, and
they will walk like the blind, for against the LORD they have
sinned', Zeph. 1:17; cf. Deut. 28:29; Isa. 59:10). They are then
subsequently treated as lepers by other nations who refuse to let
them settle among them (4:15). However, though it is not without
problems, the most probable resolution of the difficulty is that the
reference is to the fate of the prophets and priests as they too were
caught up in the conflagration and calamity.

They *wandered*, perhaps even 'staggered' (cf. Ps. 107:27),
because their expectations had been so resoundingly falsified (note
also the repetition of this word in the next verse). *Blind in the
streets* points to the stumbling progress of one without sight in an
unfamiliar environment. But physical blindness is also a metaphor
for spiritual blindness (cf. Isa. 42:18; 43:8; 56:10). Lacking true
insight into the covenant, they were incapable of giving a coherent
explanation as to why their confident forecasts of the prosperity
and inviolability of Jerusalem had proved so wide of the mark.
They were thus also unable to provide direction for the future.

Others among the people had, however, greater perceptivity as
to what had gone wrong in the land. They remembered the previous
intolerant and persecuting behaviour of the religious establishment
and realised that *they were defiled with blood*. 'Defiled' points to
cultic impurity (cf. Ezra 2:62; Neh. 7:64; Mal. 1:7, 12) which
would debar from sacred service. The passage does not accord to
priestly or prophetic garments any particular sanctity. Rather the
populace in general at last (but sadly too late) recognised the error

of their religious leaders, who had become totally defiled, and so they shunned any contact with them to avoid drawing further guilt upon themselves.

○ 4:15 'Keep away! Unclean!' they called to them.
          'Keep away! Keep away! Do not touch ⌞us⌟!'
          When they fled — indeed they wandered about —
          ⌞people⌟ among the nations said,
          'They shall not reside here any longer.'

This verse presents a twofold rejection of the former religious leaders of the community. The initial description is of the reaction within the ruined city to the priests and prophets. *Keep away/*'depart' is a general term for moving away, which is used on occasion for the separation of evildoers (cf. Pss. 6:8; 119:115; 139:19), but the addition of *Unclean!* points back to the warning which lepers were required to shout out (Lev. 13:45). This would suggest that the speakers are the religious leaders themselves, but that is improbable in that it requires that they have realised how grave their condition had become. Even though it necessitates adding 'us' as a supplement, a more probable interpretation is that these are the words of the community as they avoid their former leaders as untouchable. *Do not touch ⌞us⌟!* maintains the imagery of leprosy as the people shun contamination from the prophets and priests.

The closing part of the verse indicates that, rejected by their own community, the religious leaders *fled* from their native land. The language used does not suggest that they have been deported by the Babylonians, but that they have sought refugee status among surrounding nations. *Wandered about* pictures the prophets and priests who had shed innocent blood as condemned to reenact the tragedy of Cain, who was driven from Eden to become a wanderer (the same root as 'wandered about' here) on the earth (Gen. 4:12). However, their presence elsewhere was unwelcome, and they were treated as undesirable aliens who should be deported: *They shall not reside here any longer.*

פ 4:16 The face of the LORD has dispersed them;
          he will no longer regard them.
          The face of priests they have not honoured;
          to elders they have shown no respect.

These words[131] may continue the rejection speech of the nations from the preceding verse and, if so, this would present the reasons advanced by the others for expelling the refugees: neither their God nor their fellow countrymen want them any more. More probably, however, this is a narrator's comment to make clear that the destiny of these groups was determined by the LORD, not the nations.

Each of the two lines of the verse begins with 'the face of …' to effect a contrast between the authority of the LORD and the disrespect shown to the wandering leaders. *The face of the LORD* denotes more than 'the LORD himself' (NIV, ESV). Rather it is an anthropomorphic expression which points to his immediate presence and activity ('my face will go ∟with you⌐', Exod. 33:16, cf. Deut. 4:37; 'the angel of his presence/face', Isa. 63:9). The face of the LORD bestows well-being on those whom he would bless (Num. 6:25-26), but those who have offended him are not afforded such favour (Pss. 34:16; 80:17). So he has personally been active and *has dispersed them*, causing them to flee and dividing them into groups in various lands. Since they had been deficient and perverse in their duties, the LORD will no longer act to protect or nourish them. *He will no longer regard* ('observe', cf. 1:11) *them* as those who have special status before him, but as enemies whom he will scatter (cf. Num. 10:35; Ps. 68:1).

The absence of Yahweh's favour is clearly seen in the reaction of the nations. The prophets are not mentioned; instead, the elders are set alongside the priests. *The face of the priests they have not honoured* (literally, 'lifted up') refers to the action of a superior in lifting up the face of a subordinate who has prostrated himself, and according him a position of distinction and prestige. While this may include the disdain shown by the occupying authorities to the priests and elders who had remained in the land, the principal reference is to the hostility shown in other lands to such formerly venerable figures who sought refuge there. Those who had shown little respect to the LORD and his demands upon them are now themselves subjected to disrespectful treatment.

---

131. For the reversal of the alphabetic order in 4:16 and 4:17, see on 2:16. Some Hebrew manuscripts and the LXX transpose these verses to retain the alphabetic sequence, but thematic considerations indicate that this is unlikely to be original.

Reflection

- Adjusting to a catastrophe does not always require determining why it has occurred because the circumstances may be such that we are unable to discern what has occasioned it. But that is not the case in every situation. Many human tragedies are brought about by human error and negligence. If we are to learn from such events, we must identify the factors which have led up to them, and so be in a position to avoid repeating past errors. In the case of Zion, the poet points to the spiritual leadership of the community as being especially blameworthy (4:13).

- Whatever century is under consideration, inadequate leadership is a major misfortune both for a nation and for a fellowship of God's people. If those who hold office lack spiritual understanding, it is ruinous both for the leaders themselves and for those they are over. 'If a blind person leads a blind person, they will both fall into a pit' (Matt. 15:14).

- Leprosy was a term employed for several skin conditions, and not just leprosy in its narrower, modern sense. Though these skin conditions were attended by social stigma, contracting them was not viewed as inherently a sin. However, the disfiguring and repulsive disease was divinely specified as a symbol of sin and its effects. In particular, the leper was isolated from the rest of the community. This regulation, as well as providing a quarantine effect against the spread of the disorder, was also a picture of the socially disruptive nature of sin. 'All the days that the affliction is on him, he will be unclean. He ⌐is⌐ unclean; he ⌐is to⌐ dwell alone; his dwelling ⌐is to be⌐ outwith the camp' (Lev. 13:46).

C. Helpless is Man's Aid (4:17-20)

There is a switch in 4:17-20 to a first person plural account in which the poet identifies himself with the community as he relives the final days before the city fell: how the people kept looking for foreign intervention to relieve the siege (4:17), how they were hemmed in by the Babylonians during the siege so that their doom became inevitable (4:18), how the enemy were ever ready to frustrate any attempt to escape (4:19), and how at the end their king had been captured (4:20). No one could save them: not Egypt, not their own efforts, not the king from whom they had expected much.

ע 4:17 Our eyes ⌐were¬ continually[132] failing
⌐as we looked¬ for help, ⌐but¬ in vain;
on our watchtowers we watched
for a nation that could not save ⌐us¬.

This verse may continue the timeframe of the preceding verses and show that even after the city had fallen, the people persisted in the notion that the Egyptians would come to rescue them from Babylonian domination. However, in the light of the change of speaker at this juncture and the obvious setting of 4:20, it is more probable that this describes the expectations of the inhabitants of the beleaguered city as they awaited Egyptian intervention to see off the Babylonians. Indeed, at one point an army did advance from the south and drew the besieging forces away from Jerusalem (Jer. 37:5), but the respite was shortlived (Jer. 37:7-8).

They had strained their vision to detect any sign of assistance coming to them (cf. Pss. 69:3; 119: 82, 123; Jer. 14:6). Frantically they had scanned the horizon from their **watchtowers**,[133] whether those on the city walls or those at more remote outposts, looking for some indication of a further move from the south, but **in vain**. They detected no more than 'a puff of wind', which symbolises either what is empty or what is transitory. This was what the prophets had always said would be the outcome of relying on Egypt (cf. Isa. 30:1-5, 7; 31:1-3; Jer. 2:18, 36; Hos. 7:11; 12:1) and on foreign alliances in general. Too late the people came to realise that they could not be saved by international political intrigue. They do

132. The first word of the verse is employed in an unusual absolute construction, but the overall sense is clear. The kethibh ʿôdệnâ combines ʿôd, 'continuance/still', with a third person feminine plural suffix referring to 'our eyes'; the qere ʿôdênû reads the same word but with a first person plural suffix referring to the speakers.
133. The function of bəṣippîyātēnû is uncertain. Some versions take it as intensifying the verb, 'watching eagerly' (NRSV), but it is more probably a noun, which may signify 'watchtower' or 'place of watching'. It is from the same root as the following piel verb (ṣippînû) which it intensifies in sound. Further, use of a piel verb rather than a qal may indicate the heightened expectation associated with the action.

not as yet, however, mention the one true source of hope which had
been held out to them, namely the intervention of the LORD himself.

ש 4:18 They hounded our steps
          so that we could not walk in our open squares.
          Our end had drawn near; our days were numbered,
          for our end had come.

The experience of this verse could relate to the intense surveillance
maintained by the occupation forces after the city fell, but again it
is more probable that it is describing conditions near the end of the
siege. *They hounded* employs the language of hunting though it is
not certain if the root is one with the sense 'to lie in wait for' or
one meaning 'to hunt for',[134] which is used of the experience of the
poet himself in 3:52. *Steps*/'paces' relates to deliberate, purposive
movement, and *open squares* refers to public spaces in the city
where gatherings could be held (cf. 2:11, 12). The picture seems to
be one of the besieging forces keeping such close watch on what
went on within the walls of the city that whenever any group tried
to gather, particularly in the plazas near the city gates, they were
ready to rain down missiles upon them.

The city was living in a permanent state of fear and apprehen-
sion, and its inhabitants came to recognise the inevitability of their
doom as the enemy and famine inexorably tightened their grip.
Looking back, the people acknowledge that the word prophesied by
Ezekiel had come true: 'An end has come; the end has come; it has
been awakened against you' (Ezek. 7:6; cf. Amos 8:2). *Our end* is
not a reference to the end-time, but to the end of the existence of
the speakers who saw no future for themselves. *Our days were
numbered*/'had become full' points to the expiry of a set period,
here the quota of days allotted to their lives. Nothing more could be
expected *for our end had come.* This need not imply the death of
each and every individual, so much as the extinction of their community and all that it stood for.

---

134. The verb *ṣādû* may be derived from *ṣādâ* (I), 'to waylay, lie in wait for',
or from *ṣûd*, which is generally taken as 'to hunt for', though 'to observe
secretly' has also been suggested (*HALOT* 3:1000,1010). One might also note
the sound play between *ṣādû*, 'they hounded' and *ṣəʿādênû*, 'our steps'.

ק 4:19 Our pursuers were swifter
             than eagles in the skies.
        They hotly pursued us on the mountains;
             they laid wait for us in the wilderness.

Though this verse does reflect on the flight and imprisonment of
Zedekiah, the last king of Judah (2 Kgs. 25:3-7; Jer. 39:4-7; 52:7-
11; Ezek. 12:12-13), its scope is broader than that. No doubt there
were other groups who tried to escape from the city. Indeed,
Jeremiah urged that the people surrender to the Babylonians (Jer.
38:2) and was himself accused of defecting to the enemy (Jer.
37:11-15). When the siege was in progress, the surrounding troops
would maintain a watch for any who in desperation tried to escape.
The *eagle* was renowned for its speed of movement (cf. Jer. 48:40;
49:22), especially for the way in which it would swoop down on its
unsuspecting prey. The people felt helpless before the superior
speed of the enemy forces, particularly the cavalry.

    Wherever those escaping Jerusalem turned to avoid their con-
querors, they found that they were *hotly pursued* (cf. Ps. 10:2).
This verb has overtones of fire, referring either to how hotly
worked up the occupation forces were by their exertions or to the
speed of their movement like that of a forest fire encircling one
who tried to get away. Furthermore *they laid wait for us*, knowing
that going through the barren wilderness would be viewed as a
potential escape route.

ר 4:20 The breath of our nostrils, the LORD's anointed,
             was captured in their pits,
        of whom we said, 'Under his shadow
             we shall live among the nations.'

From the more general pursuit of the people, the focus narrows to
the capture of the king and how this had dashed their hopes. *The
breath of our nostrils* reveals the extent to which the community
derived its security and cohesion from the promises attached to the
Davidic dynasty. This phrase, which may be drawn from Egyptian
descriptions of their pharaoh, denotes that which gave vitality to
their national life. When the king was no longer at the centre of the
nation, directing its affairs, the people might continue to exist as so
many individuals, but they could no longer function as a kingdom.

The LORD's anointed (*māšîaḥ*) points to the specifically
theological (as distinct from political) dimension of their hopes.
Though the high priest and also some prophets were also anointed,
it is the king who is specifically in view in this phrase as the
successor to the promises of the Davidic covenant. At each corona-
tion, the people hoped that at last the king had come who would
fulfil the role portrayed in Psalm 72, and repeatedly they were
disappointed. And that had certainly been the case with the weak
and vacillating figure of Zedekiah, the last king of Judah (cf. Jer.
34; 38). The seizure of Zedekiah was in itself no great loss at a
personal level; he was after all a Babylonian appointee. But it also
signified the end of an epoch in the LORD's dealings with his
people as the throne of David was left vacant and the capital city
destroyed.

What is described here is Zedekiah's last-moment attempt to
escape (2 Kgs. 25:3-6; Jer. 39:1-5; 52:6-9). It has often been
suggested that the author of the poem participated in this. Certainly
he represents a viewpoint of one very well disposed towards the
king. But their hopes are dashed, because their king *was captured
in their pits*, traps which the enemy had set up to ambush and take
fugitives. The expectations of the people were thus totally
undermined. They had looked for the fulfilment of the messianic
prophecies. *Under his shadow* likens the king to a large tree which
would provide relief and protection for his people from adverse
circumstances (cf. Judg. 9:15; Ezek. 17:22-24), or to a rock which,
like God, would grant them shelter and security (cf. Isa. 32:2).
Among the nations views his success as guaranteeing the people
international status and respect. But that was not to be; the LORD
had set his face against them.

Reflection

* Dire circumstances reveal the utter ineffectiveness of mankind
  to effect ultimate remedies for human distress (cf. 4:17). We
  would do well to heed the psalmist's advice not to trust in
  princes, in a mere human ('a son of mankind') in whom there is
  no deliverance (Ps. 146:3). The prudent course of conduct is to
  take refuge in the LORD (Ps. 118:8-9), and to respond as Peter
  did when he assessed his exposed situation in the light of his
  own capacity and cried out, 'Lord, save me' (Matt. 14:30).

- The description of the king as 'the LORD's anointed'/'Messiah' (4:20) does not constitute this passage a messianic prophecy in any positive sense. Indeed, the lesson to be learned here is that of the inadequacy and failure of all those who were designated kings of Israel and Judah. Whenever a king lived up to the covenant obligations imposed on him by the LORD (cf. Deut. 17:14-20), he in measure foreshadowed the coming King — but unfortunately many kings fell far short of this ideal, and even the best of them displayed serious failings. It awaited the coming of the true son of David for there to be a king who could do all that was required as regards ruling and delivering his people. We do not now look uncertainly and obscurely into the future for the LORD's anointed. He has come and has accomplished the tasks given him (John 17:4). He now reigns as king, and we await his return and the full disclosure of the glory of his kingdom.

D. The Destiny of Edom and Zion (4:21-22)

In the light of the frustration which attached to the people's hopes, the poet now turns, albeit obliquely, to the LORD and considers how he will intervene in the present distress of Zion. What had begun as a prayer ('Let them become like me', 1:21) has now become confident, even prophetic, assurance. It is a reassertion of hope despite the reverses of the past and the defeatist attitudes of the present, and it expresses itself in the anticipated overthrow of the people's enemies.

ש 4:21 Be glad and rejoice, daughter Edom,
        you who dwell in the land of Uz.
      To you also a cup will pass;
        you will become drunk and strip yourself bare.

The words *be glad and rejoice* are addressed ironically to *daughter Edom* (for the idiom, cf. 1:4). It is significant that, when here an enemy is named for the first time, it is not Babylon that is in view, but a power much nearer home. The territory of the Edomites lay to the south of the Dead Sea. Esau, the ancestor of Edom, was the twin-brother of Jacob, and Edom's relationship with Israel had been one of longstanding enmity. At the time of Jerusalem's fall their conduct was notorious. 'On the day you stood aloof, on the day strangers carried off his wealth and foreigners entered his gates and cast lots over Jerusalem, you too were like one of them' (Obad. 11; cf. Ps. 137:7-9; Ezek. 25:12-14; 35:5, 12-15). Archaeology has confirmed that Edomite forces pressed into southern Judah in the aftermath of the capture of Jerusalem and occupied land there. The downfall of Jerusalem would indeed have been a source of satisfaction to her inveterate enemy (cf. 'rejoice', 1:21; 2:17). But she is being warned that she had better enjoy having the upper hand — it will not last.

You who dwell in the land of Uz is a parallel expression for the Edomites. Uz is distinguished from Edom in Jeremiah 25:20-21, and probably lay to the south of traditional Edomite territory. Occupation of this area may be evidence of Edom's expansionist ambitions at this period.

But their celebrations will prove premature. In prophetic language the outcome is stated: *To you also a cup will pass.* The expression 'to you' hints not only at the direction of movement, but also that it will target the Edomites. A cup was a large drinking vessel, and passing a cup was employed as a metaphor for the LORD's imposition of judgement (cf. Ps. 75:8; Isa. 51:17, 22; Jer. 25:15-28; Ezek. 23:32-34; Hab. 2:16). This verdict draws directly on the prophecies of Jeremiah where it was declared that Edom too must drink the cup of the LORD's punishment (Jer. 25:21; 49:12). Just as excessive consumption of wine deprives individuals of the ability to remain steady on their feet and to coordinate their faculties, so the imposition of the LORD's penalty will rob them of their self-control. *You will become drunk and strip yourself bare.* When what had overtaken Jerusalem (cf. 1:8) falls upon them, they in their turn will become incapacitated and, after exposing themselves, will be ridiculed by those who pass by.

ת 4:22   Your iniquity, daughter Zion, is complete;
            he will keep you in exile no longer.
         Your iniquity, daughter Edom, he shall punish;
            he shall uncover your sins.

The poet then extends a word of comfort to the people by contrasting the situation of Zion and Edom. Both lines begin with a verb followed by *your iniquity* (cf. 2:14). As has been already remarked, 'iniquity' may refer to the initial transgression, and also to the punishment imposed as a consequence (cf. 4:6). It is probable that both senses are to be found in this verse. Addressing *daughter Zion* (cf. 1:4), the poet assures her that her punishment *is complete*. The precise rendering of the perfect verb form is again difficult (cf. 3:55), though each possibility conveys in some measure an element of hope. It may be a precative perfect signifying, 'May your punishment be complete.' It may be a prophetic perfect confidently predicting the future: 'Your punishment will end' (NIV). Probably the perfect of the stative verb conveys its ordinary sense of that which is already in existence: 'It is complete.' Zion has already experienced the worst, and may now expect that *he will keep you in exile no longer*, or 'he will not send you into exile again' (cf. REB). Though grammatically feasible, the latter translation yields little comfort, and it conflicts with the subsequent history of the people. There is no need to be more specific as to who 'he' refers to: it can only be the LORD.

Over against the brighter prospect held out for Zion, the poet predicts divine punishment will come on Edom. *Your iniquity ... he shall punish.*[135] 'Punish' (traditionally 'visit') describes the action of a superior who inspects his subordinates and allots to them rewards or penalties as appropriate. The LORD's visitation of Edom will result in her ruin (cf. Jer. 9:25-26; 49:7-22). *He shall uncover your sins.* Laying bare the full nature of their misconduct the LORD will impose an appropriate penalty.

Reflection

• Both Zion and Edom were subject to divine punishment because the LORD cannot tolerate sin no matter who is the perpetrator. If God's will is defied, then there will be appropriate retribution. That is the solemn lesson presented to the people of God in every generation. While divine retribution may not now be expected in the form of political subjugation by a foreign power, the Lord is still dealing with his people individually and collectively. But there is this key difference between Zion and Edom.

---

135. Both verbs in the second line of the verse are prophetic perfects (perfects of certainty) which present the outcome as already as good as accomplished, and so are rendered by 'shall'.

In his corporate discipline of his church the Lord is aiming at restoration. Punishment for iniquity will be completed (4:22) when the Lord has removed every spot or wrinkle and has achieved his aim of making the church holy and without blemish (Eph. 5:27).

• 'In the latter stages of the history of Israel, the Edomites surpassed all their enemies in keenness and intensity of malice; and hence they naturally came to be viewed by the Spirit of prophecy as the personification of that godless malignity and pride, which would be satisfied with nothing short of the utter extermination of the cause of God—the heads and representatives of the whole army of the aliens, whose doom was to carry along with it the downfall and destruction of everything that opposed and exalted itself against the knowledge of God.'[136] 'The LORD has a day of vengeance, a year of retribution with respect to the cause of Zion' (Isa. 34:8), and that judgement will impose utter ruin on the defiant opposition of Edom (Mal. 1:4).

---

136. Patrick Fairbairn, *The Interpretation of Prophecy* (Second Edition, 1865; London: Banner of Truth, 1964), 221–2. The whole section found on pages 219-225 is an excellent presentation of prophetic hermeneutics.

Lamentations 5

OUTLINE

A. Plea for Attention (5:1-18)

(1) Petition (5:1)

(2) Economic and Political Destitution (5:2-10)

(3) Personal Humiliation and Abuse (5:11-14)

(4) Hopeless Desolation (5:15-18)

B. Restore Us! (5:19-22)

The fifth poem is noticeably different from the previous four in style. Of the alphabetic acrostic the sole trace which remains is the number of verses, twenty-two, and now each verse consists of just a single line. Whereas previously various speakers were heard alternately, here there is only one voice. The *qînâ* metre (3 stressed words + 2 stressed words) which was frequent earlier in Lamentations is no longer to be found, and instead most lines are in balanced form (3:3). Indeed, the lines contain a much higher proportion of synonymous parallelism than earlier in the book, and there is a distinct reduction in the use of metaphorical language.

These differences give rise to two questions: does this poem have the same origin as earlier chapters? and, does this poem adopt the same outlook as the remainder of the book? It is not possible to reconstruct the process by which the various poems were composed but, though chapter 5 is distinct from the others, this poem is integrated into the book as a whole and cannot be interpreted apart from what has preceded. For instance, it may be taken as providing the concluding prayer which, though present in previous chapters (1:22; 2:20-22; 3:59-66), was absent from chapter 4.

The brevity of the chapter is in part explained by the extent to which it builds on the more elaborate descriptions given earlier in the book. This can, for example, be detected in the considerable verbal and thematic echoes of chapter 1. God is called on to 'observe and see' the people's suffering (1:9, 11; 5:1). The city lies deserted (1:1; 5:18), its gates empty (1:4; 5:14). The land is now controlled by foreigners (1:5, 10; 5:2, 8), who 'pursue' the people (1:3, 6; 5:5) and show no respect for the leaders of the community (1:6; 5:12). The young of the community have not been spared in the tragedy (1:5; 5:13), and all are desperately 'seeking bread' (1:11; 5:9). There is recollection of the prosperity of 'days of old' (1:7; 5:21), but past sin is also acknowledged as the cause of their present suffering (1:5, 8; 5:16). It is thus difficult to envisage chapter 5 as having existed independently of the preceding chapters. It is plausible to suppose that it was specifically written as a conclusion for the earlier material.

Why then was it written in this particular form? Features such as its brevity and the absence of an acrostic to give it formal integration have suggested to some that a feeling of exhaustion and lack of cohesion characterises the stance of the final poem. Form critical studies, however, have found in this chapter clear evidence of it being patterned as a communal complaint with an opening plea for attention (5:1), an elaboration of the woes the community has to endure (5:2-18), and a concluding petition of adoration and request (5:19-22).[137] While one need not endorse any particular hypothesis suggested by form critical studies as to the cultic origins of the poem, the substantial agreement as to its structure shows that it is carefully crafted, following models which were customary in the community.

It is significant that the poem is not introduced by, 'Ah, how!' (1:1; 2:1; 4:1), but by three imperatives addressed to the LORD. This gives the chapter as a whole the character of prayer rather than lament. While there are descriptions of Jerusalem's intense suffering, they are thematically secondary to the prayers which are uttered at the beginning and at the end of the chapter. Furthermore, the speaker is now the community as a whole, not the poet alone. There are about 40 occurrences of first person plural forms in which the poet associates himself with the community, and speaks on their behalf.

The poem is couched in language which does not suggest chaotic exhaustion, but the emergence of a more placid, settled outlook. The situation is not indeed one where questions have been completely resolved and where the severe distress of the city has been removed, but one in which there is an acquiescence as regards how things have worked out, calamitous though the prevailing state of affairs is. Even though it remains unclear what the future holds, there is a realistic acceptance that the way out of their misery must be divinely provided. The presentation is one where the situation of the community has not been finally settled, but where in prayer they are at least looking in the right direction for relief.

The poetic structure of the chapter is not so clearly marked as it was earlier. It is significant that in 5:1-10 and 5:15-22 the language is first person plural, whereas in 5:11-14 the poem describes in the third person various groups within the city. Combining this with thematic considerations renders it appropriate to identify a major

137. See Erhard S. Gerstenberger, *Psalms, Part 2, and Lamentations*, The Forms of Old Testament Literature. Grand Rapids: Eerdmans, 2001, 501-05.

transition after 5:18, and to analyse the initial prayer as consisting of petition (5:1), followed by details of the economic and political destitution of the land (5:2-10), of the treatment of various groups in the community (5:11-14), and of the dejection which had overwhelmed the community (5:15-18). The only remedy is divine intervention, but as yet there was no convincing evidence that the LORD had heard their prayers (5:19-22). Still they do recognise his sovereignty and continue to pray. Perhaps there is a way forward.

A. Plea for Attention (5:1-18)

(1) Petition (5:1)

> 5:1   Remember, O LORD, what has happened to us;
>   observe and see our reproach!

In an urgent prayer[138] to the LORD the community jointly sets out its needs, and petitions God that he take action with respect to the adverse circumstances in which they are. ***Remember, O LORD*** asks for more than recall of facts about the past; it is a plea for active interest leading to effective intervention (cf. 3:19). ***What has happened to us*** does not just focus on the trauma of the capture of the city; it includes all that had developed subsequently. Those who speak are unsure if the LORD has abandoned his commitment to them, and this note of uncertainty about their present and their future relationship to him pervades the poem. There can be no doubt about the suffering that the city is having to endure, but what is the LORD's attitude towards them?

The second colon emphatically reinforces the initial appeal. ***Observe***[139] ***and see*** (cf. 1:9, 11) is functionally equivalent to 'remember'. If the LORD responds as desired, then it is hoped he

---

138. Chapter 5 is entitled 'A Prayer' in some Greek manuscripts, with other ancient witnesses adding 'of Jeremiah'.

139. The kethibh reads an imperative form *habbêṭ*, whereas the qere adds a paragogic *hê*, *habbîṭâ*. This may bring out the emphatic nature of the imperative, though Joüon argues that the augment is attached more for the sake of euphony than to add any particular nuance (Paul Joüon and T. Muraoka, *A Grammar of Biblical Hebrew* [Subsidia Biblica; Rome: Pontifical Bible Institute, 1991], §48d).

will be moved to act because of *our reproach,* that is, the taunts and insults which they have to endure under the oppression of the enemy (cf. Ps. 44:13-16) and which are detailed in the following verses. Terms derived from the roots 'remember' and 'reproach' are also found close together in Psalms 74:18, 22 and 89:50-51 in connection with the scornful gibes of the adversaries of the people of God, and it may be that reflection on these passages contributed to the expressions used here.

(2) Economic and Political Destitution (5:2-10)

5:2   Our inheritance has been turned over to strangers, our houses to foreigners.

The aspect of their current situation to which the speakers first draw attention is the loss of *our inheritance.* This refers to their occupation of the land which had been accorded to them by the LORD, and which was inclusive of every good gift that went along with the territory (Deut. 8:7-10), including here *our houses,* the properties built on it. The loss of the land was part of the curse imposed on those who broke the covenant (cf. 'And you will be rooted out of the land which you are entering to take possession of', Deut. 28:63b). The warnings Moses had given in this connection in the early days of the people had been subsequently reiterated by the prophets (Mic. 2:4). Now these dire predictions have been abundantly fulfilled.

The root of the verb *turned over*[140] has already been used of emotional turmoil, infliction of punishment, or destruction (cf. 1:20; 3:3; 4:6). Here it denotes an imposed change in the ownership of property. It is not only that the people have been deprived of enjoying the land and its fruits; these are now controlled by *strangers,* not family but those from a different background who lack awareness of the traditions of the community and the significance of what they found in the land. They are also described

---

140. The perfect verbs of 5:2-18 refer to past occurrences which have ongoing consequences. It is not merely that 'our inheritance was turned over to strangers', but that it 'has been turned over' in the past and the speakers are still having to endure the impact of this loss. Present perfect verb forms go some way towards conveying this in English (cf. 3:1).

as *foreigners*, with connotations of those who are unfriendly and constitute a source of danger. All this had torn the heart out of the community at a social level.

But their reproach was greater than economic loss in that what they had been deprived of was 'the land which the LORD your God is giving you as an inheritance' (Deut. 26:1). In the covenant he had made it over to his people, those who collectively constituted his firstborn. It is his gift which has been misappropriated: can he observe this and remain inactive? Indeed, in a very real sense the land remained the property of the LORD (Lev. 25:23). Can he rest content that his domain has fallen into the hands of others (cf. Jer. 12:7-13)? The alienation of the LORD from his inheritance raises questions at the deepest level regarding his relationship with the people (cf. Ps. 79:1).

5:3   We have become orphans, with no father;
       our mothers are like widows.

The widow and the orphan were recognised throughout the ancient world as especially exposed to destitution and liable to oppression because of the loss of the breadwinner and protector of the family — *with no father*.[141,142] Though the Old Testament explicitly forbade such exploitation and neglect (Exod. 22:21) and made provision to help the unfortunate (Deut. 24:17; 27:19), prophetic indictments show that it occurred all the same (Isa. 1:17, 23; Jer. 7:6; 22:3; Ezek. 22:7). Possibly the comparative in *like widows* points to families which were vulnerable because the father had been deported rather than killed,[143] but the resultant need would

---

141. There is a kethibh/qere variation here which consists of adding a *waw*, 'and', to the consonantal text to read '*and* with no father' (cf. 5:5, '*and* we have no rest'; 5:7, '*and* they are no more', and '*and* we'). This variation is most probably a scribal addition to the text on stylistic grounds. It does not affect the meaning.

142. Renkema mentions the possibility that the expression 'there is no father' (*'ên 'āb*) was originally a marginal note pointing to the absence of an alphabetic acrostic in this chapter because the letters of 'father' are the same as the first two letters of the Hebrew alphabet (*Lamentations*, 598).

143. The preposition *kə* may be taken as '*kaph* veritatis' (cf. note on 2:5), namely, 'our mothers are widows' (TNIV; cf. GNB). However, explaining the term as a comparison is by no means impossible.

have been the same.[144] Human fathers may have killed or taken off into exile, but what about Yahweh? Does he remain 'father of the fatherless and protector of widows' (Ps. 68:5; cf. Ps. 146:9)? Does he still care for the defenceless and vulnerable?

> 5:4   Our own water—by paying silver we have drunk ⌞it⌟;
>   our own wood—by paying a price they bring ⌞it⌟.

The loss of control over their inheritance meant that the people were deprived of unimpeded access to its produce. Even *water*, which they persist in thinking of as *our own*, no longer belongs to them. Since it too has been appropriated by the occupying power, it is only *by paying*[145] a price that they can obtain access to it. Even *wood*/'pieces of wood', whether timber to be used for reconstructing their homes or more simply sticks to kindle a fire, are outwith their control. This vividly illustrates how unbearably harsh life had become for the impoverished and starving community.

> 5:5   On our necks we have been pursued;
>   we have become weary; we have been allowed
>   no rest.

The description of the ongoing harassment of the population left in the land is somewhat obscure. *On our necks* may well be an idiom for close pursuit (cf. the English phrase 'at our heels' which is in fact adopted by NIV, NLT; cf. NKJV) or for complete and harsh control by their enemies (cf. Josh. 10:24).[146] *Pursued*/'persecuted'

---

144. Renkema argues on the basis of long distance parallelism with 1:1 that the reference to mothers here is to be understood as to the cities of Judah rather than the inhabitants of Judah and Jerusalem (*Lamentations*, 595–96). He then also interprets the fathers in the passage to be the local officials of these cities. However, the family orientation of the lost inheritance of 5:2 favours a personal reference here. Even Renkema acknowledges that the use of the singular 'father' rather than the plural 'fathers' does not readily cohere with his interpretation (*Lamentations*, 597).

145. In this phrase and in the next line 'by paying' renders the preposition *bə* used as '*bêth* pretii' to express the price at which a transaction occurs.

146. The similarity between *'ōl*, 'yoke', and *'al*, 'upon', led the Greek translation of Symmachus to render the first two words of the line as 'with a yoke on our necks' (cf. NRSV), but it is difficult to connect pursuit and harassment with the wearing of a yoke. So there is little merit in adopting this modification of the text.

reflects their conquerors' hostile surveillance and unremitting domination of the citizenry of Jerusalem (cf. 1:3). *We have become*
weary portrays the physical exhaustion of those who have been
compelled to work as slave-labourers. *We have been allowed no*
rest[147] picks up on a term frequently employed in descriptions of
covenant blessing, 'rest from enemies on all sides' (Deut. 12:10;
25:19; 2 Sam. 7:1, 11), but here it emphasises how they are
deprived of blessing by the interminable demands of their
taskmasters. They are the instruments through whom God imposes
his judgement on his disobedient people.

> 5:6   ⌊To⌋ Egypt we have given the hand,
>   ⌊to⌋ Assyria, to get enough bread.

At first glance this verse might well relate to the misguided foreign
policies of the past. This would lead neatly into the mention of the
sin of their fathers in the next verse. The expression *have given the*
hand to relates to confirming an agreement (Ezek. 17:18) or pledg-
ing allegiance (1 Chron. 29:24; 2 Chron. 30:8), and had there not
been various attempts at alliance with Egypt (cf. Isa. 30:1-7; 36:6;
Jer. 2:18, 36; Ezek. 17:15), and indeed with Assyria (cf. 2 Kings
16:7; Hos. 5:18)? Deliverance through international alliance had
been a feature of the false hopes entertained by Jerusalem (cf. 1:2,
19; 4:17).

Further consideration, however, makes it unlikely that this verse
reflects past political intrigue. It is clearly stated that the purpose of
the gesture is *to get enough bread*, and this relates not to the earlier
need for military assistance, but to the necessity for famine relief in
the circumstances during, and especially after, the siege. 'Give the
hand' may then be an imploring gesture, pleading for material
assistance. The balanced and emphasised mention of *Egypt* and
Assyria may well just indicate 'lands south and north'. Certainly
Assyria was no longer in existence militarily or politically, though

---

147. The hophal verb shows the situation as one imposed by their overlords
who do not permit them to rest, rather than simply one which has arisen (e.g.
'We have no rest', NKJV). The qere (supported by the LXX, Targum and Vulgate) inserts 'and' before 'we have been allowed no rest'. This is probably a
device to clarify the grammatical structure of the text rather than an original
reading (cf. footnote 141).

the term continued in use (cf. Ezra 6:22; Zech. 10:10). These pleas, however, were not addressed to the authorities of those lands, but to the Jewish refugee communities who had settled in neighbouring countries. Certainly those who went to Egypt expected to be free from famine there (cf. Jer. 42:14), and those who remained in Jerusalem might well have thought they would be in a position to send them emergency supplies.

> 5:7   Our fathers sinned; they are no more;[148]
>   ⌊but⌋ we ⌊are the ones who⌋ have borne their
>   iniquities.

For the concept involved in *sinned*, see on 1:8, and similarly for *iniquities* see on 2:14. *Our fathers* most naturally refers to previous generations of the nation.[149] The consequences of their sins continue to make themselves felt. If this is linked to the preceding verses, then what is in view is the short-term expedient they had used on entering into alliances with foreign nations. However, this verse is expressed more generally than that. Past generations have passed away, but from their misguided conduct there has arisen a legacy. *We have borne* and continue to bear the punishment of their wrongdoing. It is not a question of bearing their guilt, but of suffering the consequences of their actions. The same combination is found in Isaiah 53:11 and refers to a heavy burden of guilt. The intergenerational consequences of sin are also reflected on in Jeremiah 31:29 and Ezekiel 18:2, but here (and especially in the light of 5:16) the tone is different. It is the fact of what has occurred which is set out, and there is no attempt to avoid the complicity and guilt of the current generation (cf. Jer. 3:25). Note also the qualification in 5:16.

> 5:8   Slaves have ruled over us;
>   there is no one to rescue from their hand.

It was also hard for the people to accept and adjust to the new political regime in Judah. *Have ruled* does not emphasise the status

---

148. The qere adds the preposition 'and' before both 'they are no more' and 'we' (cf. footnote 141).

149. In the light of his previous identification of 'father' in 5:3 as a leading figure in the nation, Renkema (*Lamentations*, 605) is compelled to identify those referred to here primarily as (spiritual) leaders among the people.

of the individuals holding power, but rather the reality of the control they have been given and which they continue to exercise. Still, even these rulers are only *slaves*/'servants'. This may simply refer to the subordinate status of those put in place by the Babylonians. Judah is no longer ruled by an independent king in Jerusalem, but by the underlings of a foreign emperor. Alternatively, this verse may refer to the land as placed under the control of those from surrounding nations who had once been Judah's vassals, probably the Edomites (cf. 4:21). This was a clear indication of the humiliating reversal of fortunes that had occurred, and these petty officials were not slow to take advantage of the situation (cf. Prov. 30:21-22). The people are completely helpless, and *there is no one to rescue* them by wrenching them free from their grasp, because the officials were acting in the name of Babylon.

> 5:9   We are getting our bread by risking our lives
>   because of the sword of the wilderness.

Is this the immediate aftermath of the fall of the city? The first priority of the starving people was to get food, but because of the hostile forces occupying the land they could only venture forth *by risking*[150] *our lives*. Perhaps before the siege caches of food had been deposited in sites outside the city (cf. Jer. 41:8) but, more probably, prized possessions would have been concealed in more remote areas—a tactic often employed in the region in times of war. The enemy or marauding forces were out to snatch whatever they could, and *the sword of the wilderness* points to the violence employed even in such less well inhabited areas to rob those who had already been defeated and had gone there to recover what they had hidden (cf. 4:19).

> 5:10   Our skin has become hot like an oven
>   with bouts of fever from famine.

Though the detail of this verse is somewhat obscure, there is no doubt that it is describing the effects of famine. The Syriac Peshitta took the verb to mean 'shrivelled up', and in that case the comparison would be with the dried, cracked walls lining an ancient oven. But it is more probable that the sense is *has become hot* as

---

150. '*Bêth* pretii', 'at the price of', cf. footnote 145.

bouts of fever caused by malnutrition wrack their bodies.

(3) Personal Humiliation and Abuse (5:11-14)

This section is characterised by an absence of 'our', which gives a more impersonal tone to the harrowing catalogue of suffering. The whole population have been terrorised; no group has escaped. These scenes are not confined to the immediate aftermath of the fall of the city. What started then has not come to an end.

> 5:11 Women have been humiliated in Zion,
>   young women in the cities of Judah.

Have been humiliated/'afflicted' is a euphemism for sexual abuse, including rape (cf. Gen. 34:2; Judg. 19:24; 20:5).[151] A stronger party has misused his position to assault others. The first part of the line sets out the harrowing situation for the women in Zion (cf. 3:51), the second colon intensifies the horror. There have been ***young women*** involved (here the noun may well have the sense of 'virgins', cf. 1:4), and it has not been confined to the capital but has occurred throughout ***the cities of Judah.***

> 5:12 Rulers have been hung up by their hands;
>   the faces of elders have been shown no respect.

Rulers (cf. 1:6) refers to those who had governed Judah, perhaps those who had escaped the initial roundup but were subsequently identified and seized.

In Israel hanging was not used as a means of effecting capital punishment, but further ignominy might be heaped on one who had been stoned to death by hanging his corpse on a wooden stake (cf. Deut. 21:22-23). As the punishment referred to here is one imposed by foreigners, it is often suggested that impalement on a wooden stake is intended, since that mode of execution was employed in Egypt and Mesopotamia. Death by hanging, however, remains the most likely possibility (cf. Gen. 40:19; Est. 5:14). ***By their hands*** is not likely to refer to the rulers being hung up by their own hands, a form of execution unattested at this period. The reference is to the agency of the rulers who are oppressing the people (cf. 5:8). In this

---

151. The expression is literally 'they have humiliated' with an unspecified plural subject, a construction equivalent to a passive.

way through the instrumentality of strangers the predicted judgement of the LORD would come upon the inner circles of advisers in Jerusalem (cf. Ezek. 11:9).

Also *elders*/'old men' who had traditionally exercised a leadership role in the community (cf. 1:19; 2:10) and of whom some at any rate would have survived were *shown no respect* by the occupying regime (cf. 4:16). In Israel respect for the aged was a covenant requirement coordinate with respect for God: 'Before the face of the greyheaded you shall rise up and you shall honour the face of an old man; and you shall fear your God: I am the LORD' (Lev. 19:32). The conquerors of the land were disregarding the social structure and conventions the LORD wished to see prevailing among his people.

> 5:13 Young men have lifted up the mill-stone,
> and boys have staggered under loads of wood.

The subject of the verb 'to lift, to carry' may be the enemy as they carry off the *young men* (cf. 1:15) and compel them to engage in menial service ('they took the young men to grind', AV; cf. NLT, NRSV). That certainly was what happened, but even so the verb more probably describes the activity of the young men themselves. The grinding mill consisted of two stones: a lower heavier one, and a lighter one above it which was turned to grind the grain between the two stones. Obviously the upper stone had to be capable of being lifted to remove the ground cereal and to insert further supplies for grinding. This arduous and repetitive task was usually women's work or assigned to the lowest slave (cf. Exod. 11:5; Judg. 16:21; Isa. 47:2), but here such young men as are left in the city have been conscripted to carry out this work, and even younger *boys* are to be seen laden down with bundles of firewood which are too heavy for them so that fuel may be provided for the kitchens of their conquerors. This is a further aspect to the shame imposed on the city by the reversal of her circumstances.

> 5:14 Elders have stopped ⌊gathering⌋ at the city gate,
> young men from playing music.

The open space left inside the city gate to provide a space where troops could muster to repulse any attack also functioned as a market-place for traders and a site for public assemblies. The *elders*/'old men' would once have gathered there to debate the affairs of the land and to adjudicate in various disputes which had arisen in the community (cf. Deut. 21:18-21; 22:13-19). Now they *have stopped* doing so. The area was under enemy control, and the elders were accorded no respect by the occupying regime (5:12); so rather than suffer further ignominy they have abandoned their former habits (cf. 1:4).

Similarly the exactions of the enemy have taken their toll on the *young men.* Exhausted and drained from the burdens placed on them, they have no heart for *playing music*, and so they too have abandoned what formerly provided them with satisfaction and entertainment. This was the predicted mark of the imposition of the LORD's judgement: 'I will make to cease from the cities of Judah and from the streets of Jerusalem the voice of joy and the voice of gladness' (Jer 7:34; cf. Isa. 16:10).

(4) Hopeless Desolation (5:15-18)

The impersonal style of the previous verses is replaced in 5:15-18 with seven first person plural references. These set out the community's collective grief at the disaster which has struck every group within it.

> 5:15 The joy of our hearts has stopped;
>   our dancing has changed into mourning.

The silencing of the music of the young men (5:14) is one aspect of a general cessation of joy which is particularly described as *of our hearts.* Inwardly they are grief-stricken and bewildered, and so they have lost all motivation for exuberant performances. *Our dancing has changed into mourning.* Once they had had good reason to express joy and gladness, and such dancing formed part of their liturgy (cf. Pss. 87:7; 149:3; 150:4). But no longer. There has been a radical transformation in their circumstances, and now only expressions of grief are appropriate.

> 5:16 The crown of our head has fallen;
>   woe to us, for we have sinned!

The crown of our head may continue the thought of rejoicing in previous verses by referring to garlands worn by those at a banquet (cf. Isa. 28:1-4). Loss of the garland would indicate that the banquet was over. Another possibility is that the crown does indeed refer to royal regalia, and 'head' is used for the king (cf. Jer. 13:18). The description would then be of the way their hopes were dashed through the capture of the king (cf. 4:20). Most probably, however, the focus is now not on their temporal circumstances, but on their inward, heart aspirations. Mount Zion is explicitly mentioned in 5:18, and could well be indicated here by the phrase 'our head' with the Temple and its surrounding buildings as 'the crown'. What then is being lamented is the loss of all that Zion and the Temple stood for.

It is recognised that this change of fortune had not occurred simply through political factors. The unusual expression *woe to us!*[152] probably reflects the extreme circumstances when daughter Zion was abandoned by her allies and cried out in her death throes: 'Woe to me! for my life is fainting before murderers' (Jer. 4:31). The prophetic vision of warning had become reality for the community *for we have sinned* (cf. 1:18-22; 3:42). There is a collective acceptance that the LORD's anger had fallen on them not just because of underlying factors put in place by the failure of their fathers or because of the deficiencies of their priests and prophets. They too had to confess personal culpability: all were implicated in the guilt of the land.

> 5:17 Because of this our heart has become faint;
>   because of these ˌthingsˌ our eyes have grown
>   dim —

Because of this seems to be retrospective in its reference. Because of the community's sin, their *heart* (cf. 3:21) *has become faint.* The term 'faint' repeats that found in 1:13, 22 in reference to daughter Zion. This is not a passing swoon, but a debilitating weakness that has taken away their inner zest for life. Their vitality has been sapped.

Because of these things seems to have a prospective reference to the situation in Zion set out in 5:18. *Our eyes have grown dim* reflects the tears which have been shed and the resultant blurring of vision (cf. 1:16; 2:11; 3:49). Looking at the calamities that have

---

152. The expression *ʾ ôy-nāʾ* occurs only here and in Jer. 4:16; 45:3. The particle *nāʾ* is used to intensify the expression.

come upon Zion has caused grief and tears which have further drained them of life.

5:18 Because of mount Zion which lies desolate —
      jackals go about on it.

While the introductory phrase might mean 'on mount Zion', it is more probable that the preposition is repeated for a third time to clarify the preceding reference. Their grief is *because of mount Zion which lies desolate.* For 'desolate', see on 1:4. The Temple mountain on which there had been the visible symbol of the LORD's presence with his people is now devastated and ruined because the LORD has punished and abandoned them. To look to mount Zion for deliverance (cf. Ps. 121:1) is to be reminded that there is none, for the LORD has withdrawn. All that can be seen are *jackals* (not the term used in 4:3 but probably the same animal), which *go about on it* as they scavenge in packs through ruins. There is no one there to chase them off or frighten them away: the city is dead.

Reflection

•   In this prayer the people complain to the LORD about their grievous circumstances which they cannot accept as being normative for the future. They turn to him as the only one who is able to provide an effective remedy for their distress and, as they do so, they follow the poet's earlier exhortation to pour out their hearts to the LORD (cf. 2:19) and unreservedly set their grievances before him. That still remains the way forwards for subsequent generations, no matter what their situation. Whenever we find anxious cares affecting us about anything, we are by prayer and supplication to let our requests be made known to God (Phil. 4:6). It is instructive, however, to note the phrase which Paul adds — 'with thanksgiving'. In the light of the gospel it is possible for the believer to introduce an element of balance into any expression of need, because in Christ there is always much to give thanks for.

•   As well as enumerating the details of their anguish and hardship, the people make frank confession of their own responsibility for what has happened: 'We have sinned' (5:16). A restored relationship with God is not possible until the facts of what has gone awry in the previous situation are frankly accepted. He has said that he will return to his heavenly abode until his people in their distress acknowledge their guilt and earnestly seek his face (Hos. 5:15). Then he will be pleased to be true to the promise, 'If we confess our sins, he is faithful and just to forgive us our sins and to cleanse us from all unrighteousness' (1 John 1:9).

- The confession of 5:16 shows that the statement 'Our fathers sinned' (5:7) had not been uttered in a spirit of self-exculpation. Rather there is an underlying recognition that, while the sin of previous generations had distorted the subsequent spiritual environment, still they were paying the penalty for their personal wrongdoing (cf. Ps. 106:6; Jer. 16:10-13). Each generation has an awesome responsibility for the legacy they bestow on those who come after them, but the errors of the fathers are not to be cited as justification for the children continuing in their disobedient ways.

- The woe (5:16) and despondency ('our heart has become faint', 5:17) felt by the community are the consequences of their guilt, and their grief is intensified when they see the harmful outcome of their actions on the cause of God on earth. 'Mount Zion lies desolate' (5:18), deserted by God and man. The distressed church pleads not only for relief from its own misery but for the honour of God's name and for the glory accrues to him from the advance of the gospel.

B. Restore Us! (5:19-22)

The final section of the poem opens with a sudden switch from the detailed presentation of the suffering of the speakers who comprise the community left in Jerusalem. There is a move from description to petition in which there is unresolved tension between the expectations they tentatively cling to and the reality which confronts them on a daily basis. Their hope centres on the unending sovereignty of the LORD (5:19) and his undoubted capacity to restore the people (5:21). The reality which clouds that hope is the significance of their present condition. Does the way the LORD is currently treating them mean that they have been permanently cast aside (5:20, 22)?

5:19 ⌐But⌐ you,[153] O LORD, sit ⌐enthroned⌐ for ever;
your throne ⌐endures⌐ to generation after
generation.

From Zion which had been the earthly throne of the LORD where he
made known his presence, the community's focus rises upwards to
his heavenly throne as they resume the petition begun in 5:1. *You,
O LORD* directly and urgently addresses God as Yahweh, the
covenant King, who possesses ultimate authority and dominion as
the one who 'sits', that is, as the context makes clear, *sits
⌐enthroned⌐* in heaven (cf. 1 Kgs. 1:46; Pss. 9:11; 102:12). Though
the Temple, which had been his earthly dwelling place, had been
destroyed, that had not terminated his rule which is *for ever.* His
control is not nominal, but active and effective, and asserting its
perpetual nature implicitly calls on him to act and exercise his
sovereignty as Judge of all.

Your throne had once been visible in Zion (cf. Jer. 17:12), but
even though all that was left there was a ruin, the eye of faith sees
beyond that to the corresponding heavenly reality which it asserts
endures to generation after generation. There is permanence and
perpetuity with respect to all that God's reign stands for. What may
the next generation in Jerusalem expect from the hand of the one
whose throne is founded on righteousness and justice (Pss. 89:14;
97:2)? Indeed, the question which they may well have had in mind
was, Will there be a next generation in Jerusalem at all?

5:20 Why do you forget us continually?
⌐Why⌐ do you forsake us for length of days?

Why? expresses the tension felt by the speakers. They have
acknowledged their sin, and they have confessed their belief in the
perpetuity of the throne of the LORD and all that was involved in it.
Surely then the LORD would not maintain this hostile disengage-
ment from those whom he has permitted to survive the overthrow
of the city. *Forget us continually* does not describe a lapse of
memory, but is characteristic terminology in Israel's complaints for

---

153. 'And you'/'but you' is found in the LXX and Peshitta, but the addition
of 'and' is obviously a translator's device to bring out the significance of the
emphatic 'you' which redirects the reader's attention from the city to the
LORD.

lack of divine intervention and correction of the existing state of affairs. 'O God, why do you cast us off continually?' (Ps. 74:1; cf. Pss. 13:1; 42:9). How can the LORD rule and not act in accordance with what he is known to be?

Forsake us refers to the LORD's abandonment of the people (cf. Isa. 49:14). The King is no longer in their midst, protecting them and providing for them. The relationship they had once enjoyed with him is ruptured, and there is a sense of loneliness, isolation, insecurity, vulnerability. **For length of days** is a relatively rare expression, occurring in only two other places (Pss. 23:6; 93:5). It may not point into the indefinite future as if the speakers envisaged their present distress continuing indefinitely, but might rather signify the succession of days over time, with the thought here being a wearisome sequence of days throughout which their affliction continues, day after day.[154]

> 5:21 Bring us back to yourself, O LORD, so that we may
> come back!
> Renew our days as of old —

While **bring us back to yourself** might be a petition for return from exile to the land of promise (cf. Jer. 31:18), the concerns of the exilic community have not been highlighted in Lamentations which embodies the perspective of the community left behind. Furthermore such a return would not achieve much if the LORD himself had left Zion. Instead 'to yourself' reveals the personal as distinct from the territorial focus of their expectation so that their initial desire is not simply for their ongoing pain to be eased, but that there be restored fellowship with the LORD. They humbly acknowledge that he alone can effect such a change. This petition is thus an expression of human inability to mend a fractured relationship with God.

If, however, God is prepared to act, then their return is possible: **so that we may come back.** It is only his initiative that can achieve their restoration, and so all resolves itself into the desire and determination of God. 'Come back'/'return' (cf. 3:40), a reversal of direction and return to a point of departure, is the Old Testament metaphor used to describe repentance as a spiritual return to God

---

154. Cf. Renkema, *Lamentations*, 624.

(cf. Jer. 3:12; Hos. 14:1). Only on that basis can reconciliation be
effected, but repentance itself is dependent on the gift of God, who
alone can grant the repentance which leads to life (cf. Acts 11:18;
2 Tim. 2:25). So there is a recognition that, because they have not
the capacity to effect the renewal and restoration themselves, they
cannot begin to step out on the road towards reconciliation unless
there is a divinely granted predisposition and empowerment.

Renew our days as of old repeats the necessity of God's
sovereign action to effect restoration. It is spoken out of a background of present desolation which knows that there was a brighter
past and yearns for its resumption. The ideal period in view might
be that after the Exodus, which was on occasions looked back on in
glowing terms (Jer. 2:2-3; Hos. 2:15). In the light of 1:7, however,
it would seem that the ideal in the mind of the poet and people is
the time of the early kingdom, probably during the reign of
Solomon, when the Temple had been built and the nation enjoyed
the prosperity associated with having an empire. That time of
external splendour is viewed as one of harmony between the LORD
and his people, a time of spiritual fellowship. After all, that was the
ultimate goal of the covenant. While it is possible to contemplate
other losses occurring and life still continuing, the prospect of life
without God at its centre cannot be endured.

> 5:22 unless you have utterly rejected us,
>   for₁ you have been exceedingly furious against us.

Obviously if one is trying to trace a linear thematic development in
Lamentations, its closing verse plays a significant role in our
understanding in that it would summarise and round off the whole
argument of the book. However, even when the central section of
3:22-33 is recognised as the keystone of a concentric structure, the
final verse still has a major influence in determining the reader's
overall impression of the message of the book.

Unfortunately, despite the familiarity of the vocabulary of the
verse, the introductory terms, *kî ʾim* (here rendered 'unless') have
provided translators and commentators with problems of long-
standing. Many expedients have been adopted to render these

words,[155] of which the following certainly merit consideration.

(1) The possibility of taking the particles separately and not in combination has been again canvassed to give a sense such as, 'For if truly you have rejected us, raging bitterly against us—'.[156] While the individual terms are assigned recognised meanings, such a broken construction, deliberately providing a non-ending and refusing to follow through the implications of the thought, seems a distinctly modern imposition on the text.

(2) A concessive translation 'even if, although' has been proposed to indicate that, despite their present suffering, the people make bold to utter the prayer of 5:21.[157] However, it is stylistically unusual for such a qualification to follow, rather than precede, the main request.

(3) English translations frequently adopt the rendering 'unless', so that the preceding petition of the people is qualified by the fact of their continuing misery compelling them to recognise the unwelcome possibility that their former relationship with Yahweh

---

155. Attempts to render 5:22 which are still mentioned by commentators generally only to be rejected are: (1) that of the old Jewish Publication Society Version (1917), 'Thou canst not have utterly rejected us, and be exceeding wroth against us!' The introduction of a negative reversed the sense of the text. It reflected the same problems which led synagogue liturgy to require the penultimate verse of the chapter to be read again after 5:22 so as not to end on a sombre note, but there is no warrant for the 'not'. (2) Another proposal is to treat the statement as a question, 'Or hast thou utterly rejected us? Art thou exceedingly angry with us?' (RSV; cf. GNT, NLT). However, whatever merit such an approach has as a dynamic translation bringing out the sense of the passage, there is no evidence that *kî 'im* can be read as an interrogative. (3) A further approach is to delete *'im* since it is not represented in the Greek LXX, the Syriac Peshitta, or some medieval Hebrew manuscripts ('For you have completely rejected us …'). Absence of any corresponding term, however, appears to be a translator's expedient in making sense of a difficult passage, and the Massoretic text undoubtedly represents the original reading. For further information regarding these and other options, see R. Gordis, 'The Conclusion of the Book of Lamentations,' *Journal of Biblical Literature* 93 (1974): 289–93 and Tod Linafelt, 'The Refusal of a Conclusion in the Book of Lamentations,' *Journal of Biblical Literature* 120 (2001): 340–43.

156. See Linafelt, 'Refusal,' 343.

157. Gordis, 'Conclusion,' 291.

is now irrecoverable. The grammatical objection to this rendering focuses on the fact that *kî 'im* means 'unless' only when it follows a negative clause, which is not the case here.

(4) An adversative usage of *kî 'im* is attested elsewhere, and this would lead to a rendering such as, 'But thou hast utterly rejected us; thou art very wroth against us' (AV, following the Vulgate; cf. ASV).[158] The verse might then embody a recognition of the stark contrast between their preceding prayer and their present experience. Again, the weakness of this approach is that this meaning of *kî 'im* is only found after a preceding negative, explicit or implicit, and that is not the case here.

Neither (3) nor (4) can be said to resolve the problem, and either may be adopted with some justification. What is more important is the sense which is then attached to this verse. Even though it follows the petitions of 5:21 and contains two infinitives absolute which might be intended to heighten the contrast,[159] there is no need to view it as a plunge into utter despair. That the LORD had rejected the people was obvious; they continued to smart under the blows entailed by that rejection. What was at stake was whether the LORD had done so 'utterly'/'completely'. Their plea for repentance and renewal exhibits the desire of the people to enjoy the LORD's favour once more, but there was nothing in their experience to confirm that the LORD had entertained their prayer. As long as their misery continued, the future remained clouded by uncertainty. The measure of confidence expressed by the fact of the utterance of the petitions of 5:21 is still qualified by the 'perhaps' of 3:29. This understanding of the matter is best brought out by rendering *kî 'im* by ***unless***, though 'but' is a possibility if the infinitive absolute (rendered 'utterly') is taken in the sense 'quite', 'truly', or 'indeed'.

---

158. This approach is also advocated by Hillers, *Lamentations*, 160. It is noted that *kî 'im* may be used adversatively where there is not an explicit negative but where one may be understood from the context (cf. GKC §163b). Examples might include, 'So now let my lord the king not take the report to heart, saying, "All the king's sons have died", but rather (*kî 'im*) "Ammon alone has died".' (2 Sam. 13:33). 'But rather (*kî 'im*) Qain will be for burning' (Num. 24:21).

159. 'Since any opposition is enough to justify the use of an inf. abs. there is no need to look further for another nuance' (Joüon and Muraoka, *Grammar*, §123i).

The two parallel descriptions of their suffering are brought forward as grounds for the LORD to act in mercy.

The people are not claiming innocence or suggesting that their punishment has been undeserved. They have recognised their sinfulness and are pleading to be restored. But, because there is no evidence that the LORD has accepted them, they are still wondering where their relationship with him stands. The divine aversion expressed by *reject* undoubtedly was real, but such a reaction to their sin had never precluded subsequent reconciliation. The LORD had stated: 'They will render satisfaction for their iniquity precisely because they rejected my judgements and abhorred my statutes. Yet despite this, when they are in the land of their enemies, I will not reject them or abhor them so as to make a complete end of them and break my covenant with them, for I am the LORD their God' (Lev. 26:43b-44). Jeremiah also showed that it was a mistake on the part of the nations to interpret the LORD's punishment of his people as final rejection of them, for he would be true to the covenant he had committed himself to (Jer. 33:23-26). But it was hard to be assured of that while undergoing the blows of divine discipline. What was immediately evident to them was *you have been exceedingly furious against us* — and there had been no apparent let up in that divine displeasure because of the continuance of the chastisement to which it gave rise. Their combined outlook is at most a cautious optimism.

Reflection

• There is no contradiction between the message of chapter 3 and the concluding verses of chapter 5. The spiritual dynamic is the same in both chapters. In circumstances of suffering and confusion when there no longer seems to be any certainty in life, the only viable recourse is to look beyond human inability and sinfulness and recall the character of God. Bringing him into the picture provides a fixed point of reference that enables the contours of a way forwards to be discerned. That is no doubt why so many of the psalms of complaint point to the eternal rule of the LORD (e.g. Pss. 44:1-8; 74:12-17; 80:1-2; 89:1-18). His throne (5:19) expresses his sovereign control, and 'for ever' and 'to generation after generation' mark that control as unending and therefore unchangeably effective. 'But you, O LORD, sit

⌊enthroned⌋ for ever, and your remembrance ⌊is⌋ to generation after generation. You ⌊are the one who⌋ will arise; you will have compassion on Zion, for it is time to show her favour' (Ps. 102:12-13).

- 'Bring us back to yourself' (5:21) shows that the fundamental need is the renewal of a right relationship between God and his people. By their sin they had forfeited any right to his favour. What they are pleading for is grace, an unmerited display of compassion and acceptance. Even so, it is recognised that there must be movement on their part. They recognise that it is only as they are divinely energised that there can be an effective return, and so they plead for empowerment.

- But the dark shadow of their sin remains. The gravity of their offence has not yet been exhausted, and so their spiritual confidence falters: 'unless you have quite rejected us' (5:22). In the shattered remains of their lives there is no evidence of restoration. Faith is caught in the tension between observed reality on earth and confessed reality in heaven. The way forwards is not theirs to dictate; they can only plead.

- The subsequent history of the ethnic Israel shows that the impact of the fall of Jerusalem has not yet been exhausted. In God's providence Babylon was in her turn overthrown and permission was granted for the exiles to return home. But it was never more than a handful who returned to Jerusalem and constituted the restored community. Many lived on outside the land of promise. The glory of Zion was never restored to what it had once been (Hag. 2:3), and then history repeated itself. 'Jerusalem, Jerusalem, the one who kills the prophets and stones those sent to her, how often I wanted to gather your children in the way that a hen ⌊gathers⌋ her brood under her wings, and you wanted none ⌊of it⌋! Behold, your house is rejected!' (Luke 13:34-35; cf. Luke 19:41-44). The city which crucified her Messiah was again razed in judgement, a judgement which still persists spiritually. And yet the situation is not one without hope, for the branches that are cut off may be grafted back into their own olive tree, as Paul outlines in Romans 11.

WORKS CITED

(a)   English Translations

ASV   American Standard Version
AV   Authorised Version
ESV   English Standard Version
GNB   Good News Bible
NASB New American Standard Bible
NIV   New International Version (Anglicised Edition)
NKJV New King James Version
NLT   New Living Translation
NRSV New Revised Standard Version
REB   Revised English Bible
RSV   Revised Standard Version

(b)   Reference Works

GKC   W. Gesenius, E. Kautzsch and A. E. Cowley, *Gesenius Hebrew Grammar*. Oxford: Clarendon Press, 1910 (second edition).

HALOT *The Hebrew and Aramaic Lexicon of the Old Testament*. L. Koehler, W. Baumgartner and J. J. Stamm. Brill: Leiden, 1994–1999.

NIDOTTE *New International Dictionary of Old Testament Theology and Exegesis*. W. A. VanGemeren (ed.). Grand Rapids: Zondervan, 1997.

TDOT   *Theological Dictionary of the Old Testament*. G. J. Botterweck, H. Ringgren and H-J. Fabry (eds.) Grand Rapids: Eerdmans, 1974–.

(c)   Other Works

Berlin, Adele. *Lamentations*. Louisville: Westminster/John Knox, 2002.

Calvin, John. *Commentaries on the Book of the Prophet Jeremiah and the Lamentations*. Translated by John Owen. Edinburgh: Calvin Translation Society, 1850–55 [first published in Latin, 1559]. 5 volumes. Reprint: Edinburgh: The Banner of Truth Trust, 1989.

Cohen, Chayim. 'The "Widowed" City.' *Journal of the Ancient Near Eastern Society of Columbia University*, 5 (1973): 75–81.

Dobbs-Allsopp, F. W. *Lamentations*. Interpretation. Louisville, Kentucky: John Knox Press, 2002.

Dorsey, David A. *The Literary Structure of the Old Testament: A Commentary on Genesis–Malachi*. Grand Rapids: Baker, 1999.

Erlandsson, Seth. 'The Wrath of YHWH.' *Tyndale Bulletin* 23 (1973): 111–116.

Fairbairn, Patrick. *The Interpretation of Prophecy*. Second Edition, 1865. Reprint: London: Banner of Truth, 1964.

Freedman, D. N. 'Acrostics and Metrics in Hebrew Poetry.' *Harvard Theological Review* 65 (1972): 367–92.

Gerstenberger, Erhard S. *Psalms, Part 2, and Lamentations*. The Forms of Old Testament Literature XV. Grand Rapids: Eerdmans, 2001.

Gordis, R. 'The Conclusion of the Book of Lamentations.' *Journal of Biblical Literature* 93 (1974): 289–93.

Heim, Knut M. 'The Personification of Jerusalem and the Drama of Her Bereavement in Lamentations.' Pp. 129–69 in *Zion, City of Our God*. Edited by Richard S. Hess and Gordon J. Wenham. Grand Rapids: Eerdmans, 1999.

Hillers, Delbert R. *Lamentations: A New Translation with Introduction and Commentary*. Second ed. The Anchor Bible. New York: Doubleday, 1992.

Johnson, Bo. 'Form and Message in Lamentations.' *Zeitschrift für die Alttestamentliche Wissenschaft* 97 (1985): 58–73.

Joüon, Paul, and T. Muraoka. *A Grammar of Biblical Hebrew*. Subsidia Biblica. Rome: Pontifical Bible Institute, 1991.

Kaiser, Barbara B. 'Poet as "Female Impersonator": The Image of Daughter Zion as Speaker in Biblical Poems of Suffering.' *Journal of Religion* 67 (1987): 164–82.

Kaiser, Walter C., Jr. *A Biblical Approach to Personal Suffering*. Chicago: Moody, 1982.

Keil, C. F. *Jeremiah, Lamentations*. Translated by J. Martin. Commentary on the Old Testament. Reprint: Grand Rapids: Eerdmans, 1975 [1872].

Krašovec, Jože. 'The Source of Hope in the Book of Lamentations.' *Vetus Testamentum* 42 (1992): 223–33.

Lanahan, William F. 'The Speaking Voice in the Book of Lamentations.' *Journal of Biblical Literature* 93 (1974): 41–49.

Linafelt, Tod. 'The Refusal of a Conclusion in the Book of Lamentations.' *Journal of Biblical Literature* 120 (2001): 340–43.

Mackay, John L. *Jeremiah*. Fearn, Ross-shire: Mentor, 2004.

McDaniel, Th. F. 'Philological Studies in Lamentations.' *Biblica* 49 (1968): 29–31.

McFall, Leslie. "A Translation Guide to the Chronological Data in Kings and Chronicles." *Bibliotheca Sacra* 148 (1991): 3–45.

Mintz, Alan. 'The Rhetoric of Lamentations and the Representation of Catastrophe.' *Prooftexts* 2 (1982): 1–17.

Provan, Iain W. *Lamentations*. New Century Bible. London: Marshall Pickering, 1991.

------. 'Past, Present and Future in Lamentations III 52–66: The Case for a Precative Perfect Re-Examined.' *Vetus Testamentum* 41 (1991): 164–75.

Reimer, David J. 'Good Grief? A Psychological Reading of Lamentations.' *ZAW* 114 (2002): 542–59.

Renkema, Johan. *Lamentations*. Historical Commentary on the Old Testament. Leuven: Peeters, 1998.

------. 'The Literary Structure of Lamentations (I–IV).' Pp. 294–396 in *The Structural Analysis of Biblical and Canaanite Poetry*, JSOT-Sup 74. Edited by Willem van der Meer and Johannes C. de Moor. Sheffield: JSOT Press, 1988.

Rudolph, Wilhelm. *Das Buch Ruth—Das Höhe Lied—Die Klagelieder*. Kommentar zum Alten Testament 17. Gütersloh: Gerd Mohn, 1962.

Shea, William H. 'The *Qinah* Structure of the Book of Lamentations.' *Biblica* 60 (1979): 103–7.

Tasker, R. V. G. *The Biblical Doctrine of the Wrath of God*. London: Tyndale Press, 1951.

Thiele, Edwin R. *The Mysterious Numbers of the Hebrew Kings*. Rev. ed. Grand Rapids: Zondervan, 1983.

Thompson, J. A. 'Israel's "lovers".' *Vetus Testamentum* 27 (1977): 475–481.

Waltke, Bruce K., and Michael P. O'Connor. *An Introduction to Biblical Hebrew Syntax*. Winona Lake, Indiana: Eisenbrauns, 1990.

SUBJECT INDEX

INDEX OF SCRIPTURES QUOTED

Exodus
A MENTOR COMMENTARY

John L. Mackay

Exodus:

A Mentor Commentary

John L MacKay

The book of Exodus is about a journey: a journey out of Egypt, but more particularly a journey from a land where God's power, sovereignty and continuing interest in his people could be easily questioned, to a place where God dwelt in the midst of his people. Exodus describes God's power, his redemption of his people, his covenant requirements at Sinai, and the rules of his worship.

John L. Mackay interacts with other scholars in either text or footnotes. In addition to exploring the meaning of the text he examines the chonology, authorship, composition and structure of Exodus. In addition, at the end of each section he provides a reflective comment.

'Professor Mackay has produced a strong commentary on the Book of Exodus. It is filled with excellent material for the pastor and the serious-minded Bible student. I especially appreciate the work on application that is normally so difficult to draw out of historical literature. I recommend this work highly. It is a valuable tool for the study of this most important period in Israel's history.'

John D. Currid, Professor of Old Testament,
Reformed Theological Seminary, Charlotte, North Carolina

'A tour de force of conservative evangelical exposition. Massively researched, painstakingly explained, theologically nuanced, reliably expounded, simply expressed and sensitivly applied; this volume will be of considerable value to all preachers and Bible students. For accessible and scholarly comment Mackay's work should quickly become the standard evangelical work on the Book of Exodus.'

Stephen Dray

ISBN 978-1-85792-614-9

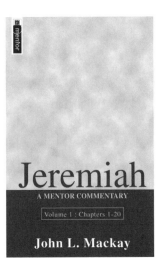

Jeremiah
A MENTOR COMMENTARY
Volume 1 : Chapters 1-20

John L. Mackay

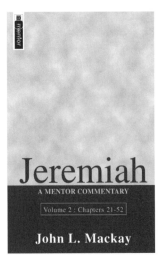

Jeremiah
A MENTOR COMMENTARY
Volume 2 : Chapters 21-52

John L. Mackay

Jeremiah Vol. 1 & 2

A Mentor Commentary

John L MacKay

'*Professor Mackay's commentary on Jeremiah is trebly welcome: first, from his earlier work on Exodus (in this series) we know that he will take the highest view of Scripture as the Word of God, ...secondly, he argues cogently for Jeremiah as author of the whole, contending that the book as we have it represents written records contemporary with the prophet's preaching... Thirdly, from the start he is concerned to handle the book of Jeremiah, not as an anthology, but as unfolding a unified message. Lovers of Hebrew will find a kindred spirit in Professor Mackay. Those without Hebrew will find a patient teacher leaving no stone unturned to make the word of God plain.*'

Alec Motyer

'*This eagerly awaited commentary on one of the longest and most taxing books of the Old Testament fulfils every expectation... The message of Jeremiah's forty-year ministry is here firmly rooted in the Old Testament history as a message from the Lord to his ancient people; but its abiding relevance is also brought out in Professor Mackay's careful application of the material. This will quickly become an indispensable tool for anyone wishing to study and preach from the Book of Jeremiah.*'

Iain D. Campbell,
Free Church of Scotland, Back, Isle of Lewis

'*...a first class explanation of the prophet... It is certain to become the first 'port of call' in my studies of the book, ...he has the ability to uncover the significance of the original message in such a way as to leave the application (almost) transparent.*'

Stephen Dray

'*The commentary is as full as is reasonably possible, verse by verse, often word by word, and covers every question likely to be raised.*'

The Gospel Magazine

ISBN 978-1-85792-937-9 (Volume 1)
ISBN 978-1-85792-938-6 (Volume 2)

Christian Focus Publications

publishes books for all ages

Our mission statement –

STAYING FAITHFUL

In dependence upon God we seek to help make His infallible Word, the Bible, relevant. Our aim is to ensure that the Lord Jesus Christ is presented as the only hope to obtain forgiveness of sin, live a useful life and look forward to heaven with Him.

REACHING OUT

Christ's last command requires us to reach out to our world with His gospel. We seek to help fulfil that by publishing books that point people towards Jesus and help them develop a Christ-like maturity. We aim to equip all levels of readers for life, work, ministry and mission.

Books in our adult range are published in three imprints.

Christian Focus contains popular works including biographies, commentaries, basic doctrine and Christian living. Our children's books are also published in this imprint.

Mentor focuses on books written at a level suitable for Bible College and seminary students, pastors, and other serious readers. The imprint includes commentaries, doctrinal studies, examination of current issues and church history.

Christian Heritage contains classic writings from the past.

Christian Focus Publications Ltd
Geanies House, Fearn,
Ross-shire, IV20 1TW, Scotland, United Kingdom
info@christianfocus.com

Our titles are available from quality bookstores and
www.christianfocus.com